Praise for *The Edge of Never*

"A heart-stopping read, *The Edge of Never* takes us beyond mountains, beyond snow and ice and danger and into the heart of family."
—Betsy Burton, The King's English Bookshop

"The ... highlight [is a] ... terrifying descent of the 55-degree Exit Couloir, which Kerig recounts grippingly."
—*Outside*

"Kerig writes about the bonds between skiers, fatherhood and his own ski ambitions ... with clear prose that delves into why skiers take such risks and why we feel compelled to document their stories."
—*Skiing*

"Kerig has a great ear for dialogue and a gift for weaving tension in and out of the plotline ... The result is both confessional and illuminating: An insider's look at a tribe of devoted—some would say fanatical—skiers in the mountains that are their lifeblood (and all too often the cause of their death)."
—Peter Shelton, author of *Climb to Conquer*

"Transcending the boundaries of sport, the book tells a deeply interpersonal and moving human story ... Kerig ... stays true to the roots and core values that define the culture of skiing."
—*Powder*

"For anyone who really wants to know what the ski life is like, this is the book for them."
—Francois Goulet, President, Rossignol North America

THE EDGE OF NEVER

A skier's story of life, death and dreams
in the world's most dangerous mountains

WILLIAM A. KERIG

Stone Creek Publications
Milford, New Jersey

Stone Creek Publications
460 Shire Road
Milford, NJ 08848
tel: 908-995-0016
screek@ptd.net
www.stonecreekpublications.com

Distributed to the book trade by Independent Publishers Group

Library of Congress Control Number: 2008929347
ISBN-13: 978-0-9656338-4-0
ISBN-10: 0-9656338-4-5

Cover photograph of Kye Petersen by Christopher Bezamat
Printed in the USA

For my family—Bel, Grace, Liam, and Huck

All men dream: but not equally. Those who dream by night in the dusty recesses of their minds wake in the day to find that it was vanity: but the dreamers of the day are dangerous men, for they may act their dream with open eyes, to make it possible.

T. E. Lawrence, *The Seven Pillars of Wisdom: A Triumph*

Prologue

Our cameras are focused on the skier. He's poised on an apron of un-tracked snow. Behind him looms a wall of ragged blue ice. The film crew and I are set up on a narrow ledge. Behind us is only pale sky and far below, already falling into shadow, the tight little town of Chamonix, France.

Sound? I yell, my breath forming a cloud in the chill air.

Sound's rolling, answers the soundman. Quiet, please.

Camera's rolling, calls the cinematographer.

The crew settles. Small movements cease. All eyes are on the skier above us. He lowers his goggles and clicks his poles together three times, snapping snow off the baskets, focusing his attention.

I count him down. Three, two, one … He plants his poles, rolls his shoulders and pushes off. He angles into his first turn, a light touch to stay in the soft new snow without driving into the hardened wind-crust beneath. His edges bite nicely.

A fine white spindrift roils over his boots and shins, flaring behind him in the glazing light. He snaps his turns, quick and precise, yet somehow carefree and light, the disciplined dance of one of the world's best skiers.

Two turns, three. His power is immense. He moves smoothly, with authority. Silken force. He speeds into the transition between the steep pitch and the flat shelf where we stand. Our lenses follow him as his weight shifts slightly forward, and one of his ski tips dives below the crust. The ski stops. He cracks at the waist, bends as if taking a bow. He drives his knee, trying to power the ski through. The ski tip plunges deeper, jerking his leg backward. Heels rising, he flies past our cameras, hands reaching into space as he disappears over the edge.

For a moment there is nothing but silence. We're frozen in time by the impossibility of what we've just witnessed. Then the moment shatters and everyone is in motion, cursing, clicking into bindings, scrambling— the chaos of sudden disaster.

I skate down the bench, stop, and inch out toward the edge. Digging in my downhill pole, I peer over. Seventy feet below is a deep crater, a hole of evil curves and wicked furrows. At the bottom of the hole is a crevasse, a gaping crack in the glacial floor. The eastern edge opens into blackness, but at its middle is a thick ice bridge. On it is his body, face down, legs and arms splayed, motionless.

Call the rescue! someone screams. Call the helicopter!

Hands dig into jackets. Cell phones come to ears. Who do we call and what's the number and, shit, who has a signal? Then one of the grips makes the connection. He speaks slowly, his French precise and measured, getting the details straight for the gendarme on the other end.

What thoughts flood a skier's mind as he feels death coming near? Does he wonder why he was drawn to the mountain life? Or does he understand that a life lived fully, lived at the edge of disaster, is worth losing? Does he feel a satisfied peace or an agonizing realization that it was all a hollow fiction, a testosterone-fueled fantasy?

Something moves behind me and I turn. Two skiers pull up and stop: Peter Pilafian, our cinematographer, and Scott Markewitz, our still photographer.

There's a moment. Something passes between us. It's a look of caring but trying not to care, fear but swallowing down the fear. A concentrated focus comes into Pilafian's eyes. He asks: Are we shooting it?

I have no answer. I'm living the nightmare I've been having since this film began. A skier, a friend, is badly injured and may be dead, and I'm responsible for it. I put him in this place. If I hadn't ginned up this whole thing, he wouldn't be lying at the bottom of a hole.

It's your call, says Markewitz.

We've tempted humble dreamers with fame and the famous with an offer of another fix. Glory for risk, that's the bargain. But this isn't some stage play, some dreamed-up script. Reality is a skier hurtling through space. Reality is a skier splatting onto an ice block, choking on his own breath in a glacial pit.

The shooters just want to do their jobs. They look to me for a decision. I look for a way out. I want to stop it, shut it all down. Nothing is worth losing a life. I think of all the other skiers and crew members I've put at risk. And for what? To make a film?

In the beginning, I'd set out to tell a story that would grab the sleepers by their lapels and shake them, that would show them what it means to live big in the face of their greatest fears, to live at the edge. I wanted real, not some sneaker slogan or soda-pop tagline. And I got real. This is real. People get broken. People die trying to make it real.

The *thwop* of helicopter blades echoes from far down the valley. A navy blue speck appears in the pale sky.

If I were a true filmmaker, a hardened director, I wouldn't be asking questions. We'd already be rolling. The filmmaker shoots first, asks questions later. But I'm not a hardened director. I'm just a guy with a lot of questions, and a skier, just like the man down there in the hole.

The thudding grows louder as the rescue chopper banks toward us.

For a long moment everyone on the mountain looks skyward. Everyone, that is, except me. I'm looking at two guys with cameras, seeing my reflection off a lens.

A Madman's Scheme

Salt Lake City, Utah
August 2004

The Wasatch Range shimmers in a thick summer haze. Down here in the valley, the city bakes in white. My only window affords a partial view of the mountains. I'm sweating in a cramped, flat-roofed office, a newly matted photograph of my wife and daughter on one wall, a ski poster that features a younger version of me on another. The poster was cutting-edge about ten years ago, back when I was a professional skier. Now it's kitsch. The clothes are dated and the skis are skinny. I'm a period piece.

Walking three parched blocks from my office, I go home to a small brick house across the street from a methamphetamine dealer whose business is thriving. Meth Boy wears a hooded sweatshirt and a bandanna under a Saints baseball cap. The belt of his trousers hangs to mid-thigh. He ambles out to waiting cars and gets in the back seat with a box of crackers in his hand—Ritz or Triscuits or Wheat Thins. The meth is in the boxes. In the time it takes to drive around the block, the car is back and Meth Boy steps out and gives the driver a soul-bro handshake. And then he's into the next car.

From our front window I watch the nightly bazaar with my wife, Bel, now pregnant with our second child. Our almost-two-year-old daughter, Grace, coos at the undercover cops who use our living room to watch Meth Boy.

Be patient, the cops tell me. Don't confront the dealer and certainly not his users. We *will* get him for you.

It's been months like this. Outside they line up for crank. Inside I hide in the draperies, wondering how the hell I got here.

When my father was my age he had three kids, a bad back and two full-time jobs. We lived in Hamilton, an affluent suburb on Boston's North Shore. We weren't rich—both my parents were teachers—but we had a green yard with woods in the back, and the speed freaks in our neighborhood raced Schwinn Sting-Rays.

It was a good childhood, one that was easy to take for granted, and I used to be so sure that I'd do a better job of providing for my kids than my old man. Now, standing in the curtains as the tweakers line up for crank, I just want to get us out of this neighborhood and away from Meth Boy.

It's been eight years since I last competed in a professional mogul skiing contest, seven since my divorce from my first wife, also a pro skier. Since then I've been in and out of the mountains, writing stories for outdoor magazines and hustling jobs in film and TV. For the last year, I've been trying to sell a pilot TV show that I produced and directed in Beirut, as well as writing the occasional magazine story. Amazingly, I've been paying the rent. But you get what you give, and though I got a living, in fits and starts, I didn't get a life. At least not the one I had imagined.

But now, things are going to be different. I have an idea for a new project, and this time it's about skiing and skiers, which is to say it's about me, my life, my extended family. I know a guy in New York who runs a film production company owned by Peter Jennings, the TV newsman. My plan – or maybe it's a delusion – is to create a documentary film about extreme skiing, sell it to my friend in New York, and use the money to move us into a better neighborhood.

Knowing it's a crazy idea, I dial Plake, the craziest and canniest skier I know.

His wife Kimberly, an ex-model, picks up the call and says she remembers me from back in the day. I remember her too: beauty-queen pretty, with luminescent skin and the glitter of diamonds at her ears. She favors platform shoes and faux leopard-skin pants, a peeking navel and feathered boas under her denim jacket.

In the skiing world, Kimberly's husband, Glen Plake, is an icon. A renegade among renegades on the mogul-skiing scene of the early 1980s, his career took a fateful detour when he was arrested in 1986 for selling psilocybin mushrooms. Released on his own recognizance, he fled to the French Alps, where he appeared in the groundbreaking ski film *The Blizzard of Aahhh's*. The movie introduced a whole generation of skiers to the idea of extreme skiing, and Plake was the movement's unlikely spokesman. With his hair cut into a two-foot-high Mohawk and a vociferously anti-establishment attitude, he became skiing's storied outlaw and later, after swearing off drugs and booze, its most flamboyant evangelist. Now he proselytizes ceaselessly for the sport that delivered his redemption.

Over the phone I tell Kimberly about Jennings, his film production company, and the idea of making a documentary about skiers who dedicate their lives to a calling and a culture that transcends sport. And no such film could exist without your husband, I add.

She makes approving noises. She says: That sounds good and won't that be something and, gee, it's nice of you to think of Glen, but no, he isn't around and would it be okay if I have him call you back?

I tell her that'll be fine, all the while knowing that he's probably standing right next to her. Kimberly is more than a wife. Along with Plake's father, who serves as his agent, Kimberly is an integral part of the apparatus that Plake has erected around himself to keep the world at bay until he's damn good and ready to step on stage.

It's days before Plake calls back, days that I don't endure well. I'm preoccupied and anxious, not only about failing to get my kids away from Meth Boy but squandering their childhood on yet another of daddy's ridiculous dreams.

On the other hand, as a skier I know that taking control requires moving toward the thing you most fear. On very steep terrain, everything in your being screams, *Back off! Get away from the edge!* But you learn to ignore those voices and move toward the emptiness because if you lean away from the void and into the slope, your ski bases tilt and you lose your edge—the only thing holding you to the hill. Lose your edge at the wrong moment, and it could be the last thing you ever do. Control comes from squaring your shoulders, reaching out and planting your pole down the hill, and moving with complete conviction toward the abyss. It's a thrilling, counterintuitive, high-stakes dance, and it's become my one enduring faith.

So what's up? Plake asks when he calls, his voice deep and gravelly. Kimberly said something about a movie?

I ask him why there isn't a big documentary about skiing like *Dogtown and Z Boys*, a film about the origins of skateboarding that a friend of mine helped make, or *Riding Giants*, another one she produced about big-wave surfing. Each film transcended the core following of the sport and spoke to a wider audience. Each brought legitimacy to alternative families, nobility to unlikely heroes, and respect to those who live on the fringes of society, daring to commit to lives of passion. I knew the mention of other sports getting that kind of respect would rile Plake. There's nothing he likes more than an excuse for righteous indignation.

We got more soul in our little fingers than some skateboard punks from Venice! Plake barks. Freakin' skiers just don't respect themselves.

We don't know where the sport's been or who came before or where it's going, so we let the dang companies tell us what's cool and who's cool and how to turn and where to ski. Stripped-down skiing is what it's all about! It's not about your dang buffalo chili at the Yellowstone Club. People think skiing's about money. Drinking $19 beer on a sundeck. Strip it down, man. Get *into* the mountains.

That's exactly what I want to make a film about, I say. I'm going to make *the* documentary about big-mountain skiing. The heart and soul of it. And I want you in it.

Plake lets out a long, thin sigh.

Yeah, I been trying to make that film ever since *Blizzard*, he says, referring to *The Blizzard of Aahh's*. But every dang time it gets sidetracked by some directing genius or freakin' money guy.

Well, that won't happen this time around, I say.

He grunts, asks what the budget is, and I tell him I don't know, which is the truth, but I'd say that anyway. Plake's years in the limelight have made him business-savvy, and I don't want our first talk to devolve into dollar wrestling.

You'll have to talk to my dad about compensation, he says, but I'm not worried about that. You remember the film *Winter Equinox*?

A 1960s ski film, right? I ask.

He refreshes my memory in exhaustive detail.

We don't want to do a remake, I say, stopping him from recounting every last scene. We're talking about a legit documentary that takes the whole program seriously.

Yeah, that would be something, he says, without conviction.

We're not making ski porn, I say, referring to the no-plot ski films that are sold on DVD from the back of ski magazines.

I tell him we'll go to Alaska to shoot a seminal set piece for the film.

Alaska? What are you smokin'? Helicopters and a thousand bucks a day? That's not the heart of skiing. What's that got to do with soul?

That's rich boys and filmers, dude. Forget it. Real and true big-mountain skiing is Chamonix. Period. Listen, you come to Cham with your crew and I'll show you heart and soul. I'll take you to where it all began. You want the history? That's the history. It all comes from Chamonix. Ski mountaineers. Pay for your turns in sweat. It's not Alaska, it's freakin' Chamonix. We'll find Anselme Baud, who wrote the book on Cham. And Sylvain Saudan is kicking around somewhere.

I tell him we need more than old guys. We need up-and-comers.

Silence on the line. Forty-year-old Plake may have ceded some of the spotlight to the youngsters, but he's still a player and protective of his turf. Nonetheless, I start listing the current crop of young pro skiers. And he stops me at one: Kye Petersen.

Trevor's son? he says. That's it, he's the one! We'll get him over to Cham.

There's a faint hissing on the line.

The Petersen name has stopped me cold. It brings me back. I see Trevor Petersen, Kye's father, lighting up a 1992 Canadian ski movie called *Carving the White*. I must have watched it forty times. I also skied in the film, but my part was small and forgettable. Trevor Petersen and his skiing partner, Eric Pehota, were the big stars. Eric was smoother and more technically impressive, but there was an animated quality to Trevor's skiing that made him irresistible. He moved with conviction, his body barely containing the power within it.

In December 1995, Trevor and I met in Vail at a ski-industry boon-doggle of seminars, speeches and workshops. Trevor came at the behest of his sponsors. His job was to ski and schmooze with journalists, retailers and corporate big shots. I was trolling for stories to write for ski magazines. He was staying at The Lodge at Vail, a five-star hotel with valet parking and a tuxedoed piano player in the bar. I stopped by his room.

Trevor's shoulder-length hair was loose and wild. He'd just woken up. His eyes were red, but he was moving and talking with intense energy. He had a group to meet at the top in less than an hour. Darting around the frilly, overdone room, he cracked a beer and offered me one. It was just after ten in the morning.

His eyes gleamed, and his movements quickened. He pulled his hair into a ponytail and whooshed out the door in front of me. Walking to the chairlift, I asked him about a new business venture he'd started with Pehota called No Wimp Tours.

The idea is to show people the real mountains, away from the lifts, he said. The title of the outfit tells you everything you need to know, eh?

His manner was wide open, as if you were welcome in his orbit and always had been. He was an invitation to adventure, his eyes promising thrilling journeys. Wild times waited just around the corner. By the time Trevor and I got to the lift, we agreed that we could help each other. He'd give me a story to tell, and I'd give him exposure for his new company. I'd join him on a five-day No Wimp Tour in the backcountry of the Coast Range in British Columbia.

We rode up the chairlift, planning the trip with building excitement. At the top, he met a group of ski-industry executives, thin-legged guys in next year's outfits. Trevor and I shook hands.

See you in Whistler this spring, he said.

I never did. Two months later Trevor's body was found in the mountains above Chamonix, his spine snapped by an avalanche. Though I'd barely known the guy, his death rattled me. The thought that such overflowing life could be so easily snuffed out left me with a profound sense of injustice and vulnerability. Now Plake had summoned up those feelings again.

You there? he asks.

Yeah, I'm here, I say.

So, Plake says, I need to see that kid again. I haven't seen him in years. We'll get him out of the park and the pipe and show him what this sport is really about. How about you call Kye and get him over to Europe with us? You want a film, that's a freakin' film, and Kye will get a chance to become a real, true skier.

The kid's gotta be, like, fifteen, I say.

It's perfect! exclaims Plake. I never heard of a fifteen-year-old skiing the big lines in Cham! And we'll get him down the run that killed Trevor. Fer sure. That's it! Call my dad and work out the details. I'll be in Europe from January on. You can meet me in France.

Plake's high-octane voice drives on. When you talk to him, you prime the pump until his engine gets running; after that, you listen to it rev. Now he's talking about France.

It's freakin' Chamonix! he exclaims, as if that explains everything, and in a way maybe it does. For serious big-mountain skiers, Chamonix's lure is undeniable. It's been called the Death Sport Capital of the World. Any number of mountains can test a skier, but none have the mythic status of Chamonix. It's Mecca and Gethsemane in one serpentine valley, a place to steal fire from the gods or get chained to a rock for eternity. The whole place is designed to usher alpinists into the high mountains so they can tempt death. And now Plake wants to bring Trevor's son there for the first time.

Can you pay Kye's expenses? Plake asks.

It's possible, I say.

Then he's there, says Plake. Trust me. This is going to be perfect. What a trippy deal getting Kye over to Cham.

He hangs up, but I can't disconnect from the idea. There's a type of narrative that, once articulated, draws you in against your better judgment. It erodes the hard foundations of logic like an underground stream. You can't control these stories. They control you. And now Plake has brought it into the light. The plot is already unfolding in my mind: A daring young man, aided by the noble elders of his tribe, faces the demon that destroyed his father and either dies or becomes a man.

It scares the hell out of me, and I know I have to do it.

I call New York, tell Tom Yellin, the president of PJ Productions, about the father-son angle, the trip to Chamonix. I talk for twenty minutes before he stops me.

Okay, you sold me, now shut up, he says. You keep selling, I'm going to wonder why you don't believe it. Write it up and send it in.

As I'm writing the proposal, my belief in the story drains away and the gravity of taking a fifteen-year-old to Chamonix fills the void. Chamonix isn't some movie backdrop. It's real and it's deadly. Official estimates vary, but most skiers and climbers who know Chamonix put the number at about sixty on-mountain deaths per year. Many more are badly injured. The idea of helping a fifteen-year-old face this mountain—the mountain that took his father's life—is terrifying. Am I really willing to risk a boy's life for the sake of a film? And what about his mother, a woman who already lost a husband to those peaks? How can I ask her to support such a scheme?

The heat of August bears down. My mind grinds through more reasons to avoid the journey. Our second child is due in March, about the time Plake wants to rendezvous in Chamonix. How can I put my own life in danger when I'm responsible for what soon will be a family of four? And what about the people I hire? Taking a New York film crew into the Alps is a dicey proposition. Sure, the New Yorkers have all skied Stowe and Vail and Whistler, but those places aren't Chamonix. And then there's the money. The expenses will be enormous, the outcome anything but assured. Even if Kye does ski well, he may not work on camera. There's a certain presence that some people have on film that can't be faked. Either you have it or you don't.

And there are other factors that are completely out of our control. We might bring Kye all the way over there and never get a chance to see the run that killed his father, much less ski it. The combination of the right snow and weather might not break for weeks or even months. I've been on film shoots where bad weather tripled the budget, and we still left empty-handed.

And what about managing the talent and crew? The skiers will pull in one direction, the New Yorkers in the other. I'll be the coupling pin between the two, each with its own agenda. The skiers will want to ski. The New Yorkers will want to *talk* about skiing. And I have both inside me: I want to ski and I want to delve into the whys of what we do, not only to share the skiing life with the world, but to justify it to a culture that considers this kind of skiing a form of lunacy. Logic tells me that Chamonix is a long shot. It's not worth the risk. You're a father now, I tell myself. You've got to make the smart call.

I call my dad to talk through the situation. He listens as I present both sides of the argument. Then, just before he asks what I think about the Boston Bruins' lineup, he says: God hates a coward, Will.

He pauses for effect—the Irish in him is undeniable—and then delivers the tag: But He also hates a damn fool.

It's a non-answer that I've heard a thousand times before. The decision is up to me. I dial Yellin again.

Forget the father-son thing, I say. It's too much money, too much of a crapshoot. We can make a history-of-skiing film with archival footage and a lot of interviews. We won't have to shoot any ski action at all. It'll be safer, cheaper, and probably give us a better, less-expensive film.

I know I'm leaning away from the abyss, but the sensible arguments are persuasive.

Sounds smart, mature, says Yellin.

It'll have a greater chance of making money, I say, knowing that money is what it all boils down to.

Write it up, he says.

Hot weeks slide by. September's cool wraps the peaks and slides slowly into the valley. I write a history of the sport from its origins in the Altai Region of Asia, through the Scandinavian period of Sondre Norheim on the Telemark Plateau, to the European expansion fueled by Matthias Zdarsky. I write about the first winter Olympics in Chamonix and the first ski films by Arnold Franck and Hannes Schneider, which starred a skiing Leni Riefenstahl, who later directed Nazi propaganda films. The narrative crawls through the migration of skiing to the Americas; Snowshoe Thompson; advancements in technique made by Dick Durrance; the films of Otto Lang; the daring ski troops of the 10th Mountain Division; and on to Sylvain Saudan, the first extreme skier. As the first snows dust the Wasatch, the pages pile up. It's not just a history, it's the genesis, the evolution of our mountain tribe.

October brings early snow and the news that Bel is carrying a boy. In celebration, we eat lamb in a restaurant with black-and-white pictures of 1950s Beirut on the walls. The wine, strong and ripe, is from Lebanon's Bekaa Valley, a place I fell in love with while shooting my television pilot there. The owner of the café, a Beirut native, congratulates us. A son! The wine's on him.

Later, at home, the phone rings. It's the middle of the night. My brother's name is on the caller ID. He never calls in the middle of the night.

Who died? I ask.

Mom, says my brother.

I fall to the floor.

The story of her death unfolds later. My mother, Elaine Kerig, was seventy and just finishing a trip down the Danube River. She was fragile when she set out weeks before, but her physical strength could not match her faith, her lack of fear. Although the days of traveling wore her down, she had no intention of going home until she had completed the journey.

It was the last day of her trip. She was in Budapest, bags packed, hours away from getting on a plane to Boston. My father was at home, madly cleaning the house so it would be up to her standards when she arrived. In Budapest, Mom turned to her friend and said, I'm so glad we came. And then she collapsed. The cause of death was never made clear. The authorities in Budapest were difficult, their system obtuse; they cremated her body.

I fly home to Boston to be with my father and family. My wife and daughter come a few days later. We stay a month. Grace turns two and I sell the option to my film treatment to PJ Productions. Just as I'd hoped, the company hires me to write, produce and direct. The money is significant and could be enough to fund a move away from Meth Boy.

It takes weeks to get my mother's ashes home from Hungary. Her wake is teary and crowded, suffused with the smell of candle wax and cough drops. It's November 2nd, election night. At home, funeral suit still on, I watch Peter Jennings, my new boss, announce the result of a presidential contest that seems to be taking place in some parallel universe. His tone is measured and reassuring. Media types call it voice-of-God authority. My mother, the cornerstone of our family, is suddenly gone, and now I'm working for the voice of God.

The western sun presses down, clear and coldly comforting. It's winter, and I'm back in Utah. The chilling East and the deathly heat of a Utah August are memories. On backcountry skis, I'm climbing new snow toward Cardiff Peak, across the road from the Alta Ski Area. The air is still. I hear the creak and clack of my touring bindings, which have a heel-piece that can be unlocked for the climb up and clamped down for an alpine descent. The bindings' creak, regular as a metronome, mixes with reggae music rising on a gentle wind from the Collins chairlift across the road. Simple sounds welcome you home.

This south-facing slope is where I go for answers. The ascent is the emptying time. My climbing skins, which are affixed to the bottom of my skis to prevent them from slipping backwards on the climb, are old and worn. To keep from backsliding, I muscle each pole plant. It's not the best way to climb a hill, but I'm not looking for easy. My backpack pulls evenly on my shoulders; the chest and waist straps, so familiar, hold me in. I'm following a trail broken by earlier skiers. The straight uphill track fills me with a sense of simple purpose: Up. I climb through six, eight inches of new snow, not enough for bottomless turns but enough to provide float, which is what I want.

My breath finds its rhythm at the start of a sustained rise. There are wind waves and curlicue furrows in the sawdust snow. Tiny ermine tracks traverse the slope and disappear into the purple-blue shadow of a tree well. In the sky above me is a red-tailed hawk. Up here, all else falls away.

The track ascends a spine where the wind has scoured the surface snow, revealing a scabby sun-crust underneath. My skis slip on the icy snow. Leaning harder into my poles, I grind over the crest. A north wind slams into me. The cold is immediate, painful and welcome.

I lower my glasses, and the fogged lenses freeze over. Through them the world is a gray-white blur. I push harder to get over the spine. As I slide down, in the low, lunging telemark position with one foot in front of the other, my lenses clear and the wind lulls. There's one more pitch to the ridge. I find my stride again, letting go and opening up on the final rise. The vacuum of my mother's death is a hollow pain deep in my gut. I clamp down on it, keeping my rhythm steady now, ascending in kicking glides.

Wind lashes the crest. Gloves in my teeth, hands moving by rote, I stretch the rubber on the climbing skins, unclip the tips, and peel each skin down. The wind snatches away the ripping sound of adhesive pulling away from the ski. I struggle to fold the skins in the wind and stow them in my pack. Clipping the heel of my binding down, snapping the buckle on the back of the boot to change from walk to ski mode, I cinch the power strap tightly across my shin. Wrenching each buckle tight, and then tighter still, my feet take on an almost painful feeling of power. There's satisfaction in these acts, a ritual of preparation.

Looping pole straps over wrists, gripping tightly, I lower fresh goggles over my eyes and inch slowly out onto the slope. Moving across the fall line, I flex my knees, bouncing as I slide, testing the stability of the snow. Nothing moves. Solid. Or solid enough.

Pointing ski tips at the valley floor, I give over to gravity. Plummeting, my skis run 11-straight, tearing through the crust. Wind presses into me, and I feel my own outline, know exactly where I begin and end. This is the perfect moment. I have yet to give in to the need for control.

I drive low and hard through the first turn. My skis rip the windcrust snow; dinner-plate shards crackle over my kneecaps and tumble past my thighs. There's no way to ski this snow slowly. Momentum is the key. Stay centered and blast the breakable crust. Great plumes of snow roil behind me. I ramp over a knoll, my skis drifting through the air, readying for touchdown. Rocking back, I land on my heels. The crust nearly stops my momentum, forcing me to take a bow.

And so it goes, on down the plunging field. All doubt disappears. I know where I am and what I'm doing. For the moment, everything makes perfect sense. This is the gift of the mountains.

The slope runs out too soon. At the trailhead, I see the simple white cross of Our Lady of the Snows Chapel. Stopping at the edge of the road, I look back to the top of the ridge where my track is alone on the headwall. The wind is already erasing the mark I've made. Such ephemeral beauty, such a sublime, pointless exercise. I've climbed a hill and skied it without a single witness. In half an hour, all evidence of my presence will be gone. The only difference this ski run has made is inside me. I feel clear. Clear enough to see that I am grieving for something more than my mother's passing.

I've brought my film project to life, but what kind of life? A safe one? A profitable one? Ten years ago, when I lived in ski towns and surrounded myself with skiers, I didn't think about profits, and I didn't shy away from risk. In the ski world, the question is not whether you take risks but whether you accept responsibility for the consequences. Sitting on the tailgate of my truck, jacket off, steam rising from my sweat-soaked shirt, I accept responsibility for wanting to make a film that gets it right—for myself, the sport, and the people in it. But I've let fear get the better of me.

I kick off my boots and dangle my legs from the tailgate. I know that the right film, a film that matches the vitality of its subject, doesn't provide an objective commentary from a safe distance. It doesn't hide in the skirts of history. And yet that's the film I've agreed to make.

Yeah, I'm grieving for my mother's death, but I'm also mourning the loss of my own nerve. As I climb behind the wheel of my old truck, I know I've surrendered something that should never be given away freely. I can shoulder the responsibility of bringing a young man to a dangerous place, but I can't accept the soul-draining knowledge that I surrendered to a fear of failure. Driving through the curves of Little Cottonwood Canyon, I pick up my cell phone and call New York. Yellin answers, and I tell him I've changed my mind.

We've got to try to tell the Kye and Trevor story, I say. We need to go to Chamonix.

Okay, he says, after a moment. Maybe we do, but first we go see the kid.

Kye

Whistler, British Columbia
December 2004

As I turn the rental car into a resort-subsidized housing development near Whistler, British Columbia, Yellin quizzes me again on whether Kye Petersen is really good enough to ski Chamonix. I've made some calls, I say. If we can set him up with guides and mentors over there, he should be okay.

You think that or you know it?

I don't know about skiing the *couloir* that killed his father, I say, using the French word for a large mountain chute. There seems to be some question about his emotional stability.

That's redundant, says Yellin. He's a teenager.

We'll ski with him, I say. I'll be able to tell.

For Kye and other skiers of his talent, skiing is a medium that transcends language. Even if he wants to hide himself, his skiing will tell me all I need to know. Skiing pits fear against faith. It reveals a person's inner strengths and weaknesses. A lifelong skier can read turning styles and techniques like a memoir.

Yellin doesn't read skiers, but he knows a good story when he hears one. During his thirty-year career, he's killed thousands of projects and accepted only a relative few. He and I met a decade ago while skiing at Vail. We've since skied together many times, but this trip is different. He's here to see if I can deliver, and if it's possible to build a multimillion-dollar narrative around a fifteen-year-old kid. In moments, Kye and I will both be on stage before a critical audience of one, but only I know the stakes.

Walking through a parking lot filled with Subarus, 4Runners and pickup trucks with snowmobiles in the back, Yellin's gaze sweeps over the balconies of the three-story condos crammed with mountain bikes, skis, snowboards and baby strollers. Water drips at the corners of the buildings. There's a light breath of wind. A ninety-pound malamute announces our arrival.

I've tried to talk to Kye on the phone, without success. He's evasive, given to one-word answers, but his story resonates with possibilities. Not only was his father a famous skier, at fifteen Kye is already making a living as a professional skier. Coming of age early, he's begun the process of leaving his mother's world in favor of the traveling troupe of skiers who chase storms and fame through the high mountains.

Up a few steps and after a quick knock, we're through an unlocked door. Snow boots and skateboard sneakers clutter a narrow foyer. Jackets hang on fat wooden pegs. Skis lean in the corner. We enter a kitchen with bottles of homemade wine on the top of the fridge, family pictures stuck to it with magnets from food delivery services. There's a dining room table of heavy oak, fat candles, and a well-used couch beneath a large framed photo of a sheer Alaskan peak.

Reclining on the couch, shirtless and bone thin, is Kye Petersen. His skin is pale and hairless. His bones look fragile, his frame slight. The potential star of our film says, Whassup, so unimpressed that he doesn't bother getting off the couch. He's barefoot, wearing a wool ski cap and a pair of sweatpants, watching a black-and-white movie on an old television.

I glance at Yellin. He's composed, blank, waiting.

I'm struck by how small Kye is. He's fifteen but looks twelve. His face is smooth, untroubled by whiskers or acne. We shake hands over the back of the couch. Yellin gives Kye a straight handshake—two times up, two times down. I fumble through an awkward transgenerational shake. There's the straight hand clasp, then the thumb hook, the finger claw and the knuckle knock, which I make a mess of.

Whatcha watching? I ask.

Dunno, some movie, says Kye.

Your mom tell you we were coming? asks Yellin, watching Kye closely.

Yeah. She's taking my sister to the hill, says Kye, turning to the television again. She should be back.

Yellin gives me a look that's opaque, but he's clearly not amused.

Under the stairs, taped to the wall, are two large pieces of poster board covered with black and red marker. At the top it reads: *Ma Rules ... no questions asked.* In a numbered list, the poster outlines rules concerning homework *(complete before play)*, curfew *(be home on time)*, bedtime and chores. The final entry reads: *No hitting.*

No hitting? That's something I've been working on with my two-year-old daughter. And this is the young man we're going to take to the Death Sport Capital of the World?

In the right margin of the poster are bullet points:

- *Help your mother, she loves you.*
- *Have good manners and be polite.*
- *Be nice to your friends and others, you never know when you may need them.*
- *Value what you have now, you may not have it tomorrow.*
- *Look to the future, live the present.*

Kye catches me staring at the poster. Our eyes meet, and I'm jarred by the intensity of his stare, the strength I read in his eyes. I'm happy to find it there—I want him to be strong-willed, driven—but there's fight there, too, anger.

He stares without blinking. I stare back. I want him to get the hell up off the couch, to let him know that this may be his big chance. But he must know that. I'd covered that much over the phone. So why the disinterested slacker pose?

How's the skiing? I ask.

You don't wanna know, he says, waving out the window at the cloudless sky, another day of sun and no snow. He shakes his head as he turns back to the TV.

Rock skis? I ask.

Rock skis with edges.

We'll make it a short day, says Yellin.

Wanted to, but I don't have any skis, says Kye.

What about those in the corner?

Kye stands to take a look. He takes his cap off, shakes his head and lets his long hair spill out. Hanging past his shoulders, halfway down his back, his hair is luminous and flowing. I'm seeing Trevor, remembering him in the film *Carving the White*, the ponytail waving like a flag. Kye is a mini Trevor. It's unnerving.

Those are my park skis, says Kye, putting his hat back on. The edges are all railed.

I think of translating for Yellin. *Railed* means dulled by sliding on the steel rails in the terrain park, an on-mountain playground similar to a skateboard park. But that'll just make us look dumb. Not that it matters. Kye could've been describing us, dull and without edge. That's how we look to this ski-town teenager. A forty- and a fifty-year-old. Ancients on the playground.

My mom let my sister take my good skis, says Kye.

Kye, put on your shirt, scolds a woman's voice. Tanya Reck-Petersen, Trevor's woman and Kye's mother, moves into the apartment with the hard, lean grace of an athlete. These guys have come all this way to see you.

Why'd you let Neve take my skis? Kye barks.

Kye, you have plenty of skis and she—

Not with edges.

Tanya tosses Kye a shirt and herds us away from him to the kitchen table where there's a pile of magazines and pictures on top of a large black portfolio.

I pulled these out to show you guys, she says. They're all shots of Trevor.

She unzips the portfolio case and begins flipping through published photographs. Trevor on the covers of *Powder* and *Skiing* magazine. Here he is on the cover of a Japanese magazine, here on a Swedish one. Trevor in Alaska. Trevor in Iceland. France. Kye puts on his shirt and walks over to us. His mother makes room at the table.

These are rad, he says. I've never seen these.

You've never seen these shots of your dad? I ask.

Oh, you have too, Kye, says Tanya. I showed them to you a long time ago.

You never showed me these, he says. Never.

Maybe not for a while, but I … Oh, come on, Kye.

I ask about the framed photograph of the Alaskan peak that hangs on the wall and seems to preside over the room.

That's Pontoon, says Tanya. It's in the Chugach, in Alaska.

Trevor was the first to ski that, says Kye.

Is that something you'd like to ski? I ask Kye, interviewing him for the sake of Yellin.

Kye gives me a look that says, you're a skier, you know the answer to that, why the hell are you asking stupid questions? But he doesn't say any of that, he just says, Someday.

An awkward pause fills the small room.

How about we head up on the hill? I say.

Have a good time, says Kye to his mother.

Kye, you're going up—

You go up there on dull skis and see.

Kye—

I'm not going, he says, as he pushes past us and goes up the stairs of the condo.

I'm sorry, says Tanya. He's just mad at me.

It happens, says Yellin with a diplomatic smile. I have teenagers, I know.

Maybe you can talk to him, Tanya says, suddenly turning to me, angling her chin toward the stairs.

I climb the stairs slowly, smelling the springlike day out an open window. I'd expected to find a kid who would love to be in a big film about skiing and a mother who's reluctant to let her kid go. But Mom's helpful and the kid is difficult. It doesn't figure. Kye has arranged his life around the sport. He doesn't go to school in winter so that he can ski. The little schoolwork he manages to do is in summer. There will probably be no college for Kye, no advanced degrees. He's already traded all that for a life of skiing. Skiing in photo shoots and films. Sponsors give him gear and money to get exposure for their products. He should be thrilled to have a shot at appearing in a wide-release ski film.

The drywall on the stairway is patched in places. The repaired holes are about the size of a fist. I stop at the door to Kye's room. Amid posters of skiers and rock stars, Kye taps at his laptop, sending an instant message to someone. His back is to me, but I can tell he knows I'm there. On the wall is a large promotional poster for Quiksilver, a brand of surfing and winter apparel. It's an airbrushed rendering of a tiny surfer on a massive wave. At the bottom of the poster, in mod 1970s lettering, is a name: Eddie Aikau. In the top left corner it reads *Eddie Would Go.*

You've got Eddie up there, I say. He was the man.

Kye turns and looks at me, then the poster, then back at his computer.

Yeah, that came from my dad. He was a big fan.

Me too, I say.

Eddie Aikau was a Hawaiian big-wave surfer and Waimea Bay life-guard. Though there were other surfers who could ride Waimea's monster waves, Eddie was a waterman, a designation reserved for a select few who possess a mastery of swimming, sailing and paddling as well as surfing. He was also one of the most widely liked people in the sport. In 1978, he was part of an ill-fated outrigger canoe trip. In the middle of the night the canoe was swamped and overturned. Eddie volunteered to paddle a surfboard to go for help. His body was never found. He was thirty-one years old.

After he died, *Eddie Would Go* became a catchphrase in the surfing world. Uttered in the face of giant waves, the pithy slogan was a reminder that life is short, filled with questions for which courage and daring are the right answers. In the beginning, just uttering those words gave you beach cred. But as time passed and stickers and T-shirts proliferated, the slogan took on the hollow ring of status seekers or, worse, marketing hype.

My dad rode for Quiksilver too, explains Kye, meaning that his father was also sponsored by the company. So after Eddie died he got all the *Eddie Would Go* stickers. That's where they got the idea for *Trevor Would Do It.*

After Trevor died, his two brothers printed stickers that read *Trevor Would Do It.* The stickers soon were all over ski towns. You'd see them on skis, truck bumpers, coffee cups and beer mugs from Whistler and Jackson Hole to Chamonix.

On the wall facing the Eddie poster is a poster of Trevor soaring off a cliff. It's taken from below, chunks of brilliant snow exploding against a purple-blue sky. He's wearing yellow pants and a red jacket, hands pressed forward, looking straight into the lens, grimacing. The caption reads, *What is altitude without attitude?*

I remember those years, I say to Kye.

He looks up, nodding, his eyes calmer now.

Yeah, that poster's the full-on, old-school poser shot. I try to do that one sometimes.

Everybody tried to do that one, I say. Your dad was one of the best.

I know, he says curtly.

I skied in one of the films he was in, I say.

Yeah, which one? Kye asks, the challenge apparent in his voice.

Carving the White, I say. I'm in the mogul sequence in Taos.

Kye turns from his small desk and the white laptop. He looks at me closer. Perhaps he's playing the moment, or playing me. Taking my measure. Then he seems to make a decision. He's in motion, striding across the room and grabbing two framed photos off the top of his bureau. He steps toward me, offering them.

These are my favorite ones, he says.

I step into the room, taking the photos of his father from his hands. The first one is dominated by a large black rock that juts into the frame like the chiseled bust of some giant, primitive statue, pushing out the pale blue sky behind it. Skiing off the end of the rock is a small figure of a man.

This is what I love doing. Exactly what my dad does, says Kye.

I take note of the present tense, wondering if it is a grammatical error or something more: A boy who can't accept his father's absence? An abiding faith in an afterlife of bottomless powder and eternal airtime?

This one is on Blackcomb, continues Kye, right by the Blackcomb Glacier. That's a sweet cliff he's about to air off right there.

Pretty big, I say. How big would you guess?

I'd say he's going to go about sixty feet, Kye says proudly.

Kye hands me another framed photo and snatches the others out of my hands. He's suddenly moving and talking very quickly, like a kid who's got too much story to tell and not enough time to tell it.

And this one is a shot of him skateboarding at the skate park a long time ago, he says. He broke his arm there.

The photo features a lean, shirtless man skateboarding in dark sunglasses, seemingly pinned to the top lip of a graffiti-covered wall. He is crouched on his board, leading with his arm, which is in a light-green cast. His other hand is grabbing the downhill rail of his skateboard. A dark ponytail flies behind him.

I always go there, says Kye. I was there every day this summer. Right there at that skate park.

Here's another one of my dad, Kye says, handing me a photograph of Trevor with a two-week growth of beard covered with ice. In it he is grimacing, as if frozen, his hair encrusted with ice crystals. He wears round, mad-scientist Oakley sunglasses.

That's for an Oakley ad he did, says Kye. They put him in a freezer for it.

In the shot, Trevor's skin is white as a corpse.

And here's this funny picture of me right here, says Kye, showing me another one. I'm wearing all my dad's gear.

I look at the shot and my heart recoils. A small, tow-headed boy stands with a thick coil of golden climbing rope slung across his chest. He's wearing Trevor's white climbing helmet and a climbing harness with a massive rack of carabiners and ice screws that pull it to the ground. Kye's fists are clenched, jaw jutting forward, a pantomime of a tough mountaineer. The boy is happy, confident, already becoming his father, or what he thinks of as dad—a steely ski mountaineer who's afraid of nothing.

Yeah, it's a sweet picture, huh? asks Kye.

Sweet, I say. How old were you when this was taken?

I was five. I've got my Power Rangers shirt on underneath.

I nod slowly, doing the math. The photo was taken less than a year before his father lost his life to the mountains. I picture a photograph of my daughter wearing her Hello Kitty T-shirt and my Red Sox cap—a cute picture, unless dad is dead. Then it's something else.

And here's my dad's ice ax, Kye continues.

The tool is blue-handled, chipped and dusty.

Do you know how to use that thing? I ask.

No, I never actually climb ice. I will, though. I need to get some crampons and learn how to climb.

I hold the ice ax. The aluminum is cold, somehow colder than the room.

And this is a poster of Everest, Kye says, pointing to a National Geographic poster that's partially obstructed by his bureau. Kye reaches behind the bureau and pulls another poster out.

And here's a project I did in a grade-four science fair. It's on avalanches.

On the brown placard are diagrams of the way an avalanche works. Magic Marker arrows represent the forces that cause the deadly slides. I look at the date, 1999, three years after Trevor died. I picture a nine-year-old school kid using a science project to come to grips with his father's baffling death.

On another wall is a poster of Canadian freestyle skier Mike Douglas. It's signed: *To Kye, the hottest 10-year-old skier in the world. Always Have Fun!*

The hottest ten-year-old skier in the world, I read aloud.

Yeah, pretty big praise, says Kye, laughing.

Here's a book from Dominique Perret, says Kye. He's a big-mountain skier who was just before my dad's time.

Yeah, I know Dominique.

You actually *know* him?

I wrote a story about him once.

Right on. Was he cool?

Yeah, very passionate. A great skier. One of the strongest you'll ever see.

He gave this book to my dad.

He opens the front cover to where Perret signed it:

> *For Trevor!*
> *Hope to share some more turns and snowy days with you. En route*
> *des de Needle. Adventure, adventure!*
> *Dominique.*
> *Chamonix, Feb. '96*

I look at the date and a tingle runs up my neck. *En route des de Needle*, he wrote, referring no doubt to the Aiguille du Midi, where Trevor lost his life. Then there's the place and time: Chamonix, 1996. Trevor was only in Chamonix for two days before he died. Perret had to have signed this the day before Trevor was killed.

Kye's eyes meet mine. I try to close down, to become an objective reporter, a world-weary documentarian, but I can't get all the way there. What comes through is empathy. Kye registers this and rears back, suddenly embarrassed to have revealed so much. His face closes down, his eyes glazing in teenage-slacker style. He pulls a thick, hooded sweatshirt on. The show is over.

So, it's pretty sketchy up there on the hill? I ask.

We haven't had snow in, like, forever, says Kye. It pretty much sucks.

So maybe you could just take a couple runs with this guy I brought from New York.

Kye pulls the hood of his sweatshirt up and over his head. Piercing eyes stare out from the shadow of the hood. A wired, five-foot monk.

Look, I'd go if I had skis, says Kye.

Ski on mine. The edges are razor. What size is your foot?

What kind of skis?

The new Monsters, I answer.

Head? I can only ski on Rossi, he says.

Kye is sponsored by Rossignol skis, along with Oakley eyewear and Leki poles, just like his father was. Each agreement pays him a small retainer, plus bonuses for appearing in magazines and films. The deals are exclusive. No using a competitor's product, not for one run, not to please a couple of ancients, not ever.

Look, there's this lady coming to see you, I say. She's the wife of Peter Jennings.

You mean Chrzanowski? he asks, mentioning the name of Canadian filmmaker Peter Chrzanowski.

Jennings, I say. The anchorman. TV news guy.

Oh yeah, him, says Kye, patronizing me, clearly not knowing or caring who I'm talking about.

He's on ABC every night, I say. He's a big deal, like, one of the most famous guys on TV.

Right on, says Kye, unimpressed.

And he's Canadian.

Oh, that's cool, says Kye.

Anyway, he has this company that makes really high-level documentary films, and they want to do one on skiing. I've told them that you might be a really good guy to have in it.

Thank you, he says, surprising me with his sudden formality.

I want this to be the best film ever made about skiing. No shit.

All right.

And we're going to be filming in Europe. Plake and some other guys. We're going to meet in Chamonix in March.

That's cool, he says, staring at me evenly with no apparent reaction to Chamonix. And for a fleeting second I realize he's assumed the detached demeanor of the professional and I'm the emotional amateur.

I take a deep breath, look around Kye's room and realize I have no right to be here. His father should be here, but he's not and I am, and there's a question on the tip of my tongue. It's *the* question, but the implications of asking it leave me momentarily speechless. Silence erupts like gushing water.

Look, Kye, if you're up for joining us in Chamonix, I say, I can probably make it happen.

All right, he says evenly, completely without emotion.

We'd film you there, I continue. But this will be different from the films you're normally in.

Different how?

Different because you're on your own. It's not like we go out and find jumps and cliffs and show you where we want you to jump. When you're there, you just do what you're gonna do and we follow you with cameras. That and a few interviews.

I'm pretty used to cameras.

I know. That's good. But if you want me to try to make it happen, I need you to do something.

I'm not skiing today, he says. I'm going over to my friend's house.

You don't have to ski. Just come meet Peter's wife. Her name is Kayce, and she's one of the decision makers. To squeeze you into her schedule, she's flown to Vancouver and is driving all the way up here to spend one hour with you before she has to turn back around and catch a plane home to New York.

Right, he says. I gotta get over to my friend's house. I'll catch you later.

Tanya Reck-Petersen skis like someone who's done the work and used to care a lot about it. She's wild and ragged but strong on her skis and fast down the hill. We've been skiing for a couple of hours, during which time she's apologized repeatedly for Kye's absence. And every time she says it, I want to ask her why she gave his skis to his sister. Why on this day? Is she trying to work against us? Is she trying to foil her son's chance to be in this film?

Not overtly, I decide, but it would come as no surprise if she's cooperating fully *and* working just as hard to sabotage the endeavor—as if she desperately wants her son both to go to Chamonix and not to go to Chamonix, ever, under any circumstances. She slaloms rocks and shrubs as she leads Yellin and me to the base of the mountain. Whistler, which normally piles more than thirty feet of snow onto its two huge mountains, is having the worst season in its history.

Sunlight slants through towering trees. A lift operator pulls an orange ribbon across the chairlift maze. Closed for the day. We're slated to leave Whistler in a few hours. I won't get to see Kye ski, won't learn what I need to know. He's showed me what he wanted to show of himself and his relationship with his father but denied me the chance to evaluate him in the way that would have been most revealing.

Après-ski tourists clog a deck warmed by the last rays of sunshine. Tanya leads us past them into Merlin's, an airy bar that smells of fried food, cigarette smoke and sunblock. Skiers drink pints of strong beer and eat deep-fried cheese sticks around high, round tables. Eighties party music plays. Televisions loop ski movies. No one ever dies in ski movies. They live on forever in ski-town bars.

See the shot of Trev? Tanya asks.

A nearly life-size ski poster of Trevor Petersen hangs in a prized spot above the pinball machine at the end of the bar. In the shot, he's flying sideways through the air, his tips crossed, his arms reaching toward the landing. His ponytail flies behind him, fanning out and catching the light like a flame. His facial expression is one of controlled confidence.

I guess no one is going to forget him in here, says Yellin as he hands a waitress a credit card to open a tab.

Yellin's casing the place, watching Tanya, watching me. Kye is late. I have no idea if he's coming. Neither does Tanya, who nervously drains her second pint.

He's just at that difficult age, she says, but I know he'd be stoked to ski in a documentary that's got Plake and Anselme and all the gurus of the sport.

Now Yellin is clearing his throat.

I know that Bill has talked to you about this before, he says softly, but what do you think about the idea of us possibly filming Kye over in Europe?

You mean Chamonix, right?

Probably, I say.

I'm nervous about it, she says. He's going to go there. He has to go there. I mean he *is* his father's son, and how am I going to stop that? Sooner or later he's going to Cham. Trevor had to go there. That's all he talked about since I first met him. And I know you guys will be more careful than the guys he usually shoots with.

We shoot documentaries, says Yellin, which means we just shoot what's happening. We don't ask anyone to do anything they're not already doing. That includes anything that happens on the mountain. And anyway, we always, always, err on the side of caution.

They're super careful, I say.

Had Kye really not seen those pictures of his dad? Yellin asks.

I catch his eye. He's watching her closely without appearing to. He has a relaxed face that almost, but not quite, hides quick, calculating eyes.

Tanya takes a long pull off her pint.

You know, I never tried to make him into his dad, she says finally. I only wanted him to know about his dad, what his dad's beliefs were. That's all I can give him. But I know how much he's got in there already.

There's definitely a part of Trevor in there.

And everyone wants to somehow keep a piece of that, I say.

Because he's like his dad, he won't do it that way, says Tanya. If you try to push him, he won't go. After Trev died, Kye became a snowboarder because everyone wanted him to be a skier like his dad. As soon as they let up and realized that he was a snowboarder, he stopped snowboarding and became a skier.

Kayce Freed, Peter Jennings' wife, strides through the door. Forcefully pretty, she wears high-heeled boots and a look of happy anticipation. She's enjoyed the scenery during the winding ride up to the mountains, she says, and only wishes she had more time to spend in this beautiful place. But wait a minute, where's the kid?

Peter's production company has purchased my treatment and retained me, but it has no obligation to make a film. Kayce's recommendation will help Peter decide whether to go forward or not. I like Kayce. We get along, but that doesn't matter. Kayce and Yellin are in the intimate business of selling stories, and I'm an outsider. I don't live on New York's Upper West Side, I live in the West. By dint of geography, my judgment is in question. Currently, I'm proving my ineptitude by failing to produce young Kye at the appointed hour.

Hey, Kye, calls Tanya. Over here.

To my amazement Kye bounds through the doorway, a slight kid in a pale-blue zippered turtleneck. He actually trots over to our table.

Sorry I'm late, he says breathlessly. You must be Kayce. I'm really glad to meet you.

He extends a hand.

Over the turtleneck Kye wears a hooded parka with fake fur on the trim, an ironic throwback lately favored by the young and rebellious, though at the moment his demeanor is anything but rebellious. Upright, shoulders back, chin up, suddenly he's as well-mannered as an English schoolboy. Respectfully attentive, he gives a cute grin as Kayce takes his hand with a wide smile. He's charmed her already. Tanya orders her son a Coke as he sits on a stool next to Kayce and rests his elbows on the table.

So, Kye, how was the skiing today? Kayce asks.

I didn't go, he says simply. He glances past her, past me, to a TV monitor. And if his simple declaration doesn't assert his control, his casual dismissal of the whole idea does.

Kayce turns to me with a questioning look.

He didn't have the right skis, I say.

I gave them to his sister to use, says Tanya.

We went up, and he didn't miss anything, says Yellin.

We need snow, explains Tanya.

Right, says Kayce, picking up on something that draws the lines of her mouth taut. Maybe I could have a glass of white wine, she says to the waitress, who's just arrived.

That's a friend of mine, Kye says to Kayce as the waitress walks away. He points at the TV monitor. That's Tanner, he says.

Kayce looks up in time to see a small skier fly off a very big jump. He spins and twists crazily through the air. Skis twirl, poles whip out to the side with centrifugal force.

Cork seven, says Kye identifying the trick. I can do those.

How do you know where you are in the air? Kayce asks, turning her shoulders to face the young man.

You just know after a while, says Kye with a shrug. You want me to teach you?

Kye grins broadly, and Kayce laughs. Yellin shakes his head. You never can tell. Kayce's wine arrives. Tanya points out the poster of Trevor. I quote a story that *Sports Illustrated* just published about Kye under the title "Here Comes the Son." Kayce soaks it all in, then jumps way ahead of all of us.

So, Kye, you're interested in skiing in Europe?

All conversation stops. I shoot a look at Yellin, listening through the barroom music for Kye's answer. Yellin's face is blank, and then a small smile forms. He's enjoying this, enjoying watching me jump, trying to figure out a teenager. Tanya leans in visibly. For a long moment, Kye's eyes are glued to the television monitor. He seems not to have heard the question.

Yeah, he says finally. I think I'm going to be over there to ski for Oakley.

I look to Tanya. This is news to her too, but she's not making it an issue right now.

Yeah, Oakley's doing a film there that I'm going to ski in, Kye continues, now lowering his gaze to Kayce. It will be my first trip to Europe. I'm super stoked.

So we could probably work out a time for you to meet us? I ask, playing my part, doing my job.

Sure, says Kye. If it's okay with my mom.

What? I want to say. Now you're asking her for permission? Where'd the petulant, shirtless teen go?

We've been talking, Tanya says to Kye. These guys are going to be safe. It's okay with me.

Tanya steps over and lays an arm around her son's shoulder. He smiles up at her as if to say, it's all good.

Yellin pulls me aside, away from the table and over to the bar. A hand on my shoulder, he speaks close to my ear to be heard above the music but not by the people at our table. He's perfect, says Yellin. I like him. This actually might work.

Never had a doubt, I say.

chapter 3

Jennings

New York City
February 2005

A dusty wind follows us from Central Park West into a small, overheated lobby. My face is flushed, boots squeaking on the shiny floor. A doorman scowls.

Tom Yellin, Bill Kerig and Brian Beck to see Peter Jennings, says Yellin.

Brian Beck is a friend and former ski jumper I know from Utah. I've asked him to help raise money for the film and for months we've used Snowbird's aerial tram to hone our pitch. With more passionate skiers per square foot than any place in North America, the tram's seven-minute ride has provided a captive audience. Much as Internet entrepreneurs practice elevator pitches, we've spent weeks polishing our tram talk. My deal with Jennings requires us to raise millions for the film, and Brian and his family have been instrumental in the effort. One brother, a passionate Montana skier, wrote the first check. Another brother referred us to his former boss and mentor, an expatriate Brit who ended up writing an even larger check. It's nice to have family; nicer still to have one that supports you.

We had been planning our Chamonix trip for weeks when Yellin phoned.

You're having dinner with Peter tomorrow night, he said. He wants to meet you before giving a final green light to the film.

We don't have a green light? I asked, reminding Yellin that we already had hotel reservations and airline tickets in hand.

Peter's agreed to do the film, says Yellin. He just needs to put his stamp of approval on the thing.

You mean his stamp of approval on me.

Pretty much, yeah.

So if he doesn't like what I'm selling, the film is off? I ask.

No, the film is happening, says Yellin. We're spending money already.

But maybe I'm not happening? I ask. By selling the rights to Jennings' company and entering into a work-for-hire agreement, I'd given Yellin or Jennings the right to fire me at any time.

No, it won't be like that, he says. Probably not, anyway. Don't worry. Just get a flight and get in here in time for dinner. We're eating at his apartment. Meet me at our office and we'll go over together.

How about I bring Brian, I say.

That's a good idea. He's raising the money, and Peter hasn't met him. Yeah, strength in numbers is good. Bring him.

Straight up, I say, is Peter going to fire me off my own project?

No, no, it's nothing like that, says Yellin, but do me a favor and don't refer to it as *your* project when we're with Peter.

Sign in, please, says the doorman in an ivory alcove. He's wedged into a small space, trapped behind a half-door.

We sign a gilt-edged ledger. A plastic pass is handed to Yellin.

The elevator operator takes the pass, and we rise in a small, wood-paneled box. It smells like lemons. A polished brass panel around the elevator buttons reflects a pinched face. Mine.

Relax, Tom says, talking as if the elevator operator weren't there. Peter probably won't be hard on you. He'll just see you as a skier. He'll ask me all the tough questions.

I nod, the face in the brass panel reflecting relief. Peter has a reputation. He demands much from his associates. Yellin has worked with him for fifteen years, won all the important awards, but is never above cross-examination. Peter, of course, can cross-examine with the best of them. I'm glad I'll be playing the supporting role in the cross-examination scene.

Kayce opens the door.

Long way from the tram, aren't you guys? she asks.

We step into a wide, woody apartment, hugs and smiles all around. It's a worldly space, filled with books and photographs, tribal masks and trinkets—small things from faraway places. The ceiling is high; large windows let a little bit of Central Park into the room. She's amused to see the skiers in her home.

Did you get to see *The Gates?* she asks, showing us to the windows.

Below, past the streaming headlights, stretched out across the park, are the saffron banners of Christo's latest project. It's just opened, and the papers are full of it. From where I stand, *The Gates* is a maze, a convoluted snake of saffron hurdles. I'm thinking emperor's new clothes, but I keep that to myself.

Peter's study is a blond room with a glass desk, soft couch and coffee table. Fruit and cheese are arranged on a tray. Kayce glances quickly at a large television—still in commercial—and offers drinks. I sit at Peter's desk, rolling his swivel chair back and to the side. On the bookcase are pictures of Peter and his family in various foreign locales but none of Peter on skis.

No skiing shots of Peter, I say to Yellin.

Guess not, but he really does ski beautifully.

Kayce reappears with wine, and Brian tries to make small talk. The opening strains of the *World News Tonight* theme hushes the conversation. No matter where she is or what she's doing, Kayce watches Peter's broadcast every night. At Snowbird, I watched her run across a snow-covered slope in ski boots to get back to her hotel room in time to watch her husband tell the world the news of the day. A great wife may be the only fan that matters.

Yellin and Kayce focus on the television. They have known each other all their lives; their fathers worked in television news together. They critique the broadcast, speaking in TV journalist shorthand as Brian and I work through the fruit and cheese. No one criticizes Peter. Peter is Peter, controlled and calm.

Half an hour later, he appears in the doorway. Tall and thin, more gaunt than on TV, he sweeps in, gives us a wave and goes down the hall to change out of his suit. In moments he's back, wearing soft, wide-wale corduroys and a cable-knit sweater.

So, you're the skiers, he says. Kayce tells me you're both really quite good.

We get down, Brian says, introducing himself and taking Peter's hand.

You're the money man, Peter says to Brian. How do you do that? How do you get people to invest?

I just tell them you're involved, says Brian.

Don't tell them that, says Peter. Tell them it's going to be a great movie that might even make money. Who *are* you taking money from?

From skiers, says Brian. There are a lot of skiers who really want to see a film like this.

And plenty of them with the money to help us make it happen, says Peter.

Brian agrees. Then Peter raises an eyebrow, a move I recognize from television. It's a signal that he's changing gears, that he's about to approach the same subject from a different angle. Here it comes, I'm thinking, the beginning of the cross-examination.

There's just one thing I need to know about this ski thing, Peter says, eyeing me intensely. He pauses and silence fills the room. I realize I'm holding my breath.

Is it too late for me to learn to ski powder? he asks.

A great exhale. Brian and I gush, no, no, no, it's never too late. Fat skis and different techniques and we'll be glad to coach you, really we will. But no, it's definitely not too late.

As it turned out, we were wrong. It was too late for Peter, but none of us could know that then.

I'm on the sofa, my spine upright, my back to Central Park. Peter's folded into an easy chair, holding the stem of a wine glass with two fingers.

So, how did you start shooting, Bill?

I shot photos for magazine stories I wrote, I say, and some video for TV shows I worked on, but I'm really not a shooter.

Peter raises an eyebrow and looks to Yellin.

I'm actually more of a writer, I add hurriedly, guiltily, though I have no reason to feel guilty.

Oh, I thought you were a shooter, he says. A writer, you say?

Now I'm defending myself, my ability to shoot, to write. I feel like I'm talking to my father, but not my own father, more of a movie father. And I'm not my father's son, I'm just Son. Another probing question knocks me back on my heels. I admit I don't know the answer. He nods gravely. Now he's a priest, and I'm in a confessional. Forgive me, Father, for I have …

I drink off the rest of my wine. I'm wired, oscillating. Peter is not firing questions at Yellin. I'm in the crosshairs.

The cook, a sporty woman in her thirties with a Down Under accent, announces dinner. We move into a dining room with avocado walls, a mahogany table and modern art, and Peter turns to me.

Bill, would you like to pick a wine for us?

I sense a trap, as if I'm being tested.

Love to, I tell him.

The cook shows me down a hall to a pantry and several racks of wine.

Nice gig, I say, hoping to make her an ally.

Most of the time, she says.

She points out the most expensive bottles. I steer away from those to a rack with the kind of wines you'd drink on a Tuesday night with colleagues from work, which is what I hope we'll soon be.

We're having tortilla soup and enchiladas, she says.

On the bottom row I find a lone Lebanese red that can stand up for itself, and I form a plan. Knowing that Peter made his career as a correspondent in Lebanon, I figure I'll present the wine and casually mention that I visited the vineyard in the Bekaa Valley during a recent trip to Lebanon. I'd refer to the famous journalist bar in Beirut's Commodore Hotel, ask his opinion of Hezbollah and Syria, compare notes on the Roman ruins at Baalbek, the temple of Bacchus, the throne of Jupiter. This shared experience, I'm sure, will afford traction in the relationship.

The cook hands me a corkscrew. I pull the cork with the confidence of a former bartender. And the damn thing crumbles. I peer in. Tiny bits of cork bob in the throat of the bottle. The cook and I strain it into a crystal decanter and taste it. It bubbles on my tongue like Cherry Coke. I watch as she pours it down the sink. With it goes my plan. I won't be talking about Lebanon, waxing worldly on the Levant. I pick an unassuming Rioja and take it to the dining room.

I present the Spanish wine without comment, and Peter nods as if to say, okay, that will do. I've dodged a bullet but missed an opportunity.

So, tell me, says Peter, as the pureed tomato soup arrives, what is this film about?

It's set in the world of big-mountain skiing, I begin, and it's about the kind of people who choose to fill up their souls, even if they have to risk everything in order to do it.

Never make it through the editing room, he says, wiping his lips with a linen napkin. What's it really about?

It's a simple question with a simple answer, but Peter delivers it with such authority that I can't keep myself from reaching.

It's about that moment when all your stars align, when your cylinders fire in sync, when you connect with something that's larger than …

Stop, he says, rolling his eyes.

It's about what you keep and what you leave behind for those who follow, I say.

That doesn't mean anything to me, he says. What's it really about?

It's about fathers and sons. Family—

He cuts me off just as I'm digging down into the truth. I want to tell him it's a documentary, and we'll find out afterwards what it's about, but he doesn't give me time for that either.

Okay, you don't know what the story is really about, he says dismissively. Why are you telling it?

Because it hasn't been told, I say, and it needs to be.

Why? Bunch of skiers suddenly need their story told? I don't see it.

I tell him about my friend, Agi Orsi, and her recent success with the films *Dogtown and Z Boys* and *Riding Giants*. I use the words nobility, respect, courage and daring, but he's not swayed.

So why don't I hire her? What's her name, Agi? Sounds like I should call her. Why do you think you're the guy to tell it?

I start to run down my résumé—downplaying my mountain life, describing in greater detail the feature film I'd written and produced, some television work—but he stops me again.

I can see that it's important to you. Why?

I stop and gather myself. I could tell him that I need a paycheck, about Meth Boy and the undercover cops, but where's the traction there? Maybe I could tell him about my new-father's interest in Kye or how my mother's death has heightened my regard for life. There are a lot of answers, but I can't find any that will play for this suddenly hostile audience of one. I'm stumped. He's derailed me expertly.

I don't know, Peter, I say. I just know that it's a story I need to tell.

What I'm asking is why you *need* to tell it, he asks. Have you thought about that?

I had. And it is a question I would continue to ask long after my dinner with Peter. A lot would happen—grave injuries, triumphs, failures, deaths—before I come to an answer.

I guess not enough, I say in surrender.

A small smile flits across Peter's lips. My eyes meet his, and something passes between us. He has affirmed his position, a status I had thought needed no affirmation. He's Peter Jennings and I most certainly am not. He's won, and I'm finished. Across the table, Brian looks concerned. He's been pitching everyone and their mothers on this film, and now it looks like the whole thing could go away. Yellin nods and smiles, a look that seems to say, you're doing fine—an assessment that is clearly incorrect. My gaze sweeps over to Kayce. She's giving Peter a look that's hard to read, but maybe, just maybe, it's saying, lighten up.

Peter's face softens, and he comes at me again from a different place. Okay, so who's in it? he asks.

Feeling like he's given me a second chance, I leap on stage again, doing impersonations of Plake and Kye, dude-speaking. My untouched soup is cleared. As the enchiladas come I'm talking Chamonix, Anselme Baud, Sylvain Saudan. I'm pitching, tap dancing, defending. My untouched enchiladas are cleared. I'm on a roll. I pause only to gulp wine between frenetic bursts of gesticulation. Key lime pie and coffee come and go.

It's actually called the Exit Couloir? Peter asks, cutting in on a torrent of Chamonix descriptors. Trevor died in the Exit Couloir?

He asks this in a way that implies I'm making something up.

Yeah, Exit Couloir, I say, stretching only a bit.

On maps its actually labeled West Couloir, but skiers commonly refer to it as the Exit. I could illuminate this fact for Peter, but now that he's connected with the irony of the Exit, that would only weaken things.

But Kye's not going to ski it, interjects Kayce. The run that killed his father.

Well, probably not, but he'll see it, I say.

That sounds weak, says Peter.

He's a kid, protests Kayce. You should see him, Peter, he's beautiful. He'll be great on camera, but he's not going to ski anything that is dangerous enough to kill him.

Well, he is a great skier, I say, not mentioning the fact that I've only seen him ski in videos. Technically, if the conditions are right, he could be capable of skiing it.

You make sure there's no pressure, Peter says to me.

I nod, taking his instruction as a confirmation of my own role in the film.

Turning to Yellin, Peter repeats himself in a deeper tone: No pressure on Kye.

Of course, Yellin says.

He does whatever he wants, continues Peter. If anyone puts any pressure—

Peter, I say, cutting him off. I won't put the kid at risk. I'm about to have a son myself.

Peter pushes back from the table, wipes his lips with a napkin, lays it in his lap, and shakes his head.

I realize I've made a mistake in mentioning my own son in the same breath as Trevor's son.

Nope. You're too close to it, Peter says. You can't be objective, so—

Now comes the part when he fires me.

No, Peter, you're wrong, I say. He's backed me to the edge of a cliff, and I'm not taking another step. I'm about to list the ways that he is wrong when I'm stopped by a grin that spreads across his face. It's a new acknowledgment, a recognition. He's found my limit, and this pleases him.

It's quite obvious, he says with quiet authority. You are too close to it. You know these people. You're friends with them. You care too much about this, and you're not going to know what's going to play with a wide audience.

That's not true, I say.

He can fire me from my own project, but I'm not going to give another inch. I reach for my wine. The glass is empty. I put it back on the table. It makes a hollow sound. Peter grins again.

So, Bill, that's where I come in, he says. I'm going to be all over you, making sure you get it right. Making sure you're going to create something that appeals to everyone, not just a bunch of skiers in a bar somewhere.

Now he's saying that he's going to work *with* me? I'm confused. He's ping-ponged my emotions back and forth, and now I don't know who scored the final point. Our eyes meet and I see something new. Something softer than before. Maybe it's empathy.

You'll do fine, he says, rising from the table, dropping his napkin on the floor and walking away from it.

Half an hour later, Brian and I are in Malachy's, an Irish bar near Peter's apartment. We're in business, Brian says, holding up a pint of black and tan. We clank glasses.

We've got a green light.

I've just ordered dinner.

Four weeks later, as I'm gripping my wife's hand in the delivery room at Cottonwood Hospital in Salt Lake City, Tanya drives Kye out of Whistler, British Columbia. As I hold my beautiful new son Liam and listen to the music of his healthy wailing, Tanya turns her car down the winding road to Vancouver. As I give my son his first bath, Tanya pulls their car off the road in Squamish and parks in front of an automotive repair shop with a billboard that reads *Pop in for some Popcorn*.

Chamonix is a long way from Whistler, too far for a mom to let her fifteen-year-old son go by himself. But there's work to do and a mortgage to pay and her daughter Neve to look after. The best Tanya can do is arrange for a chaperone. As luck would have it, Eric Iberg, a twenty-six-year-old Minnesotan with whom Kye often travels, is a filmmaker. He makes inexpensive, independent ski films. He's agreed to chaperone Kye in Europe, and I've hired him to shoot on-the-fly digital video, a backstage look at Kye's journey. It's a good fit. Iberg and Kye get along. He's cool enough to travel with Kye, yet responsible enough to please Tanya.

Waiting for Iberg to drive up from Vancouver, Tanya keeps her emotions in check by running down a list of things Kye may have forgotten.

Yeah, I've got all that, says Kye, rolling his eyes.

I can't believe you're going, she says.

It's awesome, he agrees.

Kye, this will have a lot to do with your dad, but it's also about you, yourself.

I'm not my dad, he says quickly.

You're not your dad, you're Kye, says Tanya. And it's not your dad they want out of you.

What are the chances I'll even see the run? asks Kye.

You'll definitely see it from the top of the Aiguille du Midi, says Tanya.

What are the chances of me skiing it?

There's not a chance you're going to ski that, she says. It's not something you can do on just any day of your life. That's something you have to know your shit for. Know what day it's good. Know how the snow is, all the conditions. Know what line is good. There's too much, so don't start thinking that you're going over there to ski it.

A black Ford Explorer pulls in. Iberg is at the wheel. He steps out, a digital video camera trained on mother and son. He walks with a loose bounce that pulses through his billowing, hip-hop clothes. He wears a ball cap canted sideways.

Kye gets out of the car. He wears a dun-colored Oakley hooded sweatshirt, Oakley sweatpants and an Oakley T-shirt. He wears a black, knit Oakley cap and wide unlaced sneakers. Those are Oakley too. Tanya is in a white Oakley ski jacket. Kye's sponsors have been very forthcoming with the product.

Tanya comes around the car and Kye moves into his mother's arms. Camera or not, there's no holding back, no chilled-out detachment. Kye clasps his mother tightly. Tanya rubs his back, patting it lightly, comforting him. She can feel his fear. She's trying to hide her own.

Bye. See you, have a good trip, all right? she says. You be careful and play safe and have fun.

She tells him to make sure to get in touch with some other Whistlerites who are going to be in Chamonix while he's there. He agrees to call them. She hugs him tighter.

Give me a call when you get settled and lemme know if ... Her words trail off. Tanya laughs nervously, and they break the hug. She tries again to say something that doesn't quite make it out. I guess you'll just call if you ... well ... bring me back something from Paris.

They walk to the black car. Iberg doesn't follow but zooms in with the camera. Tanya opens the door and holds it for her son. As Kye gets in, she rubs his back again. She bends into the car and kisses him on the cheek. Then she steps back and begins to shut the door. She stops, opens it again.

Be good, be well-mannered, she says. She motions with her left hand, as if hammering nails in the air. Be safe and be strong. Think about your dad. What he would do …

A logging truck speeds past. The gust tousles Tanya's hair and drowns out her words. She bends into the car and kisses Kye again.

I love you, she says. Be smart. Be mature. It's going to be a good one, all right?

Right, he says, looking up at her with a wide-open expression.

So, be smart, okay? She pounds the air again, driving home her point.

Okay, he says, nodding.

Love you, she says as she bends in and kisses his cheek again.

Love you, too, Mom, Kye says.

Tanya closes the door and moves away, straining to hold back her tears. She takes a few steps away from the car, and now there's no stopping them. She lifts her sunglasses to wipe her eyes as Iberg comes closer with the camera. Tanya laughs at herself for bawling. Iberg laughs too. They both love the kid.

Bye, Iberg, you have a good time too, she says. Look after him.

All right, he says.

Then she's gone and Iberg's behind the wheel with the camera still running.

Kye, ya all psyched? he asks.

Yeah, says Kye to the camera, dutifully. I'm psyched.

But he doesn't look psyched. He looks like a boy who's just left his home and a mother he really loves for a journey to a strange and harsh place that took from him the father he never really knew.

chapter 4

Trevor: Journey to a Strange Land

Prince George, British Columbia
1961

A rotten-egg smell permeates clothing, homes and lives in Prince George, a paper-mill town carved out of the deep woods about five hundred miles north of Vancouver. Like everyone else, Arlie Petersen has grown accustomed to the stink. He has a wife, two kids, and a job in a shoe store. Before they were married, he and his wife Beth used to win dance contests. Since their wedding day nine years ago, there hasn't been much dancing.

Closing the shoe store early, Arlie climbs into his Hillman station wagon. On the floor of the passenger side is a case of strong Canadian beer. He pulls out a can, pops the top, and puts the car in gear.

The Petersen home is warm with the tinny smell of radiator and the hearty aroma of cooked meat. Hot soup is on the table. In the playroom, Beth breaks up another brawl between her boys, Lindsay and Rick. Seven and nine, they're hellions. Great kids, the loves of her life, but they never stop whacking each other, never stop making a racket. Boys are noise, she says.

Beth looks at the clock. Arlie should be home by now.

Okay, boys, we can't wait, she says. Let's eat now before it gets cold. Dad's on his way. I'm sure he'll be here any minute.

The boys slurp their soup, finishing it with a sloppy flourish. Beth wipes the table but leaves Arlie's bowl where it sits. Sometime after midnight, soup still on the table, the front door creaks open. Beth doesn't need to smell his breath to know.

Missed you at dinner, she says.

Had to meet some people, he says, slurring his words.

Right, says Beth.

This soup is stone cold, he says.

I'm pregnant, she says.

The delivery is easy. It takes Trevor Jay Petersen less than an hour to join the world. The day is September 15th, 1962. The boy is eight pounds, with blond hair and blue eyes. Arlie passes out big cigars in the waiting room. He proudly drives Beth and Trevor to their new home. The season's first snow has dusted the trees.

The house smells of fresh varnish, and the baby room is barely ready for Trevor. Beth had hoped for a girl and dreamed that the baby would give the family a fresh start. She didn't get her girl, but for a time the baby brings a change for the better.

Arlie gets his drinking under control and becomes regional manager of a small shoe-store chain. Later, Beth credits Trevor with saving the family, if only for a short while. A spunky kid, they call him Jay, but the name never suits him.

He's not a Jay, says Beth, a few weeks later.

Yeah, he's a Trevor, says Arlie.

Like, here comes a little Trevor, says Beth. She says it in a way that sounds a bit like a little *terror*. But the kid isn't a terror. He's just a handful. A welcome handful.

Six-year-old Trevor sits up in bed. The night is dark and moonless. Treetops sway in a chill north wind. The Hillman station wagon, now showing rust spots near the wheel wells, pulls into the driveway. Arlie gets out of the car but leaves it running. It's late and the house is still; the lights are out. The stairs creak under Arlie's shoes. A crack of light cleaves the bedroom as the door swings open.

Arlie puts clothes on his young son and carries him down the stairs. Beth tries to stop them at the front door. It's the middle of the night, and the boy needs sleep. But Arlie shoves her aside and gets into his car. Beth walks slowly down the driveway, watching the car drift down the road with her youngest son in the passenger seat. Arlie is taking Trevor to drink with him, and it's not the first time. Why? She can't figure it. Trevor's only six.

From the driveway she stares down the empty street for a long moment. Beth has read books about alcoholics and talked to therapists. She knows that trying to ascribe rational motives to her husband's behavior is itself a form of madness. But one thought keeps playing in her mind: *If something happens to that boy, I'll never forgive myself.*

The cold creeps into her, and there in the darkness something breaks inside. Beth walks into the house, gathers thick blankets and goes out the back door onto a large sundeck. Bundled against the Canadian cold, she lays down on a chaise lounge. This is where she goes to still her mind. Torn between marriage vows and a mother's need to protect her children, she knows there won't be any sleep tonight. Settling in, she makes a new vow. By the end of the night, she'll choose her course and stick to it.

The sky begins to glow, to shimmer. The northern lights flash orange, purple and apple green. Beth can't remember ever seeing them so clearly. It's as if the heavens are waving a beautiful curtain in front of her, begging her to step onto the stage. She marvels at the dancing lights, their perpetual motion and ethereal beauty.

Arlie comes back at dawn. Beth meets him at the car. Trevor's asleep in the back. Arlie gets out unsteadily.

You're going to stop drinking or you're going to get out, Beth says.

Arlie gives her a long look, his eyes not quite focusing.

Beth cooks Canadian bacon, eggs and toast. Light streams into the kitchen. The house is filled with breakfast smells. She rouses her boys, gathers them around the table and fills their plates. Arlie sits down at the head of the table.

Boys, we have something to tell you, begins Beth. Your father can't live with us anymore. He's going to go live with Gram for a while. Remember that he loves you and I love you, but we cannot live together anymore.

Arlie gets up slowly, kisses each boy on the top of the head and walks out the front door.

For a moment no one says anything.

Thank goodness, says Lindsay, the oldest.

Maybe I should've gone with him, says Rick, the middle son.

Six-year-old Trevor can't shape his thoughts into words. He just cries.

It's three days later and Trevor has just skipped out of school. He runs across the field and through the woods to his house. He goes in through the back door, tussles with the dog, plays with her new puppies, and goes down to his brother's cellar bedroom. This is Lindsay's room, a cool space, a teenager's realm. There's an easel, cans of paint, brushes. Lindsay's a good painter and can draw too. There are tubes of glue in a wooden box. Model airplanes hang on white strings from the rafters. But this isn't what Trevor is looking for. He reaches under the mattress and pulls out a bag of fireworks.

The first firecracker shatters the silence. The dogs bark. He waits a long moment. No one comes. He lights a sparkler, the incandescent blue-white sparks fly about the room. Another firecracker. More sparklers. The room fills with gray-blue smoke. As the initial buzz wears off, Trevor figures he'd better stop before he gets caught. Stuffing everything back under his brother's mattress, he runs out of the house and back to school.

Beth, your house is on fire, says the caller.

Beth stares into the phone. She's a legal assistant, just back from lunch.

Driving, she can see the smoke in the sky a mile away.

Walking home from school, Lindsay and Rick Petersen hear the sirens and excitedly chase the fire trucks. Coming around the corner onto their street, they see the trucks stop in front of their house. Bubblegum lights flash red. Beth brakes and jumps out of her car as firemen spray her home with water. She scans the crowd. Lindsay and Rick run over.

I can't believe it, says Lindsay. What are we going to do now?

Where's Trevor? asks Beth.

Then she sees him. A small boy, trembling. He runs to her, tears streaming down his soot-stained cheeks. Trevor has been in the house, trying to get the dogs out.

The puppies are dead, Mother, he says. The puppies are gone.

Beth picks him up, hugs him close. He buries his head in her hair, sobbing.

It's okay, she says.

The fire started in the basement, says a firefighter. A mattress caught on fire.

Later, after the flames are doused, Beth walks into the basement to see Lindsay's model airplanes still hanging, broken and scorched, on blackened strings. The house is burned to the foundation.

It's more than four hundred miles from Prince George to the Okanagan region of southern British Columbia. Beth Petersen and her boys drive there in a pickup truck, four in the front. Arlie had stopped paying the homeowner's insurance, and with no money to rebuild, Beth saw no point in staying. The foul air and fiery memories recede in the rearview mirror.

Ahead, orchards and vineyards stretch to the horizon. After Prince George, it looks like the Garden of Eden. Beth gets a job with a legal firm that leases a small condo for her and the boys. The move is effortless. They don't have much more than the clothes on their backs, and even those are hand-me-downs from the Society of St. Vincent de Paul. Decades later, Rick can still recall the clothing's mildewy smell.

The town dump is their furniture store. The first trip yields a kitchen table. Some sandpaper and a couple of screws make it sturdy as a bank. Beth paints it bright orange. For years, the orange table centers the family. On Sundays they wear their good clothes for dinner.

Months later, Trevor comes to his mother with tear-filled eyes and a confession. Beth asks what's wrong. He tells her about the firecrackers and the fire. He says, I'm sorry, Mother, I ruined it all. I burned everything you ever had.

One Sunday there's a new face at the orange table. The man has the leather skin of an outdoorsman, and he talks funny. Peter Alder is Swiss, a former ski racer. He's befriended Beth and her boys. Lindsay latches onto the man, pressuring him to take them all skiing.

The year is 1968. Silver Star's two chairlifts, several T-bars and a Poma lift make it one of Canada's largest ski areas. To three boys on rented and borrowed skis, its 2,500 vertical feet look like the Matterhorn. Lindsay is instantly obsessed. Hungry to know everything about his newly discovered passion, he presses Alder for tips, technique, stories. Through Alder, Lindsay first hears about the almost mythic mountain town of Chamonix in the French Alps and extreme skiers Sylvain Saudan and Anselme Baud. There's something in the rebellious self-reliance of the characters in Alder's stories, something in their fierce courage, that draws him in. Borrowing gear from Alder, buying second-hand stuff at the surplus store, sixteen-year-old Lindsay suits up. He has the ice ax, the crampons, the rope. In the backcountry, he pretends he's Sylvain Saudan or Anselme Baud. He free-climbs ice and rock buttresses. He skis junk-snow in trees too thick to make a turn. His best—his only—audience is his kid brother Trevor.

Sun pours through the small windows of the condo. It's furnished now, mostly—pictures on the walls, the orange table still standing at the center of it all. It's Saturday, and the two older boys have gone out. Beth and Trevor are alone in the house. Trevor carries a large book into the kitchen where his mother pores over a legal brief, trying to get ahead on work.

What do you have there? she asks.

With effort, Trevor plunks a world atlas on top of his mother's papers. Beth smiles. This is something they do together, mother and son. The whole world opens in front of them. Together they flip through the pages.

One day, says Beth, you'll go anywhere you want. Do whatever you want to do.

Eight-year-old Trevor looks up at her and smiles.

I know where I'm going, Mum, he says.

He flips the pages and stops at Europe. He picks up a short pencil, bites on the end as he studies the map. The pencil skims over Paris, Grenoble, Geneva. It hovers over the French Alps. Then he finds what he's looking for and draws a circle around it, bearing down on his stubby little pencil, ringing the area with great force.

That's where I'm going, Mum, he says.

Beth looks down at the map, focuses on the circle he's drawn around Mont Blanc and the town of Chamonix.

Why there? she asks.

That's where the mountains are, Mum, says Trevor. That's where I'm gonna be.

Beth supports her sons' growing passion for skiing by getting a job in the marketing department at Vancouver's Grouse Mountain. The job doesn't pay much, but it comes with season passes for her family. She hopes that skiing will keep her kids off the streets. It does, for a time, but after both of his brothers leave home, Trevor finds his way off the hill and into the streets of Vancouver. Soon Beth is getting calls from the police and school guidance counselors.

The room is hot. Beth, overdressed, fidgets uncomfortably. She doesn't want to be here again, doesn't want to hear what Trevor's seventh-grade guidance counselor is telling her.

We know about the calls from the police, says the man, a pale functionary in corduroy. He's been breaking into cars now. Stealing things.

He's made some undesirable friends, says Beth.

Unless you get Trevor some help, we're going to have to send him to reform school. If that doesn't work, and it usually doesn't, his next stop will be jail.

What can I do? she asks.

You cannot be two parents.

I'm working as hard as I can.

Beth tries to hold it in, struggles to bottle it up. One small tear gets away. She wipes it with the back of her hand. Her face is filling with heat, flushing; her ears burn.

Trevor desperately needs male intervention now, says the counselor.

I can't. I don't know … There isn't anyone right now …

Beth shifts in her chair. The wool of her sweater begins to itch. Working long hours and rushing home to take care of the kids hasn't left much time to date. A single mother doesn't exactly have marriage prospects lining up.

There is a school that will give him what he needs, says the counselor. But it's not cheap.

Beth drives her old Ford through the gray stone pillars at the gates of Shawnigan Lake School. She and Trevor stare through the steady rain. Opening before them—with deep green, lightly forested hills on either side—is a small valley of well-tended hedges and gardens, a koi pond at its center. Arrayed on the surrounding hills are large Tudor-style buildings. The road forks and Beth steers to the right, where a large bronze stag rises from a grassy embankment. Twelve-point antlers and a regal bearing, flanked by towering spruces, he's looking out over the misty waters of the lake.

For grade eight, Trevor is enrolled in one of the best schools in Canada, a British-style boys' boarding school. Beth has sold their small house to pay the tuition. Angling her old Ford between the Jaguars and Mercedes, she wonders if she's done the right thing. There's a sign that identifies the different dormitories: Kayes, Duxbury, Lakes, Ripley's, Renfrew. Beth pulls up to a wide ivy-covered building at the end of a curling drive. She parks in a tight spot beside a bronze sundial, a pillar that's set off from the drive by a well-trimmed hedge. Dull and pitted by countless storms, the face of the sundial reads: *The moving finger writes and, having writ, moves on. Not all your piety nor wit shall lure it back to cancel half a line, nor all your tears wash out a word of it.*

For Beth, this is like stepping into a painting, a movie. The ivy walls, the Tudor façade, the dark wood door with a Latin motto on the transom. She tousles Trevor's long hair as they walk through the door to a boxed-in foyer of mahogany wainscoting, trophy cases and the hot dry smell of furniture wax. Footsteps echo on wood floors. High up on the wall is a wood sign carved to look like a banner. Beneath it are placards with the names and dates of each year's honored student, the so-called head boys, printed in gold.

Trevor is disdainful of the admission process. His mother mumbles deferentially. Trevor meets the barber on the first day. The electric clippers hum. In seconds his ponytail is on the floor. Sideburns shorn. His scalp is pale. And then there's the uniform. Every boy wears identical gray flannel trousers, a white shirt and a navy tie. There's a stag crest on the breast of the crimson V-neck sweater.

Beth has terrible dreams about her son. In them Trevor's being beaten, he's drowning. She's back at the school on the first Sunday, the Ford parked inconspicuously around back. She and Trevor walk the manicured grounds through rhododendron and forsythia. The air is sweet and damp.

You want to see my racing stripes, he asks. Trevor lifts up his shirt. Across his back in parallel lines are angry red welts.

The guy caned me, says Trevor, proudly.

Something pulls in Beth's stomach, collapses in her chest. It's as if she's been hit.

I'm taking you out of this school, she says.

You spent a lot of money, Mum, replies Trevor. I can stick it out.

The canings continue for a time, and then something changes in Trevor. It's not so much that they break his spirit, it's more that he allows his energy to be channeled. Small for fifteen and thin as a whip, Trevor has a large voice. The combination makes him a perfect coxswain for the rowing squad. Trevor's excitement is contagious. Every rower in the boat feeds off his energy. The team strokes to strong results. As the seasons change, he also applies his pluck to the rugby pitch and becomes the sparkplug of the team.

The curb is lined with Jags and Mercedes again, but Beth parks her Ford right up front. She doesn't care anymore. The school year is over. She thinks this will be the last time either of them are ever here. She can't afford to send Trevor for another year. It pains her, but Trevor doesn't mind. Public high school will be so much easier, and he's looking forward to having some girls to look at.

As they're cleaning out his room, a note falls out of Trevor's pocket. It tumbles lazily in the light wind, white paper on green grass. Beth walks over, picks it up, unfolds it. It's a note written in Trevor's hand, addressed to the housemaster of his dorm, the same man who caned him nine months before.

> *Dear Sir,*
> *I just want to thank you for being my father for a year.*
> *I will always remember you.*
> > *Love,*
> > *Trevor*

A massive helicopter hovers over a rugged, snow-covered hillside in northern British Columbia. A radio crackles. A long cable with a hook at the end descends toward twenty-two-year-old Trevor Petersen. Wearing a bright orange vest, standing atop a precariously stacked pile of fallen trees, he signals to the pilot to bring the cable closer. He reaches out with a handful of plastic-covered steel cables known as chokers. He hits the helicopter's cable with the chokers, discharging static electricity that's built up in the aircraft's rotors, then shoves the chokers into a slotted hook at the end of the cable. Each choker is attached to a felled tree that will be hauled off the hillside and dumped into the river, where it will be pushed by barges to a sawmill.

Trevor radios the pilot, giving the code word that signals it's clear to lift the logs. And then he slips and falls. The chopper ascends. He tries to scramble out of the way. A thousand-pound tree trunk swings toward him.

Eight hundred miles away, Beth Petersen feels a sudden jolt in her stomach. She thinks of Trevor, can see him there in his logging clothes, his eyes wide, his mouth open, screaming. She feels a twisting in her gut, a surge of something racing up the back of her neck. It takes hours to get through to the camp via satellite phone.

This is Trevor Petersen's mother, she says into the static. Is my son all right?

No, says a man on the other end. He's in an air ambulance, Mrs. Petersen. He's got a broken leg.

Canadian government statistics say that logging is one of the country's most dangerous jobs. Injury and death are part of the package, and the man who hooks the chains onto the logs, the hooker, is the most vulnerable. That's the job Trevor sought after high school. He began as a prep cook in logging camps, often on barges in remote ocean inlets. The boy who grew up without a father finds a home in the care of older, tougher men, most of whom never learn his name. They just call him the Kid.

Chamonix is another world, says twenty-six-year-old Trevor Petersen, reclining in a small Whistler condo in a development known as the Ghetto. He's talking to his live-in girlfriend, Tanya Reck. The year is 1988. This is the first apartment that Trevor and Tanya have rented together, just to themselves. There are ski posters on the wall, and milk crates and bricks stacked into shelves. There's beer in the fridge, lots of it, and not much else. Trevor is just off the phone with friend and extreme-skiing film star Scot Schmidt, who's back from Chamonix, where he filmed *The Blizzard of Aahh's* with Glen Plake, Mike Hattrup and filmmaker Greg Stump.

We have to go, Trevor says.

So what's stopping us? asks Tanya.

Tanya and Trevor share a small journal to document their trip. Tanya writes:

December 13, 1988. We arrive at Chamonix at about six o'clock and decide to call a friend of Scot Schmidt's before we freeze to death in our van. Wow, great Yank, cool guy. He gives us directions to his house.

December 14, 1988. Glen Plake has let us stay in his humble chalet until January. Then, hopefully, we can all—Glen, Beth (his girlfriend), Trevor and I—find a good cheap place to live. Today we bought our valley passes. Yahoo! Ski, ski, ski! That's all that matters now.

The season starts big. There's lots of snow, too much to ski the Aiguille du Midi. Even the out-of-bounds skiing on the Grands Montets is too unstable. Trevor and Plake ski Le Brevent, a slightly smaller ski hill on the western edge of the valley. Plake teaches Trevor to ski moguls. Trevor teaches Plake what he knows about mountaineering. At night they pore over a book about skiing in Chamonix: *Les Alpes du Nord* by Anselme Baud. It becomes their bible. Written in French, which neither of them speaks, it comes to them orally, read aloud by any translators they can find. During breaks in the weather, they hike to mountain huts known as refuges, stay overnight, and hike some more. Getting in shape, learning the lay of the land, Trevor and Plake meet like-minded skiers and before long a pack forms.

The weather breaks around Christmas. The snowpack settles. Trevor and Plake finally dare to tackle a classic stepping-stone: Glacier Rond. They load their packs—twin axes, twin ropes, ice screws clanking loudly on their harnesses. It's enough gear to climb all the way through the Alps.

They're at the tram at dawn. They take their number and get an early bin. They're at the wall at nine in the morning. The snow on the Rond is as hard as concrete. They wait hours for it to soften, a rookie mistake.

Arghh, this is bad, says Plake.

It's all right, says Trevor. I think it's soft enough.

No, man, I gotta go to the bathroom, says Plake.

No, says Trevor. We've waited all this time, you should've done it then. We're skiing now.

Okay, says Plake, let's just get it done.

Trevor prods with his pole. One poke, two. It's soft enough to get a pole in. He cuts across the top of the ramp, bouncing on his skis three times to see if he can make the slope fracture. It's stable. He makes his first hop turn, a second. Ten turns later, as the Rond rolls over, he stops and waits.

Plake makes his first turns, stops, and doubles over. Trevor shoots a look up at him. What's wrong?

I almost crapped in my dang pants, yells Plake.

Trevor's laugh rings off the cliffs.

The Blizzard of Aahhh's is a hit at home, and Glen Plake is the star. It isn't just Plake's skiing or his Mohawk haircut that makes him stand out. His punk-rock attitude and disdain for all things Establishment—especially the corporate powers that in his view have hijacked the sport of skiing—make him explode off the screen. He's dangerous, revolutionary. Greg Stump, the filmmaker, calls him to Canada to appear in his next film, *License to Thrill.*

Not wanting to go home just yet, Trevor and Tanya stay on in Chamonix. The weather is welcoming, the mountains filling with skiers and climbers. Trevor continues exploring on his own. The solitude suits him. He spends a night in a refuge, a day on the glacier. Each trip changes him, shores up a foundation. Day by day, he finds his place.

Barely a week after Plake's departure, Trevor goes back to the Glacier Rond. He describes the day in a journal entry entitled "One Spring Afternoon in Cham":

I wake to another flawlessly beautiful day in Chamonix with an urge
to do something a little bit different. A good dose of Jimi Hendrix and
Led Zep to start the blood going and I'm off to the Aiguille du Midi
téléphérique. One of the most unbelievable tram systems in the world
with the second span of the lift going a full 1,000 meters without a
single tower in between. Today I've got my eye on the west face of the
Aiguille du Midi, just along the ridge a bit from the famous Glacier
Rond. One particular gully looks most feasible so I just throw my seven
millimeter rope around a bit of existing construction cable frozen into
the ice, and off I go. At the end of a 25-meter rappel there doesn't seem
to be any place to put an anchor in, so I start kick-stepping down the
steep snow and rock. After 10 meters of descent I look to my right and
see a sling wrapped around a horn of rock just above me. Perfect rappelling for another 25 meters and then I am within reach of where I
can begin skiing. After a short sidestep through the rocks the slope widens and I can start making some righteous turns on perfect 50-degree
neve with a brand new pair of Rossis. Yeehaw, what a feeling!

After 1,000 meters of descending down this monstrous face I have
to deal with the lovely proposition of skirting alongside and in and out
of the Glacier Bossons. This is one place to be extra cautious, especially since I'm solo. About halfway through the icefall I come across a
particular crevasse that has a little island of ice wedged in the middle
of it. This chunk of ice is the key to getting across the abyss. The week
before, my buddy Glen and I had crossed it after skiing out of the
Glacier Rond, but this time I am doing it alone, with crampons, so I
must take extra care.

Just as I step on the island that is going to get me across to the other
side, the whole block cracks and moves down with me laying on top.
Very luckily the isle wedges a bit farther down, to my relief.

I thought I was a goner.

With some very awkward worming and wedging, I manage to

reach the lip of the crack and hoist myself out. Whew, that was good for a pumper.

Wasting no time to get out of this world of ice, I traverse farther along the edge of the rock wall until I can get my crampons off and my boards on. As I begin working my way on to the lower Glacier Rond I realize that conditions have changed considerably in the last week. Much more ice this time. Very carefully I traverse the midsection over the crevasses but I can't say it wasn't bloody scary. After that fun zone a little more skiing brings me to a small serac jump and then I'm home free to the trail that comes from Mont Blanc. Another hour of traversing underneath the Aiguille du Midi brings me to the Plan Aiguille or midstation. Some strange looks from Parisian tourists on the train and a beautiful sunset ride down brings me back to the reality of valley life and a cold Stella Artois on tap. This seemed a very fitting end to an entertaining spring afternoon in Chamonix.

That night Trevor returns to the chalet, where he tells Tanya that he almost died on the Glacier Rond near the Exit Couloir.

chapter 5

Death Sport Capital of the World

Chamonix, France
March 11, 2005

I love coming back, says Peter Pilafian, a wizened cinematographer with a mountaineer's mustache and a restless energy. I hired him on a recommendation. He shot *Dogtown* and *Riding Giants*, the two most successful films of the adventure genre.

We are driving to Chamonix with our soundman, Brian Whitlock, in a rental van loaded with twenty-three cases of camera gear. We flew into Geneva earlier in the day, and after stopping for lunch we've been trading tales of film shoots gone awry—the sort of I-almost-got-killed and what-an-idiot-the-producer-was stories that are common currency among people who make adventure films. But now, entering the Chamonix Valley, the conversation grows quiet.

I crane my neck for a view of the needlelike peaks closing in on either side of the road. They're broken teeth, shards of earth jutting into the heavens. My palms sweat on the steering wheel. The pale blue sky turns a shade of gray.

How many times have you been here, Bill? asks Whitlock, a peripatetic sound engineer who's financing a home in Jackson Hole with thirty-five weeks a year of recording sound on the road.

How many times? I repeat, letting the question form a bridge into thoughtful silence, as if I'm counting the visits, which I'm not. If I were, it would be an easy tally. I've never been to Chamonix. I've been close many times, skiing in neighboring resorts in France and Italy, but something has always prevented me from simply driving into Chamonix's close-walled valley. I've been drawn to the place for twenty years, but I didn't want to come as a tourist. It felt wrong, too casual, like going to Mecca to buy a hair dryer. I needed a purpose worthy of Chamonix, and now I've found it in a fifteen-year-old kid, the ghost of his famous father, and a film waiting to be shot.

Whitlock's question hangs in the air. So reverently have I recounted the legends of Chamonix that I am like the devout baseball fan who can describe the paint peeling off the Green Monster but has never set foot inside Fenway Park. Everyone I'm working with—the New Yorkers, the skiers, the crew—just assumes that I have an intimate knowledge of the place. I haven't come right out and lied, but I haven't gone out of my way to correct the misconception.

Whitlock looks at me in the rearview mirror, his eyes asking how experienced I am, how much respect I deserve. Pilafian, twenty years my senior, leans toward me from the passenger seat. We will soon be in dangerous terrain, and both he and Whitlock need to gauge how much to trust me when things get serious.

I'm asking myself the same question. Am I up to the job? Will I answer the call?

The road curves. Shafts of sun splinter through gaps in the western peaks.

Actually, I've never been here, I say, looking into the mirror. That's why I hired you two. I really need your help to make this work.

Later that evening, I take a small camera into the wide, cobbled piazza where Plake and I agreed to meet. Diamondlike refractions from the day's last light fill the lens. Men with packs and skis are given a wide berth by strolling throngs who come in by bus. At an outdoor market, men in felt caps sell fine cheese and sausage. Gray-haired women in flip-up sunglasses buy baguettes and bouquets. On the plaza, new boutiques foot old, stone buildings. Tourists take rides in horse-drawn wagons, their wood and iron wheels clacking over cobblestones.

I find Plake sitting on the edge of a stone planter, chewing a baguette and watching the crowd pass by with genuine amusement. He wears a checkered Trilby hat, his flame-colored hair spilling over the collar of a bright red T-shirt. His jeans flare over snakeskin cowboy boots. A diamond is drilled into one of his front teeth.

Next to Plake is Kimberly, in a mod suede hat and rhinestone sunglasses. A pair of crutches lean on the wall next to her. Her leopard-print trousers are slit up one leg to accommodate a fiberglass cast.

I walk over and Plake says, you made it. Kimberly kisses my cheeks in the European way, but before I can ask about her leg she spots someone else.

Look who it is, she says, pointing over my shoulder.

I turn to see a balding man in a thin mountaineering jacket, a Tibetan scarf loosely wrapped around his neck. He walks with a crutch, which he holds up for us to see.

You looked so good on yours, he says to Kimberly, I figured I'd better get one too.

No way, says Plake, with a braying laugh. You too?

It's hanging out with guys like you, says John Falkiner.

Clinging to the lowest rung on the ladder of life, says Plake.

Falkiner kisses Kimberly's cheeks, and she hikes up her trouser leg and taps on her cast.

Here's mine, where's yours? she laughs.

Falkiner turns and points to the back of his thigh.

Join the club, says Plake. Kerig, do you know Falkiner?

We've never met, I say as I shake his hand, but I know who you are.

John Falkiner, an Aussie by birth, has been skiing and guiding in the Alps for twenty-five years. He appeared with Plake in *The Blizzard of Aahhh's*. To a certain kind of skier, the kind who hike for their turns, Falkiner is a legend.

At least it's nice out, says Kimberly. Spring has sprung.

So, what'd you do? asks Plake.

Well, it was bizarre …

Noooo, it wasn't one of them freak accidents, says Plake with mock surprise.

I went through a layer of crust into some soft snow, says Falkiner. The tip augured in and I tried to power it through. I felt something go.

She was just traversing along and she got a broken leg, says Plake.

I hit some bad snow and that was it, says Kimberly.

And then, as casually as if they were talking about the weather, the conversation shifts easily to who else is in town. Injuries in this set are barely worthy of comment. Everyone has had them and knows they will probably have more. It's the price you pay. Dwelling on brief, painful episodes is quietly discouraged. Bad form. Tourists moan. Skiers endure.

Later, Kimberly brings a Sharpie marker to a bistro in Argentière, the village that's just up the hill from Chamonix, where the Plakes and I have dinner with the New Yorkers. Plake tells great and detailed stories, mostly in the first person, and everyone takes a turn signing Kimberly's cast, a ritual of inclusion that the New Yorkers seem pleased to participate in.

After dinner, I walk the empty streets of Argentière, over rounded cobblestones and past silent churches. I look above and away to the glowing lightness of Mont Blanc and its eternally creeping glaciers, and feel strangely at home.

Trevor: Return to Chamonix

Whistler, British Columbia
Chamonix, France
January 1996

The two-lane road out of Whistler makes a twisting descent toward Vancouver. Trevor drives the familiar route with a confidence bordering on recklessness. Never one to tolerate slow drivers, he passes at every opportunity. Tanya is long past criticizing his driving. Instead she spends the time talking about more important things. Trevor's headed to Europe to ski in an Oakley photo shoot, and now that the kids are growing up these long trips are getting harder on everyone. Trevor feels it too.

Trevor's fame has grown since his first trip to Chamonix six years earlier. He has appeared in half a dozen films, all with his skiing and climbing partner Eric Pehota. Together they have become the reigning duo of the big mountains. More important, they have kept each other safe by adhering to a simple pact: If one of them doesn't feel good about skiing something, neither one will do it. On this trip, however, Pehota isn't going.

Driving through Squamish, Trevor tells Tanya he's been thinking it's time to cut back on the most dangerous descents. This is something that Tanya has never heard him say before. Though she wants Trevor to take fewer risks, she hasn't said anything for fear he might misconstrue her concern for a lack of confidence.

I'll focus more on the films, he says. It's great gack.

Lately he's been doing stunts in feature films. The pay, or gack, is good, and the risks are less than those he takes on skis. Trevor and Eric Pehota have also formed No Wimp Tours to take skiers into the backcountry, and Trevor has talked to Quiksilver, his apparel sponsor, about opening a shop in Whistler.

They cross the Lions Gate Bridge, pass through Stanley Park, and drive into Vancouver's Granville district. Trevor tells Tanya that soon, maybe this summer, they'll start building a lodge on a parcel of land they bought. He has plans to turn it into a boys' camp dedicated to helping teens at risk.

Soon as I get back from Europe, says Trevor, we'll move forward together on all our plans.

Snow falls into a dark night in Italy's Susa Valley. Trevor guns a white Renault Laguna station wagon, banking it through corners, headlights finding the pavement, sweeping its snowy contours. The road is a narrow gash in the mountains. Mike Hattrup, a fellow pro skier who's traveling with Trevor, has given up on the map. Now they're at the mercy of the white arrow-shaped road signs in Italian.

Somehow they find their way to an end-of-the-road town. A five-hundred-year-old church rises in the center, its steeple disappearing into a low, fleecy sky. Feathery flakes sift downward, drifting on windowsills and into doorways. There are no ski shops, no chairlifts.

This can't be the place, says Hattrup.

Sign said Alagna, says Trevor. This must be it.

They find the hotel, the Residence Mirella, where American freeskier Gordy Peifer is already unpacked in their top-floor room. Six years younger than Hattrup and Trevor, Gordy is a Utah skier—Alta and Snowbird—who's made a name in extreme skiing competitions, films and ski magazines. Known for skiing off cliffs—freeskiers call it hucking—he broke his neck only two years earlier, but, at twenty-four, even broken necks heal. A big kid, Gordy is open-faced, blue-eyed, a member of the generation of skiers moving quickly down the tracks left by trailblazers like Hattrup, Plake and Trevor.

Thought you boys would never get here, he says to Hattrup and Trevor, helping them lug their gear up the last flight of stairs.

The three of them have been in Europe for two weeks. They've skied Serre Chevalier for an Oakley photo shoot with photographer Scott Markewitz, and caught the biggest storm in ten years and the best tree skiing in Europe. After Serre Chevalier, it was on to La Grave for more shooting with Markewitz. Though the snow was good, the sun was reluctant and teasing. They spent much of their time standing on hillsides, waiting for the sun to peek through sucker holes in the clouds. Professional skiers call such photo shoots posing. It's the toll they pay for their free gear, paltry salaries and fleeting fame.

Now Trevor, Hattrup and Gordy have come to Alagna to join Steve Casimiro, editor of *Powder* magazine, who needs photos for a story he's writing. *Powder* has a modest circulation but is considered the soul-skier's bible, and Casimiro is its greatest scribe. His story is about a little-known place he calls Valley Y. Skiers, like surfers, are always hungry for secret spots and remote, unspoiled destinations. Several years earlier, Casimiro had heard skiers talking about a location in France known only as Valley X. It turned out to be La Grave. If Casimiro's guess is right, Alagna —Valley Y—will be the next big discovery.

As morning breaks in Valley Y, the sky is gray-white with falling snow. The tram cable rises above ten thousand feet. The cabin, built in 1966, trembles as it arrives atop a three-hundred-foot cliff. Alagna has one marked run and miles of wild terrain. To lead them, Casimiro has hired

Sergio Gabbo, a lifelong guide. At the summit, Gabbo disappears into the white. With no choice but to follow, Hattrup's and Gordy's bright yellow coats disappear into the snowy curtain. Trevor's red parka trails behind.

Skiing a new area in a whiteout is like riding inside a snow globe rolling down a flight of stairs. Unanticipated drops send your stomach skyward; unexpected drifts hurl you headfirst. The world shifts, skis hiss; you descend in an opaque cocoon.

The light is too bad and the snow too thick to try any photos. Markewitz doesn't even pull his camera out. For the remainder of the day and all the next, Alagna remains a secret.

On the third day, the mountain reveals itself: a sprawling beast of cliffs and couloirs, slanted ramps and plummeting gullies enveloped in a violet-blue sky and a two-foot blanket of snow. The tram is half-empty on the most perfect day any of them can imagine.

The exuberance of sun and fresh snow brings a sudden hunger, an irrepressible mountain lust. The three skiers peer over a smooth shoulder of vast untracked curves. They plunge in, but the mountain slaps them back. The snow, wind-whipped and thick, clutches shins and tugs at the spirit.

Gordy is the first to take to the air. A seventy-foot huck. Tight and contained, he soars like a missile and comes to ground in a puff. It's so beautiful it almost makes sense. Hattrup is next, dropping sideways off a twenty-foot cliff. He's calm and controlled—a solid four-point landing. Now it's Trevor's turn. The gauntlet has been thrown down. Stepping up to the cliff, he looks over the edge.

Markewitz raises his camera. He knows Trevor, knows he's not backing down. Sidestepping back up, Trevor begins to breathe quicker, gulping in air. Enormous energy goes into his double-pole-plant, a heaving shrug of the shoulders. Skis slicing, he gains speed, his legs pumping at the edge, extending. He coils, brings it all in and soars. As he begins to descend, he reaches for the snow with his ski tips and lands in an explosion of white. He made the jump but was out-flown by the younger Gordy.

Later, on a north-facing couloir called the Malfatta, Trevor throws down his own challenge. The snowpack is stable, and unlike the wind crust they hit higher on the mountain, it's thigh-deep and downy. The pitch is easy, consistent. Seventy-four hundred vertical feet of seamless snow beneath their ski tips, it's the longest powder run any of them has ever seen. Trevor challenges them to a short-turn endurance contest. Whoever can ski the farthest without stopping, wins. Trevor pushes off first. The powerful thrust of each turn shrouds him in plumes of white smoke. Markewitz burns film, capturing Trevor in slices that can only hint at the joy, the inside-pushing-out thrill. Ten, twenty, fifty turns.

He's still going, says Gordy.

Seventy-five turns, a hundred.

He's a speck down there, says Hattrup.

Farther and farther away he skis. The mountain rolls over, and Trevor disappears. Long seconds pass, and then he's there again, a tiny dark dot moving into light.

He won, says Gordy. He already smoked us.

Malfatta means badly made. On this day, with the sun turning snow to diamond dust, the term could hardly be less fitting. It's the most perfect powder run Gordy Peifer can remember. Hattrup and Markewitz are awestruck; the Malfatta is one of the most memorable runs of their lives.

The shoot is over. Casimiro has his story. Markewitz has his photos. They have time for one cold beer. The bar at the base is rustic, with boots and a sleeping dog at the door.

Trevor steps behind the beer taps and fills a gold-rimmed glass for each of them. His ponytail pulled back, held in place by a red and white bandanna of Indian print, he's a samurai with a skier's goggle tan. Markewitz raises his camera and squeezes off one last shot. In it, Trevor stares straight down the barrel, his blue eyes electric, his intensity jumping out of the frame.

A case of Kronenbourg, in little green bottles, fuels the conversation in Trevor's car. Trevor's holding forth, and Gordy, who's new to the game and wants to know how it's done, is soaking it up. It's about money and skiing and the screwed-up nature of the ski industry. A circular dialogue—women, money, skiing—and at each turn of the wheel is Chamonix. Gordy has read about the place, seen it in ski movies. Now he's going into the thick of it with the famous Trevor Petersen, his friend and mentor. Gordy is in his element; this is a dream come true. Then Trevor starts talking about something else entirely.

You've got to have kids, Trevor tells Gordy. They're it. What the whole deal is about.

Gordy makes the right sounds, trying to convey understanding, but he's twenty-six and having kids is the farthest thing from his mind. The Renault blows past low barrier walls on high mountain passes, races through the Mont Blanc tunnel and into Chamonix.

Trevor parks downtown. Now it's time to party. Sliding down frozen stairs and running across covered bridges, the bars come and go in a blur. Up to Argentière's Tex Mex, downtown to the Jackal. Stumbling down some alley by the river, a basement bar, another narrow street. Strong smoke. Cold beer. Shots of grappa, Jägermeister. Trevor knows someone in every joint. For Gordy this is a debutante ball, his introduction to the high society of world-class skiers. For Trevor it's a homecoming.

Night pools darkly in the low corners of the valley. Trevor is behind the wheel again, piloting the Renault up the switchbacks that lead to the top of the valley. Outside, the lights of Chamonix give way to dark trees, white fields and rock walls. Gordy finishes off one last Kronenbourg as Trevor pulls the car over.

Here? asks Gordy.

This will work. Let's go.

Trevor lurches to the back of the station wagon and raises the hatch. He nearly falls in as he shuffles gear around until he finds what he's looking for. He loops a headlamp over his head and switches it on. Pulling his sleeping bag out of the car, he starts unsteadily across a meadow. Gordy grabs his sleeping bag and follows. A hundred meters in from the road is a shed of half-rotted wood, listing to the west. The door creaks. Trevor's headlamp flits over rakes, hoes, shovels. He pulls his sleeping bag out of the stuff sack and unrolls it on the dirt floor. Gordy throws his down, too. He wriggles in with all his clothes on. The cold pierces. He ducks down into his bag, covering his head with a ski hat. Drunk or not, the night is miserable.

The true measure of a hangover can't be taken until the booze drains away. At daybreak Gordy feels terrible. He puts his head back down, a rolled-up down jacket for a pillow on the hard dirt ground. At midmorning he wakes again, and the pain comes straight in, unaltered. He feels like every cell in his body has been poisoned. Stomach churning, empty and acidic, even a sip of water is a gamble. Retracing their steps back to the car, Trevor and Gordy retreat to Argentière, where they slowly chew baguettes against the nausea, sitting dazedly on a step outside a patisserie.

I'd kill for a hotel room right now, says Gordy.

I'll make some calls, says Trevor. We'll find a place to crash.

Trevor connects with a man whose real name no one seems to know. Everyone calls him the Baron. A proper gent, or the appearance of one anyway, he summers in South Africa and winters in Chamonix. There are vague allusions to nobility, but what really matters is that the Baron has a house in Montreux, and the house has couches. Trevor and Gordy spend the day sleeping.

The next day, Gordy's up with the sun. His first time in Chamonix and the guilt of missing a ski day gnaws at him.

Get up, Trev, says Gordy. We've got to get some vert today. My legs are itching.

I'm a little tweaked, says Trevor as he gets off the couch and walks a few paces.

You're limping, says Gordy.

I'm injured, he says. My groin. I'm not going to ski today.

Gordy wonders if it was the jump that he pressured Trevor into doing, or maybe making the million turns down the Malfatta.

You should go, says Trevor. I'll take today off and be good to go tomorrow.

The base of the Grands Montets is bathed in bright winter sunlight. The white Renault splashes through a puddle at the base of a snowbank as Trevor pulls up in front of the ticket office.

So I'll see you right here at five, he says.

Okay, says Gordy. What are you going to do?

I'm not going to ski, says Trevor, but I might just go up the Aiguille du Midi. Take a look around.

chapter 7

No-Fall Zone

Chamonix, France
Morning, March 13, 2005

Morning dawns thin and cold. Light trickles into the valley. Our crew has taken over a twenty-meter circle of asphalt in front of the base terminal of the Grands Montets tramway, a functional cement structure with a wooden façade and three peaked roofs. I'm off to the side of the group, putting on a climbing harness, checking my avalanche beacon.

In the middle of our piles of camera gear is Kye Petersen, wearing a camouflage one-piece ski suit with a fur collar and a black helmet. He twists his torso back and forth, bends to touch his toes, stretching his hamstrings. His body is in continuous motion, discharging nervous energy. I am standing next to Kayce. We're both watching Kye from the periphery. When he takes his helmet off, Kayce gasps.

What happened? she asks. It was such beautiful hair.

Kye's ponytail is gone, his hair now shorn nearly to the scalp. He's still pop-star pretty—there's no losing that—but without the flowing locks, his eyes are hard and intelligent in a way that dares you to disagree with him.

It could grow on me, I say to Kayce.

What neither of us says is how disappointing it is from a filmmaker's perspective. I had imagined slow dissolves from Trevor's face to Kye's, father and son nearly identical. Now, without the ponytail, you have to look harder into Kye to see his father. Maybe that's the point.

An open-faced man with dark hair and an easy manner steps up and loops the straps of an avalanche transceiver over Kye's head.

This is so we can find you under the avalanche, he says to Kye.

Stephane Dan is one of the best guides in Chamonix and the right choice to keep Kye safe. Known widely by his nickname, Fanfan, he's guided many film crews through the mountains and been a star in his own right. In addition to appearing in numerous ski films, he skied the stunts for Pierce Brosnan in the James Bond film *The World Is Not Enough*.

Fanfan pats Kye on the shoulder as the young man puts on his beacon, then hands him a climbing harness.

And this is so we can pull you out of the crevasse, he says.

I like Fanfan immediately. His calm manner puts me at ease. He has the thing you most need in the mountains: confidence. You can trust him with your life, if you're a person who can trust anyone that much. I'm trusting him with something even more dear: the life of a kid whose mother has put her trust in me.

I get to wear a harness? Kye asks, feigning excitement. He steps away from the group and tries to figure out how to get it on.

He flips it around, twists it. Where to put which leg? Which side is up? Fanfan walks over and shows him. Kye walks away from the group again to keep the others from seeing him struggle. Eric Iberg follows him with a camera. Trying to get his feet through, Kye loses his balance and falls to the pavement. Instead of getting up, he lies on his back and tries to wriggle into it.

Let me help, says a gray-haired man in a smooth white ski jacket who crouches beside Kye.

I got it, says Kye, curtly dismissing this ski-instructor-looking guy.

I'd just rather lie down because it's hard to get on.

The man's face is impassive for a moment. He wears the salt-and-pepper goatee of an academic, a sharp nose, an angular face. The professor stands up and grins down at Kye. He's seen his share of proud kids come to these hills.

Watching from a perch on a fence rail, Glen Plake is dressed completely in black. Shocks of long, orange hair poke from beneath his hat, streaming behind him as he hops off the fence and strides toward Kye.

The professor sees him coming, notes the orange hair and the saunter—Plake has a singular way of pimp-rolling in ski boots. Lifelong skiers can spot an expert skier just by his walk.

Anselme, c'est un très grand plaisir de vous rencontrer, says Plake, in careful and deliberate French. Anselme, it is a very great pleasure to meet you.

Je suis Glen Plake, he continues. I am Glen Plake.

You are American? asks Anselme.

Yes, from Lake Tahoe.

Ah, yes, Squaw Valley.

I'm from Lake Tahoe but have been in the Bishop area for sixteen years.

For skiing or snowboarding?

All skiing. I grew up in South Lake Tahoe and mainly skied Heavenly Valley. When I was fourteen or fifteen I began climbing to ski, and it opened a can of worms.

Anselme grins. From the ground Kye watches Plake, one of the most famous skiers in North America, fawn over the man Kye has just brushed off.

All of a sudden I realized that the ski resort was this, continues Plake holding his hand up, his thumb and forefinger a half-inch apart. But the mountains are this: He holds his arms out wide, cocking his head up toward the peaks.

Anselme, arms folded across his chest, nods, a don sizing up an apt pupil.

So, off I went, says Plake, pantomiming a small soldier marching. I came to Chamonix eighteen years ago. We read your book, and it gave us the information to try to become skiers in the big mountains. I've traveled a lot over the years, but always back here, eh? I've been in Chamonix for four weeks now.

Now, it's been okay, but we need more snow, says Anselme.

The southeastern aspects, the climbing routes, have been good skiing, offers Plake.

Maybe in two days, it gets very warm, says Anselme. It's not good. Maybe not safe.

Everything southeast that you would not normally ski has been quite good.

Yes, but we must be careful, eh, because with the warm, the snow comes down.

Yeah, in big fat slides, says Plake, laughing hoarsely.

Cinching the front of his harness, Kye gets off the ground.

Kye, this is Anselme Baud, says Plake.

Embarrassment sweeps over Kye's face. Anselme smiles warmly, reaching out a bare hand to shake Kye's gloved hand.

Nice to meet you, says Anselme.

Kye purses his lips, shyly dipping his head, suddenly very interested in his gloves, in fastening the Velcro just right, pushing the webbing down between each finger.

This guy's done a lot of stuff, says Plake.

Yep, I know, says Kye miserably. I've seen the book.

In addition to writing the definitive book on Chamonix's ski-mountaineering routes and notching more than a dozen first descents—among them the Arête De Peuterey from the summit of Mont Blanc and the Mallory Couloir on the Aiguille du Midi—Anselme has been

the skiing partner of some of the most famous men in the Alps: Vallencant, Saudan, Boivin, legends who warrant single-name status. Two out
of the three died quick and violent deaths. Sylvain Saudan is still alive,
still known as the skier of the impossible.

Anselme Baud has no title. He's maintained a simple life in relative
obscurity, far below the radar for all but the most ardent ski mountaineers. These days he teaches the teachers at the National School of
Alpinism and lives comfortably in a small house in Chamonix. He also
travels frequently to Nepal and Tibet to teach mountain guides there.
Anselme's father was a guide, his grandfather too.

Weeks earlier, in an effort to surround Kye with the best people
money could hire, I called Anselme and asked if we could hire him as
a guide. He said he was too busy, so I asked if we could interview him.
He was not excited. Peter Jennings' name meant nothing to him. An
American crew? Yawn. Although he and Vallencant made films of their
first descents, Anselme never sought the camera's attention.

So I told him about Kye and Trevor and the reason we were coming to Chamonix. Anselme thought maybe he remembered Trevor, but
he couldn't be sure. He's lived in Chamonix for fifty years, and with a
reputed average of sixty deaths a year there have been some three thousand corpses in his lifetime.

And he is coming here to know about his father? asked Anselme.

He's never been to Chamonix, I said.

He is a very good skier?

One of the best young skiers in North America. His father was
a pioneer. He has many first descents in British Columbia. He loved
your book.

His father, he die here?

In the Exit Couloir.

The Exit? repeated Anselme.

The West, I said, mentioning the other name for the couloir where

Trevor died.

Silence over the line meant either he was thinking or I'd lost the connection.

I will see, he said finally. Maybe I can make time to show him something between classes.

We can pay for your time, I offered. For opportunities missed.

This is the way we couched any and all compensation to the skiers in the film. Since the principals in a documentary aren't actors, you can't pay them, per se. Instead we offered to pay certain expenses—flights for Kye and Plake and a few others as well as accommodations—and then compensate them for earnings they'd forgo to ski in front of our cameras. To be sure, this approach is not up to the highest journalistic standards, but skiers make so little money as it is, and nearly all of it comes from a limited number of days on the snow. If we didn't set it up this way, we wouldn't be able to get them to take time out for us. But Anselme wasn't interested in any of this. Money is not a problem, he said on the phone.

I'd pressed on, asking how much I should budget. He exhaled audibly over the line. If we felt compelled to pay—such an American focus on money—we could give him a day's worth of his teaching salary. Wondering why he'd take the time, why Kye's story had somehow piqued his interest, I thanked him in advance.

Now I watch Anselme gaze at the young man who had dismissed him out of hand just a few minutes earlier. There's not a trace of annoyance in Anselme's expression. There's something else in his eyes, something sad and familiar.

So, we go, says Anselme.

The line into the Grands Montets tram leads inside the building and up cement stairs wet with melting snow, then through a turnstile to the tram dock where the cable car swings into place. Kye worms past a group of Japanese skiers in matching outfits and shoulders his way to a spot near a window inside the car. I follow Anselme into the tram. He moves casually, a teacher walking into a classroom. He steps in behind Kye and looks over his shoulder as the tram lifts out of the station.

When there's more snow in the valley, there is tree skiing? asks Kye as the tram car moves over steep benches of evergreens. I watch him and smile, noticing the way he's beginning to pick up the syntax of Anselme's speech.

Yes, but it is gone now, says Anselme to the back of Kye's helmet. The snow, it ran out.

Tram conversations have an awkward tension. Everyone is packed in tightly. Short people have noses at armpit height. You're surrounded by breath—the damp, hot smells of eggs, coffee, last night's Armagnac.

Anselme pulls out a pack of gum and offers Kye a piece. Wriggling his shoulders and hips, Kye turns around to accept the gum. Now that they are facing each other, Anselme puts his hand on Kye's shoulder. He points out the window.

So, this is the Aiguille du Grands Montets, says Anselme. Two thousand two hundred meters. First we will go up to the panorama so that I can show and explain the mountains. From there we can go to the Argentière Glacier. From there we will start to make some training on the glacier where it is not a big crevasse problem and it is not so steep.

Are there a lot of crevasses in the glacier?

Yes, says Anselme with a smile.

Nice, says Kye.

Nice? repeats Anselme with a chuckle. Not so nice. One time there was a guide on the Mont Blanc who fell into a deep crevasse that got narrower and narrower. And he got wedged by his head. And it was so far down they couldn't get him out. We tried with a rope and having a man go down … many things. And then he get dead. The warmth of his body made the ice melt, but as he die, his body get colder and the ice, it re-freezes. And then there is no way to get him out. It's frozen, frozen! Even pulling on his feet. So, Kye, we have to be careful.

Yeah, no doubt, says Kye.

First you have to observe the terrain and where the glacier is going. Large bumps and changes in pitch indicate maybe a crevasse. Also, if the snow is soft and there are many crevasses, you have to take the rope and tie the people together.

At what age do you usually start teaching these skills? I ask.

Probably at fifteen or sixteen, answers Anselme, but it depends on where the people are from. The people coming from the city, maybe it's later, because they do not understand snow, the pressure and movement on snow.

They need context, I say.

Yes. Mountain children, they can learn early because already they know snow from sleds and snowboards and living.

I grew up in the snow, says Kye.

And snowboarders are especially good, continues Anselme. They are always falling down and touching the snow. They are in it with their hands. They know snow better because they are in it. In the beginning we say, Aw, snowboarders do not know about snow because they are not skiers. But no. Snowboarders know more than skiers.

I've done a lot of both, says Kye.

You are a mountain child, yes?

Yes, I grew up in Whistler. My whole life.

So, for you, we start with the technique because you already know snow.

As the tram rises toward the craggy peaks, Kye chomps his gum and holds his skis the way a soldier holds a rifle at ease.

Anselme leads us out of the terminal and up five flights of metal stairs to a high observation deck. Bordered by a steel railing, the platform hovers, or seems to. From up here, the peaks crowd the horizon and jostle the sky with sharp spikes.

Have you ever seen anything like this? Anselme asks Kye.

No, says Kye, never.

Anselme names the needles: the Aiguille Verte, the Aiguille du Midi, the Plan de L'Aiguille, the Aiguille de la Gliere, and on and on. Mont Blanc, which sits in the heart of all these needles, is older, rounded by geologic time. The needles, products of more recent thrusts of the earth's crust, will someday be blunted too. Below and to the east is the Argentière Glacier, a vast creeping river of ice surrounded by walls of dark rock, striped with steep snowy chutes.

This year the World Cup was in Les Houches, says Anselme, pointing far to the west. It was in January. The snow was hard and good. Downhill and also slalom. You are skiing slalom?

No, no, never, says Kye.

You are in the bumps?

Two years I skied bumps. Now I just freeride.

And you like to ski in the trees?

Yeah, I love trees.

So it is the same style of the slalom. You have to turn. Use the edges or you hit the trees.

Yeah, I can use my edges.

This is good. We will see, but this is good.

Kye rushes ahead of us, down the long flight of stairs that descends from the Grands Montets tram. His legs and arms move with the loose grace of youth, his face a taut mask of barely contained impatience. The covered stairway ends on a small patio with a southern exposure, beach chairs and a tiny café. Skiers in the latest gear sip cappuccino, more interested in lounging than skiing. A quick glance fills Kye with disdain. Yeah, these are skiers, but they're not *skiers*.

Anselme turns the corner of the stairway and reads Kye's look. He knows the relationship between real skiers and the tourists whose money makes it possible for him—and Kye, too, for that matter—to make a living in the mountains.

This way? asks Kye as he points to another set of stairs that lead down the west side of the buttress and onto the snow.

Now, I think, says Anselme as he steps up to Kye, we have a coffee.

Kye curls his lip and gives Anselme an impatient look. Anselme responds with a smile as he turns to the small café at the north end of the patio.

Arghh, growls Kye into the collar of his coat. He follows reluctantly.

The café is nearly empty. Dust motes drift in shafts of sunlight. The smells of strong coffee and buttery pastries fill the small space. Anselme greets the smiling barista in familiar tones. In English he explains why there are three men following him with cameras and a boom mic.

It's all good, mate, she says in a twangy Australian accent.

You have coffee, Kye? Anselme asks as he turns from the bar.

Maybe iced tea? Kye says.

I don't think they have this, says Anselme.

Yeah, look, it's right there. Lipton. Anselme follows Kye's finger to a small display of candy and bottled water. On the far right is a plastic bottle of iced tea.

I never knew this one, says Anselme as he takes the bottle from the barista. Iced tea.

With lemon, says Kye, pointing to the tiny picture of the lemon amid all the French writing on the label. Anselme laughs as he steers Kye to a small table by a window with benches on either side. He sits at the head of the table, and Kye slides in by the window, taking his helmet off, placing it on the table between them. Through the window he can see all the way down to the village of Chamonix. For the youngster this is an awe-inspiring view. For the people who work here, it doesn't even warrant cleaning the window. Anselme breaks off half a chocolate bar and hands it to Kye.

Thank you, says Kye, politely.

So, how do you feel? asks Anselme.

How do I feel? repeats Kye, giving Anselme an exaggerated thumbs-up. The mountains make me happy. Jet-lagged, but happy. Tired. Nine hours difference and right now it feels like one in the morning. But I'm ready to ski.

So, you are a freestyler? Doing tricks?

Yes. I like to jump.

You spin around, like 720.

Like 1080, says Kye.

And 360, too, says Anselme.

For sure.

I do this too, says Anselme. I like the 360s.

Really? Cool.

And what is it you'd most like to learn? asks Anselme.

Well, I'd like to learn a lot more about snow danger, definitely, about avalanches, one of my main things, says Kye. The other thing I want to learn is what these mountains look like. I'd like to go and see what they're all about. And I want to see where it was that my dad skied, and where he died.

I notice the way that Kye talks without obvious emotion about the death of his father.

Yes, Anselme says as he stirs another sugar into his coffee. It was a … difficult circumstance.

Kye nods, looks down at the table, bites his thumbnail, and then looks back up to Anselme who is taking a sip of his coffee. He swirls it, letting it melt the chocolate in his mouth, and swallows it slowly.

So, anyway, says Anselme, first we must learn the technique to go down the steep slopes. To be sure, to be safe, you must never fall down. Because if we fall down, it is finished. Okay, sometimes we have a chance, but usually …

He shrugs his shoulders, offers upturned palms.

Yep. I know, says Kye.

It's better to learn all the technique and the balance and to never fall down, continues Anselme. Others learn to recover quickly after a fall, but for me it's not a good way to learn to fall and get back balance. It's not a good way.

Yeah. For sure.

So, we must never fall down, Kye, repeats Anselme, raising his feathery eyebrows. Never.

Yeah definitely, says Kye. Especially on steep stuff. On steep dangerous chutes, it can't happen.

He laughs nervously, chugs the rest of the iced tea. Anselme puts another piece of chocolate into his mouth and then takes a long pull of coffee. Chewing slowly he rests his elbow on the table, brings his fist to his cheek, and sets his chin on it. He looks past Kye, out the window to the mountains, absently tugging on his goatee. After a long moment, his gaze returns to the café and to Kye.

Your father was, um … he died … fifteen years ago? asks Anselme.

I was six, and now I'm fifteen.

Ah, yeah, sorry, says Anselme. Nine years.

Kye nods and inspects his iced tea label some more. After a moment he says: February 26th was the anniversary of the day he died. We hiked up to the peak at Whistler, a bunch of friends of his and mine. We hung out at the top …

You have a brother or a sister?

Yeah, one sister, she's thirteen.

A skier also?

Yes, she's a skier, but she's a girl. She likes the girl stuff, makeup and everything. She's into the whole scene with the friends. She doesn't ski quite as often as I do.

It's okay, eh? This skiing is not for everyone.

Anselme stands and finishes the last gulp of his espresso. Kye hikes up his baggy pants, cinches the power-strap on his boots, tightens and retightens each buckle.

Wide and well-tracked, the slope rolls over and disappears from our view. Anselme flits down it, every turn solid yet light. Wide stance, double pole-plants, he's quick from edge to edge. A spider on skis, he sticks to the hill. The skis perform; he doesn't seem to be doing anything. But he is not supple. The hard corners of his technique have never been smoothed to please the cameras. He is perfectly functional but inelegant. He edges precisely to a skidless stop.

Kye charges like a Border collie finally let off his leash. Running out on a long reach, he banks into a slippery turn. Quick splashes of snow fill with light. Steering, banking, pressing, there's joy in his shuffling dance. Feathering the edge, he lets go of a turn and spins around backward. Looking over his shoulder, angling a hip, he slips through one, two, three turns. A quick unweight and he's skiing forward again. A long skittering smudge brings him to rest next to Anselme and our film crew.

Kye looks first to Anselme and then over to me. I've finally seen him ski in person, and it pleases me greatly. There is an honesty to his movements, a truth about himself that he's not hiding. Underneath his teenage affectations, he is simple, joyful and resilient.

You are the backward man, says Anselme.

Gotta be, says Kye. It's fun.

Of course. Now, this way.

A vertical cornice runs beside a dark rock. Kye eyes it. It looks like one wall of a half-pipe, a terrain feature that he can work with. He passes

Anselme and straight-lines for the wall. The transition is smooth, and then Kye is in the air—high in the air. He turns a long, slow 180-degree spin. Flying through the air backwards, he sees Anselme take off right behind him. The spider leaves the ground, pops, extends his legs. The spin begins with a turn of the head. Anselme looks over his shoulder and keeps on looking. His body follows, rotating slowly through the sky.

Kye lands backwards. His arms touch down. He soaks up the shock and looks up the hill. Anselme finishes his 360-degree spin as his skis meet the snow. A double pole plant resets his position.

Yeeehooo! screams Anselme.

The excitement in his voice is more surprising than the jump.

Yeeehaw! hollers Kye.

He spins around to ski forward. Anselme is almost on top of him. And then he's thirty meters in front. Anselme's skis skitter, snow jetting from his edges in machine-gun bursts. He is loose now, not in perfect control. The professor has left the classroom. Anselme is alive, letting something loose that's been caged—the energy, the brio. He's skiing like a kid.

Kye ramps off a berm, floats, lands fast and fearless. This is where the kid lives. He's gaining on the old man. They've out-skied our cameras now, and I'm skiing along behind, thrilled to be watching.

Anselme drags a pole on purpose. Snow billows. Kye can't see. It's an old trick, one every skier learns as a kid. The sun is at their backs; the light turns plumes into walls of diamonds. Kye appears through the spray and passes Anselme.

So much more slope left. Kye is all heels and leaning now, his skis banking out to the side. Nothing technical, he's surfing the earth, and it's pure, ridiculous fun. Anselme hollers after Kye in French. The words are lost on me, but the tone is unmistakable—I'll get you! They eat the slope in long sweeping arcs, white smoke off skis, streaking through time.

It's noon. The sun drives shadows into our feet. We're again set up at the bottom of a long stairway that leads from the top of the tram down to the snow. Walking side by side down the stairs toward us, Anselme and Kye might be father and son.

Kye trots down the last few steps, slides across the hard snow on his boots, and slaps down his skis. One lands upside down. He kicks it over and slams his foot into the binding. The heel piece pops up and snaps loudly.

Anselme lays his skis down carefully, scrapes the snow off the underside of his boot by running it back and forth over the top of the binding's toe piece, and steps in smoothly. Kye poles off toward the piste, the groomed trail used by most of the tourists. Anselme is headed the other way, toward a boundary rope.

Where are you going? yells Kye.

Out here, answers Anselme. He ducks under the rope and herringbones up a large snowbank that's been formed by snowcats plowing excess snow out of the saddle. I watch him go, figuring he's finding a place to relieve himself.

Don't you think we could go back down there? yells Kye.

Later, says Anselme. Now I will show you something.

Kye ducks the rope and sidesteps up the berm next to Anselme.

What? asks Kye.

Over here.

Anselme pushes off and skis away from the rope, down a short steep slope and onto a large, wind-swept plateau. Kye shakes his head impatiently, drops down the short face, and skids to a stop in the middle of the saddle. The camera crew is already heading the other way. I corral them and send them after Kye and Anselme. By the time we're all moving in the same direction, Kye and Anselme are two small figures, dark against the blinding white background, dwarfed by the massive castle-topped peaks.

Stay back and start rolling, I say to Pilafian, who is operating a high-definition video camera.

Much to Kye's chagrin, Anselme seems to be pointing out more landmarks. He's back in tour-guide mode.

So, you can see the Mont Blanc, says Anselme, pointing west toward a hulking mass of blue ice and black crevasses. And before it is this couloir on the left there?

Yeah, I see it.

I skied a first descent of this with Patrick Vallencant.

Wow, says Kye, reluctantly impressed with both the feat and the mention of another legendary ski mountaineer.

And there, in front of that, continues Anselme, you see the couloir going in the shadow to the left?

Yeah, I think I see it. There's a rock in the middle.

Yes, a small rock and in the top there is the glacier.

Yes, I see it, Kye says, wanting to be done with this show-and-tell and on to more skiing.

The name is the Gervasutti Couloir, says Anselme, speaking slowly now, reverently. Seven hundred meters vertical. I have skied it many times. The first time in 1976 with Patrick. Last spring, with my son and one friend, we planned to go and ski from the top. You see where I'm pointing?

Yeah, I see it, says Kye, squinting into the sun, impatience turning into annoyance.

So we climb up that and at the top I broke my binding, says Anselme. I decide to go down. So I tell them, my son and our friend, okay, if it's good you ski it down, no problem. So I come down and join a cameraman with a radio. From the top they say they are ready to start. We say okay. One hundred meters down, my son, he calls and tells me, it's okay, the snow is good. I say, good, ski it well!

He nods at Kye who nods back, wanting Anselme to tell it faster than his halting English allows.

And you see down the cornice there? The small line of rock?

Yep.

So my son was skiing down this line and *crack!* The serac fall down. There was a big explosion just above him.

He pauses as he looks out at the far-off couloir.

And then my son was taken, says Anselme.

Kye snaps his head at Anselme.

Taken?

He went all the way down.

Shit.

He died, says Anselme, pursing his lips, holding onto himself. Kye looks from the couloir to Anselme and back to the couloir.

And you watched it? asks Kye.

Yes, says Anselme. Edouard, the name of my son, was a great skier. He was going the same line as me. He was skiing well. Skiing very, very hard. He get some first descents, and I go with him to many places. The Himalayas and such. He was twenty-four.

Kye stabs at the wind-hardened snow, his pole poking dark holes in the whiteness.

I was happy to plan many projects with him, continues Anselme. The Himalayas again. Other places. But it is finished now. Just like that.

I'm really sorry, says Kye.

Thank you, he says. It is very hard to begin again.

Anselme stares at the couloir, the terrible, beautiful face of it. His face is still, sun glaring off waxy, sunblocked skin.

Was it the cornice that broke off above him? asks Kye.

It was not the cornice, it was the serac, says Anselme, using the word for an extremely large block of ice usually formed at the edge of a glacier.

We cannot know when it is falling down, continues Anselme. Sometimes it is not falling for two months. Sometimes three or four in one week. So, we had to find him and carry him down. It is very difficult.

Kye punches more dark holes in the snow.

It is hard to speak about that and to show you that, says Anselme.

He points again to the western horizon.

But, look, this is the Gervasutti Couloir here, and the Aiguille du Midi there, he says, pointing with his ski pole. And behind the Aiguille du Midi is the Glacier Rond, where your father died. We supposed he fell down in there and the rescue, they find him. So, my son get killed in the Gervasutti Couloir, right there, and your father on the Glacier Rond, right there. They die very close. It is difficult to observe that.

Kye swallows hard.

Definitely, he says.

I tell that story, I speak about that bad experience, to say, be careful. We have to be sure about our observation of snow quality and technique. Even if we have many good tracks to follow, and we are ready to go, maybe it's not a good time because maybe avalanche is here. Just because there is one track or many tracks—

That doesn't make it safe, says Kye, somber now.

This is a bad story, says Anselme.

Kye nods in agreement.

But it is a beautiful life, sometimes, says Anselme. And anyway the mountain is here. We have to take the best of the mountain and follow life.

Jordan Kronick, a thirty-something, New York-based producer, taps me on the shoulder. Efficient and energetic, he's along to make sure I don't overlook any details. A Canadian who's done his time in Whistler and skis well enough to keep up, he's a stalwart member of the PJ Productions team. Mostly he watches and makes suggestions—different angles, more coverage. He does this in a way that is not annoying. His diplomatic skills are considerable.

Ah, Bill, he says, in a way that's meant to remind me of something.

Right, I say, knowing what he's referring to.

Anselme, can you come back here? I ask.

Anselme and Kye turn, annoyed looks on their faces.

I just need to get a couple more things before we move on, I explain. Can you come back and stand in the same place for a moment?

Kye's shaking his head as they move back to where they'd been standing. I explain that I need to get a few more shots, what film people call coverage. Unless I reconstruct the scene, the editor will only have a limited point of view, which makes it difficult to cut. I ask Anselme to point to the Gervasutti Couloir again so that I can film a close shot of his ski pole pointing to the area. Then I have him mimic his earlier movement and point to the Glacier Rond, where Trevor died. We shoot from behind his shoulder. Then we move back and shoot medium shots of the two of them in frame as well as a master of them standing alone on the saddle. All these shots—cutaways, in the parlance of the filmmaker—are necessary to allow the editor to heighten the drama of the scene.

Okay, Kye, I just need one close-up of you looking out at the couloir to make this work, I say.

Kye gives me a *whatever* look, and Pilafian moves in close enough to see his reflection in Kye's goggles.

Goggles up, I say.

The sun's too bright, Kye says as he squints at me.

Just for a minute.

Dude, I'm burning my eyes, he says, pinching his eyes shut.

And I realize I've gone too far. Kye's just been moved by his new mentor, just connected with him, and now I'm asking him to playact. He's not going to re-enact the scene, and I'm ashamed of myself for asking.

Leading Kye across the saddle toward the piste on the summit of the

Grands Montets, Anselme spots a lone figure in black standing on top of the snowcat-made ramp: Plake.

Kye, your dad would be stoked to see you skiing next to that guy, Plake says as they arrive.

Kye smiles at Anselme, who returns the look. I motion for Pilafian to get into place with his camera. Another spontaneous scene may be unfolding, and I want to cover it while it does.

Did he show you the turn? Plake asks.

I don't think so, Kye says. Anselme shakes his head.

This one, says Plake as he makes an exaggerated motion to lift his uphill ski. He pushes forward, stomps the uphill ski and, shifting all his weight to it, presses it through a smooth turn.

The Anselme turn, says Plake.

I quietly direct Beat Steiner, a Super-16mm shooter, to get close shots of their skis, their pole plants. This time, if anything worthwhile happens, I'll get the cutaways on the fly and not have to ask them to re-enact anything.

This is good, Glen, says Anselme. He sidesteps up the small ramp.

This is a special turn for a narrow couloir, says Anselme. So, your weight is all on the downhill ski. Your feet are wide. And it's just so.

Anselme raises his uphill ski, pushes forward, and steps all of his weight onto the uphill ski. The ski responds beautifully, coming around in a tight arc. It looks like the easiest thing Kye has ever seen. Why are these guys making a big deal of it?

Kye sidesteps up. He plants his poles and makes a fast hop turn, his skis leaving the snow as he changes direction.

This is not the one, says Anselme.

Don't jump, just stamp, Plake says. Plant both poles and unweight.

Kye tries again and falls.

Another attempt, this time he rocks back on the tails of his skis.

Be careful, you have to finish your turn on your downhill ski, says

Anselme.

He tries again.

Arghh! Kye yells.

You leaned in, says Plake. The key is to get on the uphill ski first. No hop.

Another.

Anselme: No rotate. You rotated.

Plake: Step and slip. Every turn counts, man.

Anselme: It is a lazy technique.

Plake: But it works the best.

Anselme: Use the least amount of energy when you ski.

Plake: The gravity is the power, not your body.

Another attempt leaves Kye twisted.

You're still jumping, says Plake. If you're skiing down, that's where you want to be looking. Not where you've been. Where you're going. Look where you're going.

The last one is worse than his first. Kye collapses, smacks his hand into the snow.

I can't learn this turn, says Kye. I'm really sorry.

You're all right, says Plake. We'll go someplace where it's steeper and less static and you'll be right.

Hopefully, or else I'm never going to ski nothin', says Kye.

What about this, can you do this? asks Plake. He plants both poles to one side of his skis, springs, and drives his tips into the snow. He rides up and over his tips, using them as a pivot, and lands facing the other way.

Tip roll, says Anselme. He pushes off and snaps up on his tips, executing the old trick perfectly.

Hey! yells Plake. All right!

Kye pushes off, springs, drives his tips into the snow, and falls.

Plake's laughing. Get up!

I'll be fine, says Kye. I'll just have to learn how to ski.

My father taught me the tip roll, says Plake. It was what the ski in-
structor used to do at the bottom of the hill. He'd come down and *bop*,
do it right in front of the lodge. Hello everyone, I'm here, I've arrived!

On the shoulder of the Grands Montets, the snow is hard, smooth as
a hockey rink and slanting down steeply. The town of Chamonix, dark
and delicate, is far below. Kye stands on the steep face. The surface is
blank, the wind calm, the shadows a ghostly blue.

Okay, we work all the way down this, says Anselme. You will get it
here, I think.

Kye kicks his edges into the surface. They barely shave off any snow.

It's hard, he says.

Perfect practice, says Plake. Nail it here and you're good to go.

There is nothing but snow below them—a half mile of linoleum-
hard snow, a kitchen table tipped on edge. If Kye falls here, he will slide
a long, long way, but he won't crash into rocks, fall off a cliff or into a
crevasse. This is a training hill for experts.

Anselme makes three turns, each one ending in a complete stop. Kye
follows; his first turn is nearly as tight as Anselme's, but the next ones
are sloppy, off-balance.

Now, you must get this, says Anselme more sternly than before.

There are other techniques for descending steep slopes that work as
well, but technique is not what Anselme and Plake are really teaching.
They need Kye to learn this turn because with it will come confidence,
which is more important. To stick to the steepest faces, a skier must
believe it is possible. When Kye can make the turn every time, he will
believe in himself. Technique is just a tool. Belief and courage are what
make it work. Sliding back on his heels, he nearly tumbles.

Right there, Plake says. It's right there.

Kye looks at him as if to say, Where?

It's right there in front of you, says Plake. You can do this.

Kye tries again, and again.

Just take it, says Plake. It's yours.

And then something happens, a surprising suppleness. The key is in the initiation of the turn, and Kye's found it. No hop. All edge and pressure. The hill relents; gravity becomes a lubricant. His skis caress rather than chop, and he carves to a complete stop.

Good, says Anselme.

Another turn, smoother still.

Now do another five hundred more of those and you'll be right, says Plake.

Small in a Strong Place

Chamonix, France
Evening, March 13, 2005

Cold night pours into the Chamonix Valley as the last light of day retracts behind stone spires. Far up the hill from Chamonix's cobbled streets, tucked into a fold between the serpentine road and the abrupt rise of the Grands Montets, is the Grand Roc bar, a creaky tavern of rough-hewn wood, free-flowing Stella Artois and framed photographs of French mono-skiers.

I walk in with Kronick, the producer who accompanied me on the hill. Around a varnished wooden table are Yellin and his team. The top director in the production company, Mark Obenhaus, a white-haired fifty-something guy who stands six feet four inches in his skateboard sneakers, is here with his even taller son, Sam, a good-natured kid who's introduced as someone who watches ski films continuously in his college dorm room. Sam is part of the core audience, I'm told. He has suggestions, ideas. Son and father are sunburned, happy from a day on the hill, and enjoying a pleasant après ski.

The older Obenhaus has made films for television about the Kennedy assassination, jazz, opera. Yellin is keen to have his longtime friend and colleague involved in the film, but at this point Obenhaus is uncommitted and my relationship with him is ill-defined. I once skied with Obenhaus at Alta, but since then I haven't had much contact with him. Knowing that Yellin is a careful planner, I assume our vaguely structured working relationship is by design. My contract, the only thing concrete in the shifting world of film production, reads co-producer, writer and co-director. It would seem that I'm supposed to be co-directing with Obenhaus, but I've barely spoken with him since this project began. He's been busy directing a documentary about UFOs.

Give him time to get up to speed, Yellin had said earlier.

The Chamonix trip with his son and wife are part of his getting-up-to-speed process. Kayce is here too. She's spent the day skiing the Grands Montets with Yellin. They're loose, happy and awed.

Any word from Peter? I ask.

It doesn't look like Peter's going to make the trip, reports Gabrielle Tenenbaum, a get-it-done producer for the company, who completes the team.

He's not feeling well, says Kayce.

So, how'd we do today? asks Obenhaus. He and Sam lean forward, clearly excited.

Fine, I say. Plake and Anselme taught Kye some stuff. It was good. Long day.

There's beer on the table, an empty pitcher next to one that's half full.

And how did Kye do? asks Kayce.

I think he did pretty well, I say. Anyone else hungry?

Tell me what you did, where you went, says Obenhaus. Everything.

Then I get it. This isn't a kick-back-and-have-a-beer moment. This is a download, a postmortem on the shoot. Cooked by the sun and sore from carrying a backpack filled with cameras all day, I'm not in a story-telling mood. It's eight o'clock, and I'm still in ski boots.

You tell 'em, Jordan, I say.

Kronick is good. He gives the whole update, scene-by-scene, everything boiled down to essentials. A lawyer by training, he knows how to build a case. When he's done, they're excited. They want to know about the Glacier Rond: Is there any chance Kye might ski it?

If it happens, we're going to need a helicopter to shoot it, I say.

That's completely wrong, says Obenhaus. It's an intimate moment for Kye, and you're going to go blazing in there with a helicopter?

It's a tough place to shoot, I say, bending to unbuckle my boots. Our guys won't be able to ski it. It's fifty, fifty-five degrees.

Can you ski it? asks Kayce.

Probably, I say. But we need a better shooter than I am. We need one of our guys in a chopper.

That just feels wrong, says Obenhaus. Kye has his father's ashes. This is his private moment. You're going to ruin it with a helicopter hovering there.

Maybe we could just have one standing by, I say.

How much is *that* going to cost? asks Gabrielle.

No, I don't think so, says Obenhaus. No helicopter.

I look over at Yellin. He's just watching the dynamic. It's clear he's not going to step in.

I think Obenhaus is wrong, but it's late, I want out of these ski boots, and I don't want to kick off our working relationship by fighting over something that's probably not going to happen anyway. Despite the fact that Kye's trying hard, I know he's not ready for something as steep as the Rond. He'll have to improve an awful lot, and so many other variables will have to come together—weather, snow, schedules—that it's not worth arguing about now. I figure we have a week, maybe two, to sort it out.

Okay, I say. Forget it.

And then I add, Dumb idea.

It's one of the things I will most regret saying.

The next morning, Plake, Fanfan, the film crew and I are at the top of the Grands Montets. The wind is up, the first high, thin clouds slipping in from the west. Anselme is back in his classroom.

Kye is in his skis at the base of the stairway. Plake checks his edges by running his hand slowly down the ski. Kye slides up next to him. Another day of practice on hard snow has given Kye the turn. Whether he has belief is another question.

So, if the weather's warm and the light is correct, says Plake to Kye, we might ski what we skied in *The Blizzard of Aahhh's*: the Poubelle Couloir. It might be a perfect way for you to have your first real run. We'll go down and look at it.

Kye nods.

The Poubelle is a look-in, continues Plake. It's not like hike up and then rappel down and go around the corner and lower in and all of a sudden you go, oh, we're going to ski there? No, this is, ski to the top and look in to see if it's right.

I'm ready for something like that, right? says Kye.

Yeah, you can do it. Heck, you can go in first. But we gotta see if the snow gets nice.

Let's go now, says Kye.

Fanfan is a few meters away, checking his gear, and listening carefully to Kye's tone.

No, it's an afternoon thing, says Plake. We need to wait for the snow to soften some.

If it doesn't happen, I want to find someplace else, says Kye. I'm going crazy.

You gotta wait until the snow gets right.

Now Fanfan slides over, his helmet on, pack straps cinched tight. A cream-colored silk scarf dangles from his pack. Given to him by a monk in Tibet, he told me it protects him more than any helmet ever could. It's one of his secret weapons, one of the ways he finds belief.

Kye, we need to explain to you the place where we are, says Fanfan. This is the big mountain. We need to go over the things we can do and the things that we don't do.

Okay, but can we find a place to jump?

Fanfan just grins and shakes his head as he leads them east, off the saddle and into a massive valley of high, jagged walls. At the head of the valley is L'Argentière Peak. Two high ridges extend northward from the peak, their walls stippled with rock, ice, tongues of snow. The valley floor is moving an inch an hour. The Argentière Glacier is a river of hundred-year-old ice a mile wide, cracked and blue at the edges.

Fanfan skis down through a heavily trafficked funnel formed by snow fences, and then angles off to the right. Kye whips toward the funnel, hits a small mogul, and spins around backward. He hits an ice patch and spins forward again, slashing a quick turn to make it through the fences.

Save the tricks for later, says Plake.

Kye just gives him a wave and a grin, which Plake can't help but return. Fanfan pushes powerfully through a long right-hand turn, driving against the fall line. He stops at a boundary rope with a sign in French that says: Beyond this point you are on your own. Kye pulls up, then Plake.

So it's okay to duck this rope? asks Kye, edging forward as if to take the lead.

Of course, says Fanfan.

Here it's your responsibility, says Plake.

After this line we are entering off-piste, says Fanfan. There is no help here. We have to be careful of everything. For example, see those broken pieces of snow?

He points to refrigerator-sized blocks of snow that look like they've been dumped by a truck.

This is coming from a big avalanche, continues Fanfan. Everywhere we go we have to understand where we are. Kye, you must always be looking above you to see what could come down on your head.

Kye looks up the hill at the shadowy wall that runs down the western side of the valley. He pushes back on his poles, subtly backing away from the rope.

Okay, duuuude? asks Fanfan, doing his best Glen Plake impersonation.

Plake gives him a *very funny* look. Kye laughs as they duck the rope. Skiing fast, they cross a long traverse under craggy rock spires, truncated glaciers, hanging seracs. Sun shafts poke through irregular openings in the serrated ridgeline. Skis clatter across wind-scoured patches of ice.

Glory glory, who's that man who's trying to fly, sings Plake as he straight-runs the traverse. *Glory, glory, that's a sport I'll never try.*

Plake sings long-forgotten songs about skiing and sometimes writes his own. There's a singer in Chamonix who performs his tunes at local bars.

Fanfan arcs up a ridge, glances quickly up the hill to the cliff faces above, and snaps to a stop. Plake greases in next to him. Kye slides to a snow-spraying, skittery stop, the kind you use to impress the après-ski deck. Fanfan and Plake just grin.

So, Kye, now we are off the piste and on the Argentière Glacier. It is a very, very beautiful place, yes?

Fanfan glances over at me and the two cameras that are trained on him. Then he sweeps his hand around to display the mountains like some high-elevation game show host. He indicates an immense natural cathedral, towering spires, walls a mile high, and the otherworldly blue of glacial ice. The grandeur of the place is almost too much.

It's awesome, says Kye, using the word properly, for once.

But there is something I need to explain to you, continues Fanfan, becoming serious, turning away from the cameras and focusing completely on Kye. The mountain is very big, and we are very small here. The one thing you must do in the big mountains is realize that you are a very small thing in a place that is more stronger than you.

Much more, says Plake.

You have to learn to be not pushing every time, continues Fanfan. If you want to do something strong, you can do it, but you have to wait until the mountain is ready for you.

Kye nods, reluctantly.

So, if you stop somewhere, you have to look up, says Fanfan. Never stop somewhere where something can happen to you. For example, this serac, you never stop under it because we never know when it is going to come down.

Kye looks to where Fanfan is pointing. A blue-gray ice block sits precariously at the edge of a nearly vertical wall. The serac is the size of a house.

When they fall, they just explode, says Plake. It looks like a bomb went off. They cover the glacier from edge to edge with debris. It's almost like you have to have a sixth sense about them. When airplanes fly over, there isn't one person on this crew who won't look up the hill because we're never sure if it's one of those things coming down.

You need to smell it, says Fanfan, touching his nose. You need to feel it.

Time is part of it too, says Plake. You have to be in the rhythm of the mountains. Sometimes we could go across this glacier and nothing would happen, but other times this could be the craziest place you could go. It's like you have to be in the same breath as the hills. You have to feel it. Does the mountain want you here or not right now? It's true, believe it or not.

Kye is withdrawing, pulling into himself. There's a limit to how much cautionary advice a young man can take.

The big difference in Chamonix, says Fanfan, is that most of the time we ski the big glaciers. Here the most dangerous thing is the crevasse. So you must learn where you can ski and where you can't ski.

He points with his pole.

Here we can see that the glacier follows the movement of the ground, and most of the time the crevasses form where the glacier gets steeper.

He holds his arm horizontally, cocking his wrist downward to show a slope that suddenly gets steep.

It's like water in a creek, says Plake. When the slope goes down quickly you get rapids, and when it goes down really quick you get a waterfall. It's the same here. When it gets steep the river breaks into frozen pieces.

But often you cannot see the crevasse because it is covered with snow, says Fanfan. Snow makes bridges across the crevasse, but it may be ready to break. With speed you cross the crevasse no problem, but if you stop you could be on top of the crevasse and maybe you broke the bridge.

Okay, says Kye, trying to absorb as much information as possible.

That's why we're wearing our harnesses, says Plake. If you do fall in, it's a lot easier to pull you out.

Anselme told me about a guy who fell into one and got frozen in for good, offers Kye.

There are terrible stories, says Plake, tapping Kye's shins with his pole. Sometimes, when you fall into a crevasse, you break both legs automatically. Or you break your hips.

In some places we'll be roped though, right? asks Kye.

Right, says Plake. Let's say we have to cross this glacier. Fanfan will have a rope that's tied to you and, fifty or sixty feet behind you, I will have a rope, too. Fanfan will go first, and then you and then me. Chances are we're not all going to fall into a crevasse at the same time. So he may fall in. Then you break, you know, by putting your skis sideways. Then I hit the deck and you and I are the anchors. Then we need to set up a formation to get him out. On the other hand, if you fall in, in the middle, then we have an interesting rescue because we have anchors on both sides. Different techniques. It's all rope skills and mountaineering skills. But if we're traveling through the glacier, for sure, we'll rope up.

So, just to see, says Fanfan, which way do you think you can take from here?

Kye looks down the hill. They're on a large, rounded hump. Straight down the hill from them it drops off quickly. Inside, I'm rooting for Kye, urging him to pick the right line.

That looks like a problem zone, says Kye, pointing at the steep spill of slope beneath them. It looks like right through there is the least roll-over, so it should be safest.

That's good, Kye, says Fanfan.

From where I stand, behind one of the cameras, I want to cheer.

Yeah? says Kye, sounding a little surprised. Right on.

Oh, one more thing, Kye, says Plake. See that mountain over there?

Kye follows Plake's ski pole to a single, slightly curved fang.

Yeah.

That's the Matterhorn. You ever seen the Matterhorn?

Only in pictures.

Well, there it is, dude, the Matterhorn!

Wow, says Kye.

Fanfan begins laughing.

I'm just messing with you, says Plake. That's not the freakin' Matterhorn. That's what you hear the tourists say at the top of the Aiguille du Midi. Every sharp peak they'll look at and say, honey, there's the Matterhorn!

The glacier opens beneath us. The skiers are skirting one of the walls, traversing deeper into the glacier, far downhill from the seracs and cornices. Fanfan drops in; the snow is as dense and stiff as month-old cream cheese. He makes angular turns, his stance upright, arms quiet, ski edges slicing cleanly.

Plake is looser, smoother, flowing through turns like a swimmer. Kye can't resist flipping to ski around backward, covering the long slope in great hip-leaning carves.

As he pulls up to the others, Plake and Fanfan are laughing. Backwards skiing is a generational thing. Only kids do it. The men smile.

Kye deliberately looks up, scanning the chutes that empty onto the glacier. Fanfan takes notice. They're standing on the hard edge of a dark shadow off the western ridge of the valley. Kye points up at one of the chutes that's draped in shadow.

Anselme did the first descent on that one, Kye says proudly.

That's right, says Fanfan. A lot of those he did first. Those cols are huge.

There are seven or eight direct chutes, all eight hundred to a thousand meters, says Plake, longer than most ski areas back in the States. And you get to stand on your edge the whole way down. Most ski films don't show this type of skiing. You can't straight-line these, thinking you're cool. It's not Alaska.

I've seen movies of guys skiing this stuff and I was like, What are those guys doing? says Kye

They're surviving on every turn is what they're doing, says Plake.

The hard shadow of the ridge suddenly disappears as clouds close out the sun. In seconds the light goes completely flat. The porcelain blue of the French sky is suddenly swathed in gauze. The glacier surface is a blank page, out of focus.

Okay, now we must go off this, says Fanfan. I don't like being on the glacier when the light is this way. Follow me exactly, Kye. The same track, eh?

I'm on it, says Kye.

We can see nothing, says Fanfan as he begins to traverse. It looks very safe, but you see this small hole?

He points to a dark hole about the size of a football.

I think that down this hole, there could be a crevasse about fifty meters. He begins sidestepping up around it, giving the hole a wide berth. Kye hikes right in his tracks. He's moving sharply, responsibly, taking charge of his own destiny.

Fanfan stops as he crests a knoll. He's spotted something farther out on the glacier. He waves me over to him. Hiking in his tracks I step up next to him.

Okay, I change my mind, he says, lifting his arm and pointing. I take you out to this area to show you something special, but you keep all your crew behind me. Don't let anyone move off my track.

Fanfan leads us to a spot just below a gaping crevasse twenty meters across, its walls dirty and hard with old ice. Its base is dark, unfathomable. We get there just as a skier drops in above the crevasse. The man's edges bite pleasingly into glacial snow. Kye, Plake and Fanfan watch as the skier makes turns right up to the lip of the crevasse, and falls in. Plummeting toward blackness, he grabs futilely at the side of the crevasse, then jerks to a stop. Above, a rope pulls taut, and a man heaves backward, digging the tails of his skis into the snow.

There are cheers from the fallen man's friends.

Kye stares wide-eyed.

These are the gendarmes, says Fanfan. Training for crevasse rescue.

Look at that up there, says Plake, pointing to the single track in the snow above the crevasse. You'd be like, hey, great powder snow, and no tracks, but guess what? These things could be five feet. They could be ten feet. Or you could fall and go all the way down into never.

Plake, Fanfan and Kye stand at the edge of never, gazing into the black heart of the abyss. The man on the rope dangles, snow falling off his skis, disappearing below. He swings himself over to a small shelf. Reaching over his shoulder, he releases an ice ax from his pack. He drives the tip into the ice. *Clonk.* The sound is hollow. The man pulls himself up as his partner on the rope above takes in slack.

The gendarme, they are very good, says Fanfan. They get a lot of practice in getting people out of very bad places. Sometimes they use helicopters, sometimes they just use ropes, but they are never not busy.

Yeah, hopefully we don't have to call these guys, says Plake with a laugh.

chapter **9**

The Eagle's Lair

Chamonix, France
March 14, 2005

At lunch in the cafeteria at mid-mountain on the Grands Montets, Plake is making the rounds, glad-handing, greeting friends he's never met. Kye and Iberg sit with Anselme, talking quietly. Kronick, who's become my filmmaker conscience, nods toward them and asks me if I want to shoot. It's not so much a question as a suggestion. I look over at them again, just as Kye laughs at something that Anselme or Iberg has said. There's ketchup on his face.

Let's let them be, I say. Let them develop a real relationship without cameras on them, and it will be better when we're shooting. Besides, the crew is starving.

Kronick disagrees, but he's hungry too, so he lets it go and heads off to the cafeteria line.

How's it going? asks Yellin, as he sits down.

Between mouthfuls I describe the crevasse rescue. Yellin nods. Outside, the sky is streaked with high, thin clouds, scudding fast across the horizon.

Looks like a little front moving in, I say. We're probably not going to get much more today. The light's too flat.

Shoot what you can, says Yellin.

Plake and Fanfan want to do a reconnaissance of the Poubelle Couloir, I say.

If they're doing, we're shooting, says Yellin.

Of course, I say, not bothering to add the inverse to his dictum: If we're shooting, they're doing.

Low, gray clouds fill the open spaces between dark peaks. The afternoon sky has closed out and the wind has picked up. The only run off the Grands Montets is clogged. Nearly everyone on the mountain is beating a hasty retreat, but Fanfan, Plake and Kye are going for one more. Chairlifts are empty and the tram has stopped running, but the gondola continues to move uphill, its cars lurching in the gusts coming out of the west. This sort of wind would shut down the lifts at most North American ski resorts. The safety concerns and potential lawsuits would be too much, but here at the summit terminus of the gondola, the attendant, a man in his mid-fifties with a heavily pocked face and a bored slouch, casually smokes a cigarette and watches the gondola cabins swing sideways. Most arrive empty. Kye, Fanfan and Plake step out of their car, grab skis from the outside rack, and walk out of the building and into the wind.

Fanfan's Tibetan scarf streams from his backpack, Plake's orange hair flutters beneath his black hat, and the fur on Kye's collar flattens in the gale. The skiers skate across a small plateau toward a boundary line marked with hollow steel poles strung with cables. Beyond the boundary is a long, deep gash in the mountain. This is the Poubelle Couloir. The wind whistles mournfully over the tops of the poles. The cables vibrate and hum.

Aigle, aigle, yells Fanfan as he points to the sky.

A large eagle soars up the chute.

Oh, it's huge, man, says Kye.

The eagle rises above our heads, moving through the air at high speed, perfectly still, sailing on fast-moving currents. Kye watches intently. Wings outstretched, the bird cranes its neck and looks down on Kye and Plake and Fanfan. It banks through a tight circle, floating lazily over the throat of the chute.

Beautiful. We are lucky to see this, says Fanfan.

That's pretty rare for Europe, says Plake.

The eagle catches an updraft and soars over Kye. It keeps on rising, motionless, approaching the highest peaks.

Kye watches the eagle, but Plake is more intent on the couloir that opens on the other side of the steel cables. It's a classic of ski mountaineering. Rock walls rise two hundred feet, forming a deep V, their faces craggy and dark. The couloir entry is narrow, perhaps 240 centimeters across—hardly enough for a pair of skis. On either side are sharp rocks, some barely pushing through the snow, others poking several feet above the surface. Twenty meters downhill from the entry, fins of rock rise ten to twenty feet. A fall on the upper portion will send a skier sliding into the fins—not fatal, unless someone is unlucky, but there is certainly a risk of injury. This is known as a cheese grater.

So what do you think? asks Plake. You all right?

Yeah, I'm stoked, says Kye. I think my dad is stoked, too. I think he was just flying over us.

Yeah, I saw it, says Plake. It's funny to think about those things, huh? Kye nods and smiles.

I skied this with your dad a couple times, says Plake. It was easy access. You just go up this lift and slide over.

It's a good tune-up, says Fanfan. There's not really much exposure.

What Fanfan means is that if Kye falls, he won't tumble off a cliff. The principal dangers in the Poubelle Couloir are slamming into one of the couloir walls, tumbling into the cheese grater, or getting caught in an avalanche. Beyond the cheese grater, farther down into the chute, the narrow lane of snow widens to six or seven meters. It plummets straight down before it makes the first bend. With new or sun-baked snow, this section is bound to slough and can easily toss a skier into the wall where the chute bends. Below the first bend, the chute doglegs and narrows twice more before it opens in a wide meadow far below.

What does Poubelle mean? asks Kye.

This couloir is very close to the civilization, says Fanfan. Everybody gets out of the cable car and comes here for a look. And some of the guys, they throw the garbage. So they call it garbage can. Poubelle means garbage can. So you have to be careful when you ski.

Yeah, that no one throws garbage on me, says Kye.

There's lots of poubelles, says Plake. This is the poubelle on the Grands Montets. There's one on the Aiguille du Midi. We did this one in *Blizzard*. It was our first, and this will be your first thing with a name.

He points past the couloir to a wide ravine of steeply sloping powder, flanked on all sides by dark, irregular spires.

When you're skiing the Alps, Plake says, places with names mean more. The chute ends on the Pas de Chevre, which means goat path, but it's quite a lot of space for a goat. It's one of the most famous powder runs in Europe.

When it's good and when it's powder, this is the most beautiful run you can have in Chamonix, says Fanfan. It's a dreamland.

Let's hike up here and get a better look, says Plake.

The whistling of the wind through the poles grows louder—a flute elevated to the pitch of a siren. Kicking out of their skis, the three men hike up a short knob. The wind flings loose pellets, skimming the surface, blurring the line between sky and snow. Kye pulls up his hood.

At the top of the rise, Fanfan ducks under the boundary cable and steps out on a high fang of rock. Plake follows him carefully. Kye looks to Fanfan.

It is okay, Glen will put you on a line, says Fanfan.

We're just going to let you look it over, says Plake. We'll clip you 'cause the wind's blowin'. Take your time.

The sky presses down, low clouds coming in harder now. It's a fast-moving front. The first flakes are small and sharp, and any exposed skin feels the sting. Kye ducks under the cables and carefully inches out onto the rock next to Plake, who clips Kye's harness into a strap that he's attached to one of the boundary poles. As Kye climbs onto the rock, Plake holds a hand on his back.

You're all right, he says. You're tied in, so if you want to throw a leg over there it's all right.

Kye wiggles up on the rock. He carefully moves his leg over the edge so that he's sitting on it like a saddle.

There you go, ride it like a horse, says Plake.

Below Kye, it's a hundred feet straight down to the snow.

It looks sick from here, says Kye. I'll tell you that.

From this perch, almost directly above the couloir, it looks like a thin canal of frozen water, tipped on edge. Fanfan steps gingerly onto the rock next to Kye. Kye glances over at him: plastic ski boots on hard rock, no rope, no protection. The wind gusts, shoving at the three men. One slip and Fanfan will fall a hundred feet. Noticing the look from Kye, Fanfan arches his back and pounds his chest like Tarzan. Kye laughs and Fanfan, having had his moment, climbs down and sits casually next to Kye. He gestures toward the chute like a man feeding pigeons.

At the entry you have to be very careful, says Fanfan. It is very steep at the top.

Yeah, I see that, says Kye.

We might have you rappel in, says Plake. With your twin tips you can just get the cord set, lean back, and go fakey right into the thing.

You are happy skiing backwards, eh Kye? adds Fanfan.

Kye laughs and then looks again at the entry. I think I can get down that without rappelling, he says.

Good. Just make sure that you don't make a turn until you feel it, says Fanfan. If you make a turn, you do it. There's no …

He waggles his hand and shrugs his shoulders to suggest indecision.

If you do it, you do it.

This is too narrow to use the Anselme turn, says Plake. You have to hop-turn it.

If you're not sure, says Fanfan, we don't do it.

If the snow's good, says Kye, I think I can.

That's it, says Plake. Get used to waiting. Maybe tomorrow.

Plake and Fanfan back away from the edge and duck back under the boundary line. For a moment Kye is alone on the high, thin knife-edge. Straddling the rock, he rests his upper body and then his head on the edge of the rock as if he were hugging it. His whole body supported by the mountain, he looks all the way down the chute, nodding to himself, visualizing every turn he'll make.

The film production team—Yellin, Obenhaus, Kayce and Gabrielle— has our usual table in the Grand Roc bar. Obenhaus offers beer from a pitcher. I decline, and Yellin asks if I've quit drinking. I tell him I'm not having a drink until this thing is over. What I don't tell him is about the pain in my stomach that's been with me since I set out on this trip. Alcohol only makes it worse. I sit for the download.

I've accepted this daily summit as a necessary part of the day's work. Everyone in the world has someone to answer to, why shouldn't I? Kronick and I take turns telling them about the Poubelle recon, and the plans for Kye's first big test. Obenhaus asks how I intend to film it.

I'll have the high-def crew at the top, I say, the Super-16 camera roped in on a fin of rock right above the couloir. We'll have a long lens across the valley at the hotel at the top of the train tracks, a helmet cam on Fanfan, and I'll film the chute with them.

You're going to ski it? asks Kayce.

Yeah, I say, why should they have all the fun?

What about the crew? asks Obenhaus. You probably should stay with them.

They'll ski down the Grands Montets, I say. Down the piste. Jordan can ski it with them.

If they want, says Jordan Kronick, they can ride down on the gondola.

Okay, says Yellin. Sounds okay.

Let's hope the kid can ski it, says Obenhaus.

I'd bet on him, I say—which is exactly what I've done.

chapter 10

The Cheese Grater

Chamonix, France
Morning, March 15, 2005

The sky is clear, sun rising warmly. Fifteen centimeters of snow have fallen, and the garbage chute is a thin white strip of unsoiled beauty. The harsh light turns the couloir into an overexposed photograph. The rocks are the colorless black of deep space, and the white seems lit from within. I'm there early with the film crew. Plake and Anselme are the first skiers to arrive.

I think that the new snow has melted into the old snow, Plake says. How do you say, *adhesion?*

He uses the English word with a heavy French accent, rubbing his palms together. Anselme looks at him with amusement.

The two layers have come together, Plake offers. Anyway, it's better than dust on crust.

Plake laughs at himself.

At the top it is good, says Anselme. But in the middle, it is crusty and then slushy. And all the way down, *shhhhhh,* water is coming down. Sometimes the sun is heating the rocks, and maybe you have rock slides at the bottom.

Fanfan arrives with Kye. Both wear helmets.

Kye shakes Anselme's hand.

You are doing well I hear, says Anselme. This is good.

Kye shrugs, smiling, clearly buoyed by the praise.

The snow looks very good, says Fanfan. I am a little bit surprised.

But we must not take too long, says Anselme to Fanfan. The sun, eh?

Fanfan agrees, and Anselme ducks under the boundary cable to set up his skis. As he does, on-piste skiers from the gondola begin to take notice and slide over to see what the group is doing.

Kye looks down the chute. The Poubelle is a rifle site that's pointed straight at the base of Mont Blanc, the Aiguille du Midi and the Glacier Rond. He kicks off his skis and walks uphill to find a place to relieve himself.

Anselme gives Fanfan instructions in French. Then he turns to Plake, who's been trying to follow it, and explains in English: It's better that Kye ski down and Fanfan holds the rope, says Anselme. He does not have a solid enough technique to rappel.

Kye holds the cable and stares at the chute. Plake steps up next to him.

I've skied similar chutes in Whistler but none as steep as this is at the top, says Kye.

So, we'll get you on the cord, says Plake. Make sure you talk to Fanfan because he's going to feed you rope. You say, Okay, I'm going to turn, and he gives you rope to make the turn.

Okay, so I'll just yell.

Anselme hums a song as he ties the knot to one of the steel poles that hold the boundary lines.

Remember, it's real long, so don't blow everything here at the top, cautions Plake. We'll do this right. We'll ski it in sections, one at a time.

Anselme clips a carabiner to Kye's harness. *Voila*, he says.

Thanks, says Kye.

Lock 'n' load, send the kid in, says Nate Wallace, an expatriate American who we've hired to carry camera gear. Don't worry, kid, you're young, you'll bounce.

Kye gives him a look but doesn't say a word.

They call him super skier and he swore he'd never spill, sings Plake.

Anselme checks the rope by tugging on it.

Use the turn like we do the other day, says Anselme. A little stop at the end of each. And you stop after each part, okay? You don't go fast. No attacking the couloir.

You okay, Kye? asks Fanfan as he picks up the rope.

Yep, I'm happy more than nervous.

Don't do it! You'll all die! screams a man from the uphill side of the crowd. Turn around! What do you think this wire is here for? Are you guys crazy? Are you drunk or what? You're all gonna die!

The yelling man bears a striking resemblance to Jack Nicholson. Plake recognizes him and laughs. He's an American bar singer who sometimes sings the songs that Plake writes.

There are a lot of people, says Kye to Fanfan. I didn't expect it to be like this.

It's okay, says Fanfan, and then with a laugh he adds, no pressure.

Kye lowers his goggles and looks intently down the couloir.

You want to bet how many turns we can make through the rocks? asks Plake. Anselme just smiles at him.

Kye, only if there is room enough, you turn, if you're not sure, don't, because there are rocks, says Anselme. We'll rendezvous below the rocks where it's safe for everybody.

So, you can ski exactly like you don't have the rope, says Fanfan. But don't go too fast. If you feel you can make a turn because you have the security of the rope, it is okay. And then we put you off the rope. Then you have to ski. Really. So don't go fakey in the couloir.

No, I won't.

Just make sure your turns are one by one, says Anselme. Each one right. You can do this.

The crowd is now two, three deep along the boundary line—kids squeezing through their parents' legs to look. A man in a dark, one-piece ski suit pulls a small video camera out of his coat. Then another appears and a third. Snapshot cameras bloom.

Anselme wears no helmet, no goggles, just a pair of sunglasses—the glass kind that pilots wear—and a black ball cap. He looks over at Kye and nods. Kye nods back. And then Anselme takes his poles and holds them together, digging them both in on the uphill side, like a man at the tiller of a boat. With a roll of his ankles he releases his edges and starts side-slipping. He leans hard on his ski poles, digging the tips into the snow. As he feels the surface, he lets up on the poles slightly, rights his stance by a few degrees, and lets his slide pick up speed.

The crowd goes quiet.

Be careful, Kye, because it is scratchy under this, says Anselme.

He moves through the narrow chute perfectly, his tips and tails clearing the protruding rock fins by mere inches. As the chute widens by a foot, then two, he rolls his feet into a quick turn. Twist, hop, snap, he turns the other way. Then he stops and stabs something with his pole.

There is a rock in the middle! he yells back up to the other skiers.

He hops sideways over the rock. Rolling his ankles and knees toward the hill, Anselme traverses left and slides to a smooth stop in a protected pocket under an overhang. He kicks his downhill leg forward until the tail of the ski is above the snow. He drops the tail into the snow and twists his tip until it is pointing behind him. Then, completing the kick turn, he steps around the twisted leg and brings his whole body to face the couloir. Out of the direct path of falling rocks or an avalanche, he will wait here for the other skiers to join him.

A man in the crowd yells: *Vous êtes toujours l'homme*—you are still the man!

Ski gloves thud in low, pounding applause. Kye nervously kicks his boot toe into the snow.

I've never seen that technique before, he says. That was rad, the way he used his poles like an anchor.

You just use what you know, says Fanfan.

Am I next? Kye is shaking.

Scott and Bill must get into position and then Glen is next, says Fanfan.

Still photographer Scott Markewitz is a former pro skier who was also a close friend of Trevor's. He and I duck under the cable and pick our way carefully into the chute. It's not pretty—we're both carrying heavy packs and not trying to put on a show—but we get down and find a safe nook to shoot from.

Plake slips under the line next.

Good to go, Kye? he asks. You've got your dancing shoes on?

Lock and load, says Kye.

Plake sets up right where Anselme started. He prods the snow under his downhill ski with his pole, then bounces on his edges to get a feel for the surface.

I've got my short skis on, says Plake.

I'm excited to see this, says Kye to Fanfan.

Plake springs into the air. He spins his skis 180 degrees, lands solidly, both poles driving into the snow, a flex of his knees to test the surface. Now he's in the air again, snapping his skis into another 180-degree turn. With each hop he descends fifteen feet down the hill, but his line stays straight. Six inches forward or aft will put him into the rocks.

Glen Plake, there it is, says Fanfan.

Yep, that style, you can see it a hundred miles away, agrees Kye.

The rocks pass his tips, orange hair flying. Plake moves tightly, within himself. He's performing now. The mountain is his stage. It's as if he leaves a little doubt behind on each turn. You can't take your eyes off Plake because you sense that he might, just might, overextend and crash big. It never happens, but he lets you *think* it could. It's part of his gift, why the cameras still follow him after twenty years.

The eagle's back, says Kye.

The crowd presses tight to the wire.

Okay, Kye, now we go, says Fanfan, coiling the extra rope neatly near his feet.

That was my dad's favorite animal, Kye says to Fanfan. The eagle.

Okay, so now you can put on your skis, says Fanfan, not interested in birds right now.

Kye ducks under the cable, and Fanfan grabs his harness to make sure it's on tight.

Make sure you have nothing on your boot, Fanfan cautions.

Kye scrapes the underside of his boot on the toe piece of his binding.

Okay, one by one. Make sure each binding is okay, says Fanfan.

Kye steps in with one foot, then the other. He looks to the sky, scanning for the eagle, but it's gone. Then he drops his gaze to the cheese grater and shuffles his feet nervously. The crowd is still. Three, four, five video cameras are aimed at him. Five documentary cameras are rolling.

Kye bends over and reaches down the hill with his pole. His skis slip. He drives his downhill edge to stop. He nods his head. Just testing.

For the first half you are on the rope and you are safe, so no problem, says Fanfan. But then we put you off the rope. And when you put off the rope, you have to ski for real. It is just you and your skis. Go slowly. If you want to make a turn, you tell me, but if you want to slide, you slide.

Kye steps into place. The snow is harder now. Anselme and Plake have scraped all the new snow off. Kye begins to side-slip. His uphill ski catches and rocks him sideways, down the hill toward the cheese grater. The eagle banks above the crowd, but all eyes are on Kye. He's about to cartwheel down the chute. He heaves his downhill ski out of the snow, jumps up, and hops both skis into the air. He covers two meters in a blink, and then sets his skis down hard. The edges find purchase. Kye skitters to a stop and collects himself.

Little bit of slack! he yells.

Fanfan lets the rope run through his hands as Kye leaps free of the snow. He spins his skis 180 degrees, floats, and returns to the surface, both edges biting, both poles stabbing. The crowd yelps.

Yeah! Kye! screams Eric Iberg.

Bolstered, confidence building, he hops into the air again, spinning his skis effortlessly, quicker even than Plake with his longer skis. One turn, another, gaining momentum. Spring, spin, stab the landing. Spring, spin, stab. Each turn sends a platoon of snowballs tumbling down, smashing off rocks, skittering out of sight. The chute is alive. The crowd chatters excitedly. The eagle circles. Fanfan closes his hands on the rope and pulls it taut.

Kye, Kye, Kye, listen to me! yells Fanfan. Be careful of the rock.

Got it, yells Kye as he hops over it, landing solidly, his knee ramming into his chin.

Okay, good, yells Fanfan. You have one more turn with the rope, and after, you stop and put off the rope. Be careful with the rock on the right side. And go slowly. Make sure.

Kye makes one more turn. Most of the jagged rocks are above him, but he is still in a no-fall zone. He carefully unclips the carabiner from his harness.

I'm off! he yells.

Anselme clenches his jaw, watching.

He'll be right, Plake says quietly.

Kye adjusts his pole straps, looks down the chute, then up to the sky. The rope recedes as, far above, Fanfan slowly coils it. The crowd is quiet. Heat comes off the black rocks. Through the lens, I see sweat beads in the sunblock on Kye's chin. Small strips of fog climb up his goggles.

Kye stabs his downhill pole into the snow and tests it. Solid. He pivots around the pole into a smooth Anselme turn. Another pole-plant starts the next turn. Smooth and solid. One at a time.

There's a contained confidence in each leap, a focused edging on every landing. He is living the moment we came here for. The mountain yields; the chute widens.

Yeah, Kye! says Plake.

Kye skis off to the side into the safety zone where his mentors are waiting. Anselme nods and smiles softly as he begins to breathe again.

Now Kye is beaming, his smile unconstrained. I try to zoom in on him, but Plake moves into my way. He is stripping off a layer, stuffing a sweat-soaked shirt into his pack. He's already on to the next.

Okay, Kye, this was good, says Anselme. I think you will be okay. He lowers his sunglasses and taps his poles together.

Wait, are you leaving? asks Kye.

Yes, I must go to the school. You are with good people.

I'll catch you later, says Kye hopefully.

Anselme smiles as he slides backwards on his skis, nudging the tips into the fall line.

I'll bring the book, says Kye.

Good, says Anselme as he rides the uphill ski and shears the snow with a smooth, effortless turn. The spider is in motion—one arc, two, and then he's gone.

Above, Fanfan stows the rope in his pack. He uses the tip of his ski pole to shave shreds of hanging wax off the bases of his skis. Ducking under the wire, he gently lays down his skis.

It is getting warm, he says to a man in the crowd. Could be a problem down below.

He scrapes his boot sole on a rock to clear any ice. He steps into his bindings and loops pole straps over his wrists.

I have too long skis for this, he says, meaning his skis are almost as long as the opening is wide.

He clicks his poles together three times—snapping sticky snow off his baskets and signaling himself to focus—and steps into his first turn with a simple and smooth springing motion. Not exactly a hop, nothing showy about it. He lands and allows his skis to slip backwards to give him room for the next turn. Another hop, another backslide. He has power in his skiing that Plake and Anselme don't have. There is no separation between who he is and what he's doing.

Not bad, he says as he arrives in the safety zone.

That eagle's been flying, says Plake.

Really, where? Kye cranes his neck.

I think this is his place, says Fanfan.

Kye scans the sky, unable to spot the bird.

Looking down, the middle section of the couloir widens as it doglegs to the right. For a hundred meters it is wide enough to make giant-slalom turns. A fall here will send a skier sliding into the rock wall at the bend. Injury is possible but unlikely in this section. Relative to the danger they've just skied through, it feels like a playground. Kye loosens his harness.

Hey Kye, you know what a danglebanger is? asks Plake.

A what? says Kye.

Danglebanger, Fanfan? Plake asks again as he pushes off.

Fanfan just stares at the strange American skiing toward him. Plake coils, plants his downhill pole, and springs into the air. He drives his up-hill shoulder, a dive straight down the fall line. The bottoms of his skis flash white. Plake is weightless. He's doing a front flip in the couloir!

Landing on his shoulder, bending his knees, he tucks into a perfect shoulder roll. And he's up. Moving flawlessly into another turn.

He's crazy, says Fanfan.

What the hell was that? asks Kye.

Doppel ... how does he say? Doppeldangler?

Bangledopper.

Kye and Fanfan share a laugh.

Now, Bill, I think it is okay for us to ski this section together, Fanfan tells me. I ski behind him to get the shot, eh?

Fanfan has a tiny camera strapped to his helmet. He figures he can film Kye without putting either one of them in much danger.

If you think it's safe, I say.

It's okay, says Fanfan. Now, Kye, I am right behind you. Just keep moving.

Kye shakes his goggles, forcing air through the lenses to clear them, and then pushes off fast. He pulls quickly away from Fanfan, off the cord and on his own. Pent-up energy drives his edges. Pole plants snap like punches. Snow flies. Fanfan has to straight-run to catch the kid. When he does they drop into a synchronized rhythm. The effect on film is jittery and alive.

Okay, Kye, now out to the right, yells Fanfan.

Fanfan turns past Kye and ramps out into a safety zone that has opened in the dogleg of the chute. Kye pulls up as he looks down the last section: straight down, narrower with a double fall line, and a constriction at the end of the chute.

Kye, be careful here because I think that the snow is changing a lot, says Fanfan. At the bottom I think it is sketchy.

Suddenly we hear a low booming sound, like the distant thunder of storm surf. This is the sound of avalanche. Plake and Fanfan share a look. Fanfan looks at me.

I think we have to go now. It is very warm and ...

Don't worry about the cameras, I say. We'll get what we can.

Yeah, I think we need to move, says Plake.

Fanfan pokes his ski pole into the snow. It disappears easily down to its middle. The snow is very soft, half-melted, slushy under the top layer, rotten.

Okay, we keep moving but not too fast now, Kye, says Fanfan. The snow is changing. I think we can go all the way down now. Don't stop. Very smooth, okay? But no stops here.

Something wrong? asks Kye.

No, says Plake, lying to keep Kye from panicking. But we need to move, that's all. You guys go first. Hit it now.

Kye nods and pushes off. He smooths into a short-radius turn, his skis sinking deeply. As his uphill ski comes around, he shifts his weight, getting into the turn early, the way Anselme showed him. Two more smooth turns. He is confident, but behind him a wet slough—a three-foot wall of slush—is picking up speed.

Kye, go on the right. Now! yells Fanfan.

Kye steers hard to the right of the couloir.

The hip-high slough rolls past, crashing against the downhill wall, washing down the chute.

Kye watches it go and then turns to Fanfan with a questioning look.

Now go, says Fanfan. No stopping. Do four turns and go to the right. Let the snow pass and go again.

Hearing the tension in Fanfan's voice, Kye heaves himself up off the snow into a forceful jump turn. He spins his skis 180 degrees and then reaches with his legs for the landing. Extending, his legs meet the snow and drive down into the mashed potato slop. His feet are buried, but his momentum pushes him down the hill. He tumbles forward, helmet driving into the snow, a fulcrum for his whole body to continue its revolution. He uses the motion to propel himself right back up on his skis before his slough can wash over him. He skis out to the high side of the chute and stops.

Fanfan pulls up to him. That's what I said, you know. Don't go very fast, but smooth in the snow now. It is too soft and we must keep going.

Off in the distance, another rumble. The mountain is shedding layers in the heat.

Four turns and to the right, says Fanfan.

Kye responds immediately. Four smooth turns and a quick cut out to the right. His slough rolls by each time.

Very good, Kye! yells Fanfan.

The couloir pinches as it finishes, and Kye banks a long turn through the narrow opening, flying out into the open apron. Below him is a wide-open meadow. He surfs through a long, fluid turn and pulls up. Fanfan cuts the other way to avoid sending his slough down onto Kye and stops below him.

That was very good, Kye. You do exactly what we said. This is excellent.

Behind them are cliffs hundreds of feet high. In front of them is the lower flank of the Aiguille du Midi, two miles of meadows and, way down below, the town of Chamonix.

Plake skis smooth and fast out of the chute. Markewitz and I are the last ones out. We stop beside them at the base. Fanfan scans the cliffs.

I think we must traverse now because here is not good, he says. Now it is very warm, and we never know what is happening up there. Go there, everyone, to the high place.

Plake leads the way with Kye right behind him. We hurry onto a ridge, away from the cliffs at the mouth of the couloir, in the middle of the Mer de Glace. The snow is crystalline here. Sunlight reflects off fields of diamond chips. Fanfan pulls his helmet off, hair wet with sweat, forehead glistening. He lights a cigarette.

Hey, he had a good style, huh? Fanfan says to Plake.

Kye pulls a bottle of water out and takes a long pull.

Look at what you just skied, Plake says to Kye.

We turn and look back. The Poubelle looks like a vertical strip in a fortress of jagged rock.

See all the people up there still? asks Plake.

At the top of the strip, the people look like insects. High up on a cliff near the base of the couloir, a plume of white breaks free and rushes toward the valley. It careens over rock and ice, picks up speed and size, and ramps off a cliff into the air, a waterfall of wet snow, ice and rock. It explodes on the ground. The *boom* takes a second to reach us.

That's pretty close to where we were just standing, says Kye.

Yeah, like *real* close, says Plake.

Now you know what I mean, eh? says Fanfan. We have to have eyes all over our head.

A stillness settles over the three skiers. I pull my camera out and begin shooting. Fanfan takes notice and slips into tour-guide mode.

Up there, Kye, is Le Dru, says Fanfan, pointing away from the Grands Montets toward a staggeringly abrupt peak in the center of the valley. This is a very good wall for climbing.

Le Dru, says Plake. Very heavy, very dangerous.

And you see that over there? says Fanfan, turning and pointing with his pole to the west where a low stone building is perched on the skirt of a mountain on the horizon. This is the hotel and train station on the Aiguille du Midi.

We're moving from the Grands Montets to the Aiguille du Midi, says Plake. Slowly but surely we're moving that way.

Kye nods. He knows what waits for him on the Aiguille du Midi. Fanfan takes a long drag on his cigarette, the orange tip burning through the white paper.

That eagle we saw was the same one as yesterday, says Plake after a moment.

That is his couloir, says Fanfan.

I think he's living there, says Plake. Waiting for the cheese to be thrown down.

The eagle was my dad's favorite animal, says Kye, repeating what he tried to tell them before. My mom believes that if he were to be reincarnated he'd come back as that.

I understand, says Fanfan. There is a superstition from old days. All the birds you see in the hills are the spirits of dead mountaineers, coming back.

Kye looks back up the hill, scanning the empty sky for the eagle.

After a moment, Plake says: I think all of us that ski in the hills would probably come back as birds. Then we wouldn't have to climb no more.

The uphill slog to the Grand Roc bar feels downhill tonight. We're all exhausted but buoyed by the day's events. Kye is learning his lessons well and rising to the challenge. He is becoming a real skier, a man among his father's peers. He skied the chute well and confidently, no one got hurt, and we shot the hell out of it. Tonight I won't mind reporting to the New Yorkers. Tonight I'll tell Obenhaus and Yellin that we had all the angles covered. Kronick will agree. Kayce will want a play-by-play, and I'll be happy to give it. There will be beer, smiles. Maybe I'll have a couple, unwind a little. Perhaps Peter has arrived. I can see myself sitting in the bar with him, recounting our victory in the Poubelle.

But as soon as I walk into the Grand Roc, I know something is wrong. Yellin is standing next to Plake at the bar, and he doesn't look pleased.

You know about this? he asks immediately.

What? I look from Yellin to Plake.

Fanfan and I have been talking about it, says Plake, and this could be our one and only shot. It's not ideal that it comes after today, but when you get it, you get it. We're gonna do it. We're skiing the Rond tomorrow.

Yellin nods and looks at me, waiting for a reaction. I'm poleaxed by the news. My first reaction is all about me. I'm not ready. I want a break before we double-down on the stress and danger.

Then I have another thought: If I'm not ready, what about Kye? Sure, he skied well and proved he can handle steep couloirs, but tension takes its toll. It's not even seven, and I wouldn't be surprised if he's asleep already.

But in the Alps, the weather deals the cards. You plan and plan, only to have the weather turn on you. Sometimes the right conditions never come. The days slide by. You miss the objective, wait for another season. More rare are the times when the weather is right before you want it to be. This is one of those times. We can seize the opportunity or wait for another chance and risk getting closed out. Plake and Fanfan have decided to take it.

Fanfan said that? I ask. He said tomorrow's our only chance?

It's going to get real warm starting tomorrow night, says Plake. The sun beats on that thing and it's cooked.

I don't need to translate for Yellin. A quickly warming snowpack greatly increases avalanche danger, especially in a western-facing chute like the Exit Couloir. He's got the gist. If we're going to do it, it has to be tomorrow.

And Kye said he's ready? I ask.

I haven't told him yet, says Plake. Fanfan's getting the radios charged and his team ready.

Haven't told him, I repeat, rolling the words over in my head.

Have *you* talked to Kye? Yellin asks me.

Not since we got off the hill. I was helping the camera guys unload.

He's ready, says Plake. You see him in there today?

I saw him, I say. He was good.

Yellin nods, keeping his own counsel, thinking.

Right, so he's skiing as good as he's going to be skiing, says Plake. It's time to do it. It's what we're here for.

I realize that for Plake, the idea of Kye skiing the run that killed his father is a foregone conclusion. I ask myself why I'm so surprised. This is the idea that hooked me on the story in the first place, the undeniable energy of it. But that was back when this thing was a loose plot for a documentary film. At the time, Kye was just a character in my head, a generic kid. Now he's real, and I've promised his mother to keep him safe.

We're here to film whatever you guys decide to do, says Yellin. But don't do it for us.

I watch Yellin as he says this, and I imagine him repeating the line many times. If you make documentaries, it's what you say, what you have to say. The real situation is far more subtle—an elaborate dance between the observed and the observers. The principals perform actions and we make judgments on the worthiness of each one by how and when we turn the cameras on and off.

We're doing it, says Plake. With or without you guys.

I don't say a word because I sense his honesty and focus. Without a trace of ambivalence, Plake knows what he's here to do. He's here to guide his friend's son down the avalanche chute that killed his father. And he's here to make a film about it. If he has any qualms about it, he dealt with them long ago.

We're not going to shoot anything that's reckless, Yellin says.

Yellin is completely still. I watch for tics. There are none. Comfortable in his producer role, he knows where his boundaries begin and end. He knows that his only responsibility is to turn the production switch on or off, not to try to direct the actions of the people we're filming. I envy but don't share his well-drawn boundaries, his sense of certainty.

Kye'll ski it on the cord if it's sketchy, adds Plake.

Yellin nods and looks to me. What do you think?

What I think is that Plake and Fanfan are skiers. They know that they can ski the run and get Kye down it, too. That's why I've chosen them, why I've put Kye in their care. Fanfan, in particular, offers the greatest insurance policy against something going wrong. Although I've known him only a week, I have complete faith in his abilities. He won't let anything happen to Kye. Of course, skiing the Rond was well within Trevor's ability too.

I also know that the crew and I are tired. Kye must be exhausted.

We've been pushing hard all week, and now we're all going to have to ratchet up our focus. I want to err on the side of caution and just say no. But that feels wrong too. So I say the line I'm supposed to say: If they're doing it, we're shooting it.

All right, so I'm going to go talk to Kye, says Plake. We're meeting at the Aiguille du Midi at eight.

After Plake is gone, Yellin looks at me.

You ready for this?

Hell no, I say.

Trevor: Exit Couloir

Chamonix, France
February 26, 1996

On the western shoulder of the Aiguille du Midi are the ruins of the Col du Midi Téléphérique, Chamonix's first tram, built before World War II. Once there was a forty-square-meter structure of concrete and iron that served as the terminus. Today all that's left are a few steel towers, some collapsed wooden beams and the westernmost wall. Built of granite blocks, the castlelike wall rises some seventy feet from the top of the Glacier Rond, an iron ladder leading down the side to the glacier below.

Though he complained of an injury earlier in the day, Trevor Petersen has decided to ski after all. It's warm, really warm, due in part to a dry, down-slope wind known in the Alps as a foehn. Associated in folklore with madness and misfortune, the foehn has been known to raise temperatures as much as fifty degrees in only a few hours.

Trevor walks onto the wall and climbs down the ladder onto a knife-edged ridge at the top of the Rond. To the right is the sheer, staggering openness of the Glacier Rond, the most perfectly slanted ramp in Chamonix. Shaped like an upside-down funnel, the Rond starts out narrow, then widens dramatically before terminating at a cliff a thousand feet high. The only way around the cliff is the Exit Couloir. Wide as an interstate, hemmed in by hundred-foot-tall walls of dark rock, the Exit faces directly into the setting sun.

The foehn wind would have softened the top layer to a meringue. Snowpack accumulates in layers, as one storm follows another. The key to stability is bonding between layers. Gradual warming can help. As the snowpack undergoes cycles of warming and cooling, the layers bond together to form a more stable slab. Rapid warming has the opposite effect. The top layer warms first, and moisture from the melting snow acts like a lubricant between the crystals. If there is weak fusion between layers, the top layer is more likely to succumb to gravity and slide down the hill. A trigger event, like a 170-pound skier pressing down on it, can cause an avalanche.

Trevor knows all this and more. According to his longtime skiing partner, Eric Pehota, Trevor would have cut across the slope in a cautious traverse, thrusting his legs into the hill, preparing for a slab to release. But the Rond doesn't release. It's stable, or at least the top of it is.

Grinding, slow-moving glaciers compact snow crystals into ice. Much of it never melts. The Italians have a name for it: *neve*, never-ending snow. Trevor always liked the sound of that, the idea of snow that never melts. He gave the name to his daughter, Neve Petersen. He has a picture of her in his wallet—brown eyes, round cheeks, the flawless skin of a four-year-old.

The wallet is in his pack. The pack is cinched snugly to his waist and shoulders, ice ax lashed to the outside. He won't be needing the ax today. The neve is buried under new snow. It's been snowing in Chamonix for weeks. The thin tips of his 203-centimeter Rossignol Vipers dive into the fluff. His feet drive through thick snow the texture of *crème fraiche*. Between pole plants his hands rise high; his pole baskets clear the deep snow before plunging in again. In the swish of white velvet, the whisper of parting snow, Trevor leaves his last tracks on the Rond.

The Exit Couloir begins in a deep V formed by high rock buttresses. The first pitch is wide, less steep than the Glacier Rond. Constricted by the rock walls, the chute narrows into a formation that skiers call a choke. Trevor would've stopped uphill of it, assessing it from a safe distance.

The foehn and western sun have warmed the cliffs, increasing the chances of a slide coming down from above. Trevor drives the tips of his Rossis into the snow with confidence. The crazy wind blows as he nails one turn after another. For long, precious moments, it's just him and the mountain.

He slows, navigates the choke, traverses to his left. There's a bulge in the slope and beyond it a steeper section. He pushes over the bulge, the sun shining on his face.

This is how it feels: The first *shhhhhhh* comes from under your skis. Suddenly the world is moving. The surface begins to heave and roll. You try to stay on your feet, try to get out to the side, but the walls hem you in. There are no islands of safety in sight. You have only one option: Try to outrun the slide. You point your skis straight down the chute and go like hell. But the mountain won't let you go.

The slide catches Trevor, and by the time it lets him go, his back and neck are broken. He comes to rest in a seated position above the settling snow. His posture suggests relaxation, as if he had decided to sit down and admire the view. No one knows if he died instantly in the tumble, or if his life slipped away slowly as he gazed at Mont Blanc.

chapter 12

Into the Mess

Chamonix, France
Evening, March 15, 2005

Glen Plake bangs on Kye's door. Inside, in a warm space with a low ceiling of exposed pine beams, soft yellow light pours over piles of ski gear—gloves and helmets and ski boot liners stacked up by the heater, sunglasses and goggles, radios and avalanche beacons strewn across a heavy table. At the periphery of this mess, slumped on a couch and staring into the darkness outside the sliding door, is Kye Petersen. He's wearing a loose T-shirt and sweatpants fraying at the cuff where they drag on the floor.

His day in the Poubelle Couloir, his first real big-mountain test, has left him wrung out, too tired to drag himself to the restaurant. Listening to music through big, DJ-style headphones, he can't hear the insistent pounding on the door.

Kye's roommate and chaperone, Eric Iberg, finally gets up. He's been catching a disco-nap before mounting an assault on Chamonix's nightclubs. Stalking past Kye, he opens the door.

Whassup, Plake? he mumbles, taking note of the head-to-toe black ski outfit that Plake still wears. It must be eight o'clock, and the guy hasn't gone home to change yet. Plake moves comfortably into the cramped quarters as Iberg subtly sets a camera on the table and hits the record button.

Kye pulls off the headphones and nervously gets up to greet him.

What did you think about that today? Plake asks with a big-brotherly slap on the back. Fun, huh?

Yeah, that was super fun, says Kye, with forced enthusiasm. Thanks, Plake.

Plake sits without bothering to unzip his jacket or take off his hat.

Getting into the big hills now, says Plake. It's a different type of skiing, huh?

It was a big step, says Kye as he puts the headphones on the table, picks up his knit cap, and slouches back down into the couch.

Definitely a big step, and tomorrow will be another step, says Plake. A big, big step.

Kye sits up a little straighter and leans toward Plake.

Tomorrow will be like skipping four steps, he says. The weather's right, so tomorrow we go straight up the Aiguille du Midi.

Kye knows that going up the Aiguille du Midi means skiing the Glacier Rond, and skiing the Rond means facing the Exit Couloir. He swallows visibly and nods at Plake.

Tomorrow is no Grands Montets, continues Plake. It's straight into the mess, right off the bat.

Am I ready? Kye asks Plake, turning his small face to look up into Plake's tired eyes.

Yeah, says Plake without conviction as he stands and turns away from the boy. Moving toward the door, he leans on a post that holds up the sleeping loft. You'll be fine, he says, absently fiddling with a light switch. Suddenly, the room goes dark. Plake has inadvertently turned off the light. He quickly snaps it back on.

Whoops, he says. Anyway, there's always the rope. We could rope a truck down if we had to.

Kye nods, not sure how to respond. Is Plake being positive, negative, or just realistic?

But today you figured it out, eh? continues Plake, turning away from the light switch and facing Kye again. You gotta become finite. He draws a six-foot plot in the air with his finger. That's the only piece of snow, right?

Exactly, says Kye, enthusiastically.

You can't just go whoopin' on down, says Plake. You got to be right there. He draws the imaginary box of snow again. That's all there is, right?

Yeah, definitely, says Kye, looking up at Plake and crossing his arms across his chest, rubbing his left arm as if trying to keep a chill out. Plake gives him a long look that seems to say, I'm serious about this. Kye nods to assure him that indeed he understands and that, yeah, he's serious too.

Plake sits down, turns to face Kye again.

Okay, so, eight o'clock out front, ready to go, says Plake. Harnesses on. Everything ready. I tell you right now, going up there is going to be a mess, a freakin' circus. Everybody will be freaking out because it's a pretty trippy place. They'll be oohing and ahhing all over the place. And people fainting.

Fainting? Really? asks Kye, sharing a look with Iberg.

Yeah, people faint up there all the time, says Plake. They go on up the cable car, and you're in there and you hear them go *fwunk*. Right in the bottom of the cable car, they faint. You got your average Joe straight off the dang tourist bus, and up they go 10,000 feet in a half hour.

Nice, says Kye, clearly excited at the prospect of seeing someone faint, never entertaining the notion that it could be him.

But anyway, continues Plake, we'll get up there and get over to the Cosmiques Refuge and start setting up our rappels. And wear the tightest pants you got.

Kye gives him a look that says, tight pants? Is that a joke? He looks at Iberg. All their clothes are stylishly loose-fitting, mountain hip-hop chic.

You gotta wear pants that are tight because we'll probably have to crampon, and you can't crampon with baggy pants, says Plake. He doesn't bother to explain that loose pants aren't used with crampons because the spikes catch in the folds and can cause you to trip in places where tripping isn't an option.

Where are we going to crampon? asks Kye.

Out and around the ridge, he says. We may or may not. But you need to be ready.

Kye looks at Iberg, who shrugs and shakes his head.

Okay, you got any tape? Plake asks. Duct tape? We can tape 'em up.

Plake looks at Iberg, who says, no tape.

So, it's going to be a neat deal up there, Plake says, trying for a more positive tone. For all of us. It's what brought this whole project together. They started mentioning places and started mentioning your name, and I said if we're going to Chamonix, we need to bring in Anselme because it was his book that led your father and me to the Glacier Rond.

Is Anselme coming? asks Kye, clearly hoping.

I don't think Anselme is coming, answers Plake, and then seeing Kye's disappointment, he adds: But we got plenty of people who are surefooted in these places. I think we're going to have perfect weather. I think it's going to be a really good day. We go to 13,000 feet right off the bat. So let's talk about the … for now, I'm going to call it a memorial or dedication.

Plake picks up a two-euro coin off the table and begins slowly rolling it between his fingers.

Right, says Kye, shaking his head.

I think we're going to do it on the arête, says Plake, tapping the coin on the table. Does that work for you?

What's an arête? asks Kye.

That's the knife edge that we're going to be standing on above the Glacier Rond, says Plake, as he stops tapping and puts his palms together, fingers pointing upward, showing what the arête looks like. For an instant, with his palms pressed together, he's a pantomime of a man praying.

Okay, says Kye, consciously adding the word arête to his big-mountain vocabulary.

So, you should start trippin' out on what you want to do up there on the ridge. Have you thought about that?

I brought some ashes, Kye says. That's about all I've thought about.

Plake rocks back in his chair, pushing the front two feet off the floor.

Think about something you want to do, he says. This is your moment.

Kye puts his head into his hands, rubs his temples and then his eyes as if to stimulate thought … or hide from it.

I want to get a cool shot of me throwing some ashes, he says after a moment.

But it's even more than that, says Plake.

Yeah, you've got to be in the right spot, too—

We've done moments of silence before, suggests Plake. We've told stories.

A moment of silence, I think, says Kye, testing the idea on Plake.

Yeah, come up with something, says Plake. It's going to be a moment shared by everybody, but it should be led by you.

Okay, uh-huh, for sure, says Kye, shaking his head, nodding to himself as if to say, I can do that. I'm capable.

If you believe in God, say a prayer, or if you want us all to be quiet for a minute, tell us, you know? I think you should lead this.

Good, says Kye as he puts on his hat and pulls it down to his eyebrows.

I'm more than willing to help, says Plake. I've been to plenty of funerals ... and graduations.

Plake busts out a braying, embarrassed laugh that shatters the tension. He's named something that, until now, no one has said outright: The ceremony they plan to do on the arête is both a funeral for Trevor and a graduation for Kye.

So if you want help on that, I'm here, continues Plake. Just ask me and maybe I can help. It would be cool for you to say, this is that, or I want to say a prayer, or I want everybody to be silent for a second, or I want everyone to think of my dad on every turn, you know? 'Cause that's your opportunity there.

Sure, on the arête, says Kye, looking down at his bare feet.

Exactly. I think everybody will have a lot of moments going on up there, says Plake. You know, I skied my first turns there with your dad.

Now Kye glances up from his feet and meets Plake's gaze. Plake nods before he continues.

Yeah, me and your dad.

Plake pauses, and for a moment it is easy to imagine that his thoughts run to Trevor or to a much younger version of himself. Maybe he remembers how inexperienced they were, all the extra gear they carried. Or maybe he's reflecting on how it could've just as easily been him who didn't come back and wondering why it wasn't.

But, you know, everybody who'll be up there has lost people.

Yep, Kye says attentively.

You know these guys from Cham lost three friends just this year. So everybody up there has gone through these moments.

Definitely, says Kye, tapping his knee lightly with his fist.

So it could be very ... it *will* be very ... it's just one of those emotional roller coasters we get to go on every now and then, for better or for worse. Plake laughs his high, harsh laugh again, and Kye tries to match it with a throaty chortle of his own.

And then, down we go, says Plake, abruptly getting back to business. Depending on the snow, we'll either put you on a cord or not. We'll probably set up a rappel that will be sixty or seventy meters. That will be your first section. Fanfan will probably go. I'll send you down the first section, and you'll meet up with Fanfan. If things are looking good, that might be it. But if they're still sketchy, we'll hook up another rappel. We're going to just make it until we get you right.

Kye glances at Iberg, who's murmuring in agreement, and gives him a *holy shit* look.

You'll be fine, says Plake, catching the look. It will be fun. You'll dig it. It's a rush. It's a rush for all of us, no matter how many times we do it. It's not like, oh wow, check me out! I'm so rad! It's not like that, he adds. It's so steep you just go … Plake lifts up his leg and raises his arms like a bird taking wing, then steps down with his right leg to simulate moving through the turn. He turns his torso and makes a sound like a bird whooshing past. His arms carve a hawklike arc through the air.

It's a neat feeling, says Plake, you don't have any pressure.

That's awesome, says Kye.

And then later, says Plake, some of us who have been there and know a little bit about what happened to your father can explain that as we go, but I don't think it's going to be a major production.

Okay, yeah, says Kye, riding an emotional roller coaster just by talking about it.

As we get to the Exit Couloir, we can create our own idea of what possibly might have happened that day. Some of us know where the slide pulled out. We have an idea of where he was found. None of us were there, but we've all been in this place.

Kye pulls his hat low over his eyes for a second, pushes it up on his head, and turns his attention back to Plake.

Anyway, think about it, says Plake as he gets up and heads for the door. It's an opportunity. Dream on it tonight. If you want to talk about it tomorrow, we'll have plenty of time.

Thanks, Plake, says Kye, with true feeling.

Like I said, everybody up there's been through this type of stuff, says Plake, avoiding the emotion and stepping into the dark hallway.

For sure, says Kye, looking over at Iberg for assurance. When he turns back, Plake is gone.

In a cramped condo devoted to camera gear, I work with Peter Pilafian and Beat Steiner, two of our shooters. Amid packs and tripods and innumerable Pelican cases, we storyboard as much as we can about the day ahead. Based on descriptions from Fanfan and Plake, we draw a map in my notebook of what we think the Glacier Rond looks like, and then we diagram camera positions. It's now too late to line up a helicopter even if I could convince Obenhaus that it is the right way to shoot it. Nonetheless, by the time we're done talking, we've convinced each other that we have a handle on the shoot.

It's nearly midnight by the time we finish, but instead of going back to my apartment I head up the hill and into an Internet café. Wreathed in blue cigarette smoke, I open an e-mail attachment. My wife has sent pictures of our new son, Liam. Here he is, two weeks old now, fat-faced, big-eyed. And here's our two-year-old daughter, Grace, hugging him, letting him know that he belongs in this world. They are younger than Trevor's kids were when he left them, nine years ago, a thought that I find heartbreaking. It's unimaginable to me that I could make a wrong turn and never see my family again. As I look at their pictures, I tell myself that tomorrow I will make every decision with them in mind.

Back at my own apartment, Greg Stump, who is sharing my flat, comes in and wants me to have a beer with him. I tell him no thanks, not bothering to mention that I doubt my nervous stomach will keep it down. Back in the day, I would've welcomed the chance to have a cold one with Greg Stump, as would most people in the ski world. A legendary ski filmmaker, Stumpy, as he was known to friends and wannabe friends (and there were plenty of those), captured the spirit of the anti-resort skiers of the late 1980s. With *The Blizzard of Aahhh's*, he introduced extreme skiing to a North American audience in a way that reverberated with mythic overtones and allowed a million Walter Mittys to project themselves into the lives of some of America's best skiers. Stump's genius, whether conscious or not, was the way he cast the skiers for his films. Selected for their personalities as much as their skiing, Stump tapped into universally recognizable archetypes—outlandish Glen Plake was the trickster; quiet Scot Schmidt was the loner hero; beautiful and dangerous Chamonix was the femme fatale; and everyman Mike Hattrup was the herald who could tell us what it all meant.

The Blizzard of Aahhh's told a story (albeit simple and contrived) that changed ski filmmaking and skiing itself. Before *Blizzard*, aspiring pro skiers looked to mogul skiing or ski racing to make their mark. After *Blizzard*, North America's best skiers wanted to become extreme skiers. Stump, Plake, Hattrup and Schmidt paved the way and now, twenty years later, so-called freeskiers dominate the pro scene, and the roots of virtually every ski filmmaking company (there are dozens) can be traced back to Stump.

But Stumpy didn't take the whole ride. In 1995, while filming in Siberia, avalanches nearly killed two of his stars. With the skiers stranded on a remote mountain, Stump prayed: God, if you let those guys live, I will never, ever, put people's lives in danger again. The skiers survived, and Stump quit making ski movies.

Fame, even modest fame, has a way of opening doors, and Greg Stump soon found plenty to fill his spare time. Retreating from the high mountains to the low nightclubs, he and his girlfriend, Ace, a beautiful go-go dancer and talented cinematographer, became central figures in Whistler's underground party scene. When the snow melted, they took the party to Hawaii.

Years later, he came back to the high country to make a film about mogul skiing, and it seemed his dalliance with flatland living had ended. He showcased *A Fistful of Moguls* in a nightclub in Park City, Utah, during the Sundance Film Festival. A Who's Who of freestyle skiers showed up, and I was there to film a television piece on the event. Stump and I had a few laughs, and, as a former pro mogul skier, I thanked him for bringing the sport back into the limelight. I thought, and indeed hoped, that *Fistful* signaled the long-awaited return of one of the sport's best filmmakers. After *Fistful*, however, he went back to the islands and returned to directing commercials for a Los Angeles production company.

When I set out to film Kye's story, Plake urged me to track down Stump. He said Stump was ready for a change.

I called Stump in Maui, and he regaled me with stories about poker games with singer Willie Nelson, outrageous parties, famous people. Beautiful women still came calling. Life was wild and, no, he didn't really miss the ski stuff.

I'm making a documentary about skiing, I said. I thought maybe there was a way you might help.

Really? he said. Huh.

It's about something much bigger than sliding on snow, I said. I'm doing it with Peter Jennings, his production company.

Well, I do *need* to get back to the mountains, Stump said. I need to get things back on track. Get back *my soul*. I've been thinking it was time. I'm serious, I want to come back.

Good, it's about time, I said.

Nobody ever leaves the ski world, he said. Once you're in, you're in.

Amen, brother, I said.

Now, three months later, we're roommates in Chamonix, and he's telling me about the new film he's writing (working title: *Snow White Trash*) about his own return to the ski world. He cracks a beer and wants to talk about James Joyce and Ernest Hemingway and why doesn't anyone write anything worth a shit about the ski life? It's a conversation I would love to have at another place and time, but our morning call is in five hours and, besides, I'd rather call my wife.

I have no intention of telling Bel about the Glacier Rond and the Exit Couloir. I just want to see how she and the kids are doing and tell them that I love them. But once I get her on the phone, I can't help myself. I tell her everything.

At first I'm feigning confidence that I don't really feel, but as we talk, my confidence ceases to be an act. In the telling, it all begins to make sense again. I can see the successful completion of our objective as I speak. And I realize that the crew and I are ready. This is what we've come for, and I feel sure that we can do it safely, that everyone will get off the mountain in one piece. Bel believes, or says she does. It's not until much later that she admits our talk scared the hell out of her.

Ascending the Spire

Chamonix, France
Morning, March 16, 2005

Dawn. The Aiguille du Midi tram descends smoothly out of golden light into the still-dark valley. Sunlight won't reach the valley floor for another hour, but already the tram terminus—a utilitarian building of exposed steel beams and a faded sign, *Téléphérique de l'Aiguille du Midi, 3,842 metres*—is crowded with expectant riders. Serious ski mountaineers with ice axes and crampons strapped to their packs stand apart from the tourists. A cluster of British skiers, wide-eyed and obedient, follow instructions from French guides with badges pinned to their jackets. Diesel smoke from delivery trucks mixes with the sweet smells of bread and coffee.

Around the corner, in a parking lot clogged with tour buses, Kye Petersen wriggles into his harness, confidently cinching it tight. In gray camouflage pants and a black parka with a fake-fur collar, he leans casually on the open door of a minivan in the center of a small staging area. The crew is busy with harnesses, ice axes, skis and backpacks. Kye sees me watching and smiles, and I smile back. He's come a long way in only a few days.

Plake digs through a backpack. Nate, you bring any extra crampons for Kye? he asks.

Nate, a burly American friend of Plake's who we hired to hump camera gear for the film crew, shakes his head.

I've got some sevens or eights, but they might not work, says Plake.

I'll keep looking, says Nate.

Greg Stump aims a small digital camera at Kye and zooms in on his face. Later, the tape will reveal dark circles under Kye's eyes, his pale skin pulled tight.

What's up, captain? asks Stump. I've met you before. I don't know if you remember me. I'm Greg.

Yeah, Greg Stump from Whistler, says Kye.

What grade are you in now?

Grade nine, almost.

Did you bring all your schoolwork with you? asks Stump.

Nope, says Kye with a smile.

How'd you get out of school? asks Stump with obvious amusement.

I just have to do that sometimes, says a self-satisfied Kye.

You got a girlfriend?

No, not right now.

That will be easy, won't it?

Kye bows his head, zips his jacket up to his chin. The air is damp.

I heard you're skiing great, Stump says to Kye.

Yeah? asks Kye. Cool.

You're way into the tricks, right?

I like everything, says Kye. I'm way into *this*.

How nervous are you, Kye? asks Iberg.

Kye gives him an annoyed look—how dare you question my composure.

Iberg presses: C'mon, scale of one to ten.

Kye cracks a smile. Nine and a half, he says.

Fanfan steps around the corner, looking calm and purposeful in an orange jacket and his usual goofy blue hat, the kind with ear flaps. He kneels in front of Kye and tests his harness. Plake steps behind Kye and checks the leg straps. Fanfan yanks a strap tight, knocking Kye off balance. Plake catches him. Then Plake yanks on one of the leg straps. This time Fanfan steadies the young man.

You done good this time, Kye, says Plake.

Check? Kye asks Fanfan, holding a questioning thumbs-up to him.

Fanfan stands up and pats Kye on the shoulder. Check, it's good, says Fanfan, returning the thumbs-up.

Fanfan opens the day's first pack of Gauloise cigarettes, tearing the cellophane with his teeth. He lights up and inhales deeply. Satisfaction, he says to Kye, exaggerating as if doing a TV commercial. Kye laughs, pleased to be in on the adult joke.

Plake picks up a rack of ice screws.

Here, these make a lot of noise, he says, clipping the dangling chain of metal to Kye's harness.

Make 'em jingle, Kye, coaches Iberg.

Kye jogs in place. The climbing hardware rattles and clacks.

I did that when I was a little kid, Kye says excitedly. I put on all of my dad's climbing gear and was walking around the house. In my room I have a picture of me with all his equipment on.

I remember the photo, the little boy in his father's equipment with the Power Rangers T-shirt underneath.

What do you think, Fanfan, are these enough? asks Plake, clearly making a joke.

I think we need some more, says Fanfan.

Anybody got a B-flat screw on them? yells Plake as he adds a ridiculous amount of hardware to Kye's harness. These are all C-minor.

Kye jogs in place again, making the metal jingle, and they all laugh. Kye is completely in on the joke. In Chamonix it's not uncommon to see inexperienced skiers jangle onto the tram, their harnesses hung with excessive hardware. *All that equipment, all that stuff! He must be goooood!* Of course, real experts carry as little as possible—only what experience tells them they need.

Hey, that's the guy with the Mohawk! says a tall, thin man in a light mountaineering jacket with two ice screws clanking on his harness.

Plake growls a laugh and reaches for the man's hand.

What are you doin' here? asks Plake.

I came to ski. We're doing Glacier Rond, right?

He scans the group, his gaze falling on Kye, who is quietly watching the exchange.

This must be Kye. C'mere, let me shake your hand.

Plake makes the introduction.

Kye, this is Mike Hattrup.

Kye steps up and reaches for Hattrup's hand.

Nice to meet you, says Kye, carefully, respectfully. He looks up into Hattrup's face, making sure not to mistakenly insult one of the sport's luminaries … again. A member of the U.S. Ski Team in the 1980s, Mike Hattrup was one of Plake's co-stars in *The Blizzard of Aahhh's*. He'd had a good run as a ski film star and now directs the telemark division for K2 Sports. Hattrup's face has thinned and aged since the movie days. Instead of his famous golden locks, he now sports a shaved head. But his smile is as boy-next-door as ever.

I skied a lot with your dad, says Hattrup to Kye. I had some awesome adventures with your dad.

Yeah? Kye takes a step back.

In fact every time I skied with your dad, it was an awesome adventure. So I'm really stoked to be here with you.

Yeah, says Kye, me too.

Well, this is going to be a cool day, says Plake, taking a step away from Kye, putting his hand on Hattrup's shoulder, leading him away from the group. Kye watches intently. Plake explains the plan for the Glacier Rond, and Hattrup asks how well the youngster is skiing. Plake nods as if to say, all right, then adds: With any luck the snow will be soft.

Kye can't hear what they're saying, but he doesn't need to. He can feel the tension. Pulling his gloves on tight, he fidgets with his poles as Hattrup and Plake separate to get themselves ready. Now no one is talking. Hattrup pulls a screwdriver out of his pack, turns his skis upside-down, and begins tightening the DIN settings on his alpine-touring bindings.

Kye looks down at his own bindings.

The most common injuries for resort skiers are broken legs or blown knees, usually caused by a binding that doesn't release soon enough to discharge the pressure. But when you're skiing where a fall means death, the risk of a binding releasing prematurely is more serious than the threat of torn ligaments or a fracture. Kye's DIN settings are on eight, the recommended level for an advanced skier weighing 150 pounds. Kye weighs only 110. He should be fine.

Hey guys, yells Fanfan from the periphery. We are in different cars going up. So we meet at the bridge, yes?

Fanfan steps up next to Kye. Ready to do this, Kye? asks Fanfan quietly.

Yeah, I think so, says Kye, steeling himself visibly.

A loudspeaker blares in French. Fanfan translates, and the crew is in motion.

Let's go, five o'clock comes early! yells Plake in his best foreman voice.

Kye laughs because, like many things that come out of Plake's mouth, it just sounds funny. Packs are hefted, skis shouldered, and a platoon of men clomp across the asphalt toward the Aiguille du Midi tram.

It's nine in the morning and the tram climbs steeply into bright sunlight that sends most of the riders digging for their sunglasses. Outside, the town gathers itself and recedes in our wake. The overhead cables drone eerily.

Kye, Iberg and Stump are squeezed in the middle of the car. Hangover breath and stale cigarette smoke cling to clothes like yesterday's mistakes. Stump widens out his camera's lens and focuses on Kye.

I want to see someone faint, says Kye.

What do you want to be when you grow up? asks Stump, doing his rote ski-film interview.

Kye turns toward Stump, grinning broadly, happy to have the answer to his question: Skier, he says with complete certainty.

And if you could be any animal in the world, which one would you be? asks Stump.

Bird, says Kye quickly.

What kind of bird?

An eagle, says Kye. Yeah, eagle, for sure.

Man it reeked in there, says Kye, breathing deeply and hurrying out of the tram car and into the Plan de l'Aiguille midstation. His boots echo on the concrete as he elbows through another turnstile. He walks onto an outdoor tram platform and lifts his eyes to the fluted, rock-and-snow face of the Aiguille du Midi. Off to the right, barely visible, is the sickeningly steep ramp of the Glacier Rond and behind it, Mont Blanc.

Holy shit, Kye says to Fanfan.

Hunched and hulking, Mont Blanc spreads its massive shoulders. A true mountaineer's mountain, Mont Blanc engulfs your imagination. It *is* the horizon. Blue seracs and pearl-colored ice floes glisten with life-ending finality. Here, too, are the sirens of soft powder just waiting for a reason to avalanche. But the most dangerous of Mont Blanc's traps are the ones that you can't see—hidden crevasses, false ice bridges, thousand-year-old glacier ice lurking just beneath a scrim of powder that defies any ski edge.

But Mont Blanc doesn't rush at you. It stands back, content to play the quiet heavy to the Aiguille du Midi. Rising out of the narrow crease of the Chamonix Valley, the twin-finned Aiguille is made all the more menacing by a man-made, ten-story spire that stands at the rocky summit.

The tram midstation sits low in a natural amphitheater of rock and snow. Sounds bounce eerily off the cliffs. A small ice fall spilling down the eastern shoulder half a mile away sounds like wine bottles breaking underfoot.

Fanfan pulls a cigarette out of an already crumpled pack.

I thought you quit, says Plake as he joins us on the deck.

I will quit again tomorrow … after this day, eh?

Fanfan's voice seems a mile away. Kye laughs nervously, his eyes never leaving the peak, the mountain, the sheer, threatening verticality of it. The sun is already high and harsh. Kye pulls his goggles down, shading sensitive pale blue eyes. The wind sucks away the strong smoke from Fanfan's cigarette.

The tram car arrives, and a door clanks open. It's 9:30 and Kye's time has come. He gets in next to Stump, and the bin begins to climb. The cable hangs slack; the tram rises five thousand feet without a single securing tower.

It looks like we're going to crash into the rocks, says Kye.

And indeed it does look that way. From inside the tram, you're sure the cabin is going to swing straight into the face of the Aiguille du Midi. It's only at the last moment that the tram climbs abruptly up and over the rock through a gaping hole in a sheer face called the Piton Nord. The car bumps to a stop, bounces backward, and falls half a foot. Several people scream. Even experienced skiers grab something to hold. The car moves up the cable, bangs the dock, and slips back again. The tram operator, a small man on a hard stool, grimaces and punches another button. On the third approach, the car rises up again but is still a good six inches below the level of the dock. Close enough. The operator opens the door.

Faites attention ou vous mettez les pieds. Montez, says the tram operator. Be careful. Step up.

Kye, Iberg and Stump hustle out of the car and into a dim tunnel that leads to a steel bridge spanning thirty meters to the other pinnacle, the Piton Central. The bridge has high steel railings with sheer drops on both sides. I step aside, taking in the tourists who line the rail. They snap pictures and back away. Then I notice a man who is clearly not a tourist. A head taller than the rest, wearing a red bandanna and dark, wraparound sunglasses, he leans casually against the rail. I recognize him almost immediately—Doug Coombs, arguably the best big-mountain skier in the world. Running into him here is like running into Tiger Woods on the back nine. I didn't orchestrate this. So what's he doing here? I never get to ask him.

A chorus of Japanese women squeal as they walk out of the darkness onto the metal grate of the bridge, nothing but ice and rock seventy feet below. They join the other tourists who hustle across the bridge into a second tunnel, then up an elevator to an observation deck at the top of the Aiguille du Midi.

Kye steps carefully onto the bridge, plastic ski boots slipping on cold steel. He shuffles to the railing and looks over the edge—a nearly vertical chute that ends abruptly in a massive cliff over the Glacier Rond.

We're not in Kansas anymore, says Iberg.

No, shit no, says Kye, as he steps back from the railing, his eyes wide, his face lit.

Let's get the pictures for your mom out of the way, says Iberg as he pulls out a small camera. She told me I gotta get shots of you.

Definitely, says Kye. She'd kill me if I didn't get a few shots for her.

Later I learn that although Kye had been in constant communication with his mother, he hadn't called her the night before the Rond. He didn't want to worry her.

Iberg pulls off his backpack, sets it on the grate, and starts digging for his camera. Coombs steps smoothly past the tourists. He looks down at Kye, and for a moment the youngster looks up at him.

Hey Kye, Doug Coombs, he says, extending his hand. I met you when you were two or three. I heard you were coming. You having a good time?

Yeah, an awesome time.

Yeah, isn't this place the best? Coombs looks out toward Mont Blanc with genuine affection.

It's incredible, says Kye, following Coombs' gaze.

You're gonna want to move here, says Coombs, turning back to Kye.

Yeah, exactly, says Kye, shaking his head excitedly.

When I first came here I was like, that's it, I've got to come back. Now I always come back. You'll be back.

Oh yeah, there's no doubt.

At this point, Stump, who's been filming the exchange, steps up and reacquaints himself with Coombs. They haven't seen each other in ten years.

How about little Kye? says Stump.

He's not that little any more, says Coombs.

Eric Iberg introduces himself to Coombs and asks if he can take a photo of Coombs and Kye. The two strike a pose. Kye's head barely comes up to Coombs' ribs. The boy looks into the camera, a beaming smile that seems to be a lot more than just a good pose for the picture. As Iberg's camera flashes, Coombs turns to face Kye.

You know, I skied here with your dad a bunch of times. And up in Alaska I did twenty or thirty first descents with him back in the early 1990s. When I could find him. He got lost, like all of us.

Kye cocks his head and looks up at Coombs, not knowing what to make of the remark. I, too, wait for Coombs to elaborate, to tell us what he means. Sure, Trevor got lost, literally, but Coombs seems like the least lost person you'll ever meet. Does he mean that they got lost in the commerciality of it? The ski movies and photos shoots and magazine covers? The ego trip of being a big-mountain skier?

Anyway, you'll never get tired of it, Coombs says as he turns toward the end of the bridge. I'll see you later.

Yeah, see you, Doug, says Kye with an easy familiarity that makes Coombs smile as he walks toward the dark tunnel at the end of the bridge.

The final tunnel is low and round, the air still and damp. It curves organically, like the innards of a frozen beast. Dirty yellow lights hang from the roof. The floor is uneven and slick with hard ice. Kye, Plake, Fanfan and Hattrup carry their skis in their hands tips up, using them like canes to keep from slipping. The skiers don't talk, moving quietly, almost reverently, through the darkness toward a faint light at the far end.

As the light becomes brighter, the tunnel splits. To the right, through the dimness, is the tourist elevator to the viewing platform. Skiers turn left into a bright, hand-hewn tunnel of white ice that leads outside. Fanfan turns to see the wonder on Kye's face.

Here we go, says Plake as they step into the light. Now we got something to play with.

The four of them stop at a triangular sign. It's an icon of a skier with a slash through it: No skiing allowed on this section. To the left is the sheer face of the Aiguille, unskiable for all but a handful of the best ski mountaineers and only then in rare and perfect conditions. Even skiers of Anselme's or Fanfan's caliber have to wait years until it's right to ski. To the right is a steep slide into a rock wall. A long stairway is dug deeply into the snow along the spine, with steel poles planted at regular intervals. Thick ropes strung through the eyelets form a handrail.

Let me put a small rope on you, Kye, says Fanfan.

While Fanfan ropes up Kye, Hattrup and Plake point out the Vallee

Blanche and the Italian border. Then a group of Brits carrying helmets and short skis push past. They walk in a straight line, each holding a rope in the left hand, skis in the right. They will be led down the ridge to the glacier. From there they will be guided down twenty miles of the Vallee Blanche. The skiing is not demanding—an intermediate pitch—but it requires weaving around crevasses and seracs. A guide is a must for inexperienced skiers. A rope is looped through each Brit's harness. The first and last men in the train are guides. The lead guide turns to Fanfan.

Petit garçon pour ici-haut, he says. A small boy for up here.

Il est petit mais un très bon skieur, says Fanfan. He is small but a very good skier.

Oui, says Plake. *Très bon*. Yes, very good.

Est-il français? asks the man. Is he French?

American, answers Plake proudly, and incorrectly, since Kye is Canadian. The exchange is lost on Kye. He is too busy trying to breathe.

All right. Are we ready? asks Hattrup. Can we go now?

We are just waiting for this group, says Fanfan. They are moving slow.

As the Brits move down the line, Hattrup starts humming a song. Then, in a quiet moment, he begins to sing.

Oh he skied quite well, he skied like hell, but he didn't have a bend in his knees.

Plake joins in: *No, he didn't have a bend in his knees. He skied quite well, he skied like hell, but the thing he was taught, he soon forgot, was to get a little bend in the knees.*

Hattrup: *Oh, he skied quite well, he skied like hell, but he ended up in the trees.*

Together: *No, he didn't have a bend in his knees. He skied quite well, he skied like hell, till he said, send the toboggan, please.*

Plake: *Now he can't make haste with a cast to his waist, and he still doesn't have a bend in his knees.*

And then, with the men humming, Fanfan says it's time. Put your skis over the right shoulder and your left hand on the rope, he tells Kye.

They start down the mountain. Plake leads the way, Hattrup next, then Kye. He trails a thin rope that leads to Fanfan.

Have fun, you guys! shouts Stump with a camera in his hand. Be safe!

See you later, says Kye, hopefully.

14

The Wall

Aiguille du Midi, Chamonix, France
Early afternoon, March 16, 2005

The sun is near its apex as Hattrup and Plake take a warm-up run down the shoulder of a steep ramp at the end of the arête. Fanfan takes Kye around it to a less steep pitch.

Okay, Kye, we do not need the rope on you now, he says. We use this warm-up to feel the snow, eh? Here, on every turn, is a different snow. You must be on your feet, not your heels, and you must pay attention to each turn, okay?

Is that a crevasse down there? asks Kye. He points to where the steep skirt of the arête meets the more gently sloping glacier. From a thousand vertical feet above, it looks like a pencil line, but once they are down below, they will see it's wide enough to fall into.

Yes, Kye, this is good that you see this. That is the bergschrund. So when we cross it, we have to go straight and no stops, okay?

And Kye, remember to have fun, says Fanfan as he traverses into the middle of the steep slope. Kye follows Fanfan's tracks, making his turns on the hard pack that Fanfan has scrubbed off. After four turns, the helmet that Fanfan has strapped to his backpack suddenly breaks loose.

Helmet! yells Kye as he stops in a hard, skittering spray.

Shit! yells Fanfan as he pulls up to a stop.

The helmet bounces crazily until it comes to rest on the uphill side of the crevasse.

Okay, Kye, I will have to stop and get it, says Fanfan. But you must not stop. You will make turns until before the bergschrund and then go straight and jump over it without turning, okay? You are a flier man, eh? So it will not be a problem.

With that, Fanfan skis smoothly down the face and makes quick turns right up to the crevasse. He sidesteps near the edge, hooks his helmet with an outstretched ski pole, shakes the snow out of it, and puts it on. Carefully now, he traverses the crevasse until he gains enough speed to jump over its dark opening.

Fanfan is gone; Kye is on his own. He holds onto each turn until he has almost stopped. He's not as smooth as Anselme or Plake, and there's a slight hop at each transition, but his control is complete. Uphill of the dark line, he sets his skis in parallel, making a perfect eleven. He shoots toward the crevasse, hops slightly, and flies over it. He lands lightly, sweeps through a right-hander, and follows Hattrup, Fanfan and Plake toward a long, low saddle between the Aiguille du Midi and the Mont Blanc du Tacul, the easternmost of Mont Blanc's summits.

While I help Peter Pilafian break down the heavy tripod he's been using, I watch Kye disappear from sight. The sun is warm on my back, and, as I work, my jacket exhales gusts of hot, moist air. I'm sweating freely but tingling with excitement. Kye is rising to the challenge, and the family of skiers is closing tightly around him. Even Doug Coombs, the king of big-mountain skiing, has arrived spontaneously to bless the operation. The weather is cooperating, and we are about to confront what until now has been just an idea. Everything is going so damn well that I have to remind myself that we haven't gotten to the dangerous part yet.

I catch up to the group as Mike Hattrup hikes up the saddle between the south-facing cliffs of the Aiguille du Midi and a climbing hut known as the Cosmiques Refuge. Even after hours of morning sun, this south aspect is granite-hard. The Glacier Rond faces north, which means it will be harder still, unless the weather changes. A chill wind smacks Hattrup as he crests the ridge. In seconds his jacket is zipped, hood up. Plake and Kye pull up their hoods and set down their skis next to him on the saddle.

Now we take a short break here, says Fanfan. I want to go look at the Rond. We will see, maybe it is not a good day for it today.

My heart sinks. Not a good day? Today *is* the day. I can feel it. The story is coming together. It is all going to be right. I barely restrain myself from telling Fanfan this. Instead, I watch as he straps crampons to his ski boots and walks around the rock to the north, traversing carefully above a sheer slope that, if he were to fall, would send him into a cheese grater on the east wall of the Cosmiques Couloir.

On the saddle, Hattrup unpacks sandwiches, cheese, nuts and dry sausage. Kye walks away from the group toward me. I ask if he's okay. Yeah, he says, just a little cold. I offer my puffy down jacket and he takes it, wrapping it around his shoulders as he steps away from me to gaze out toward Mont Blanc. I watch him, trying to imagine what he sees. The mountain is wide at top. It doesn't just loom, it pulls down the sky and blots out the horizon. Crevasses spider-web the skirts. The ice floes are enamel-white, seracs pale blue. Kye must know the story of Trevor circling Mont Blanc on a map when he was a boy. He must know that this is where his father had always wanted to be. He must know how, after the avalanche snapped Trevor's spine, he'd come to rest in a seated position as if taking in a view of Mont Blanc. The mountain that Kye is staring at now was the last thing that Trevor saw.

Beside me, Plake watches Kye with a concerned look. After a while, he walks over to him.

So, you've seen Anselme enough, you've seen me enough, he says. You've seen how we do it. Little by little. Turn by turn, right?

Yeah, I'm okay, Plake, says Kye quietly.

Every step is just that, says Plake, choosing to talk about skiing instead of the young man's emotions.

One step at a time, Plake continues. Don't rush. You're gonna feel the fear, but don't rush. Right?

I got it, says Kye, as he picks up his skis and starts running his hand down the edges, making sure they're sharp enough.

What Plake doesn't say is this: If you feel like you can't do it, just tell me. Fanfan hasn't said it, nor has Hattrup. No one is offering Kye a face-saving way out.

Fanfan stomps back around the corner. He takes one of Kye's skis and looks at the settings on the bindings.

Eight, says Fanfan, reading the DIN setting on Kye's binding. I think we better put it a little more.

Hattrup asks Fanfan how it looks, and Fanfan shrugs.

I think we can be okay, he says. It is too hard now, but the sun is coming. I will have to set up ropes and this will take some time. We will wait perhaps one hour but not longer.

So it can soften, says Plake.

Yes, but not longer than one hour, says Fanfan.

Plake digs a Leatherman tool out of his pack. Fanfan grabs his pack and rope and heads back to the top of the Glacier Rond to anchor ropes that will keep everyone safe. Plake takes Kye's skis and goes to work tightening the DIN setting.

I usually use safety straps because your brakes aren't going to work out there, says Plake. Some people disagree with that, but I want my skis with me at all times. I can hook 'em to my leg, and I'll never have to worry. If you hit a rock and kick a ski off it's gone.

What are you putting them at? asks Kye.

Ten, says Plake.

Kye nods and I notice again that no one is asking him if it's okay. Plake is just doing it. The time for collaboration is over. Plake and Fanfan and Hattrup are taking charge. And Kye is giving over to them, trusting them completely.

I am, too.

Are we going down the ladder on the wall? asks Kye, who's been told that there are two ways onto the Glacier Rond—one is down a long ladder, the other involves traversing above cliffs in crampons.

Yeah, the ladder's the best way onto this, says Plake, who continues to twist the DIN screw on Kye's binding. Besides, we don't have crampons for you.

How big is it? asks Kye.

Big, says Plake. It's going to be scarier than the run. Well, maybe …

Plake's bare hand turns an angry red as he holds onto the cold steel of the Leatherman.

I should get some food into me, says Kye.

Yeah, you're gonna need it, Plake says.

I haven't been able to eat, he says. My stomach's just not good.

I nod silently. I am not the only one whose gut has been in knots over this.

Hattrup doles out food and water. Kye sits on a mound sheltered from the wind by a tusk of rock. Iberg is by his side, trying to keep it light. Plake rarely sits. He paces. Five steps this way, six back. Talking, chewing. He throws food to black birds that have arrived, looking for a handout. Jordan Kronick steps between me and a view of Mont Blanc.

We have to interview them before they ski it, he says.

Kronick is thorough. Up here on the mountain, he is the eyes and ears of Obenhaus, Yellin and Jennings.

You're probably right, I say, not moving.

Downtime makes production people nervous. It's easy to believe that if the cameras aren't rolling, then nothing is happening. From a production standpoint, Kronick is absolutely right about the interviews, but from a skier's point of view it just feels wrong. I don't want to intrude on the moment. I tell him I want to let the guys relax before they tackle the Rond.

He disagrees, and we talk it over. Kronick is earnest. He has a list of questions. Eventually I relent, saying that as soon as Fanfan says it's time to go, we wrap the interviews, even if we're right in the middle of one. This makes Kronick happy and allows me to feel like I'm doing my job. Hattrup, who's heard the exchange, steps forward. He knows the game, and he's happy to be the lead-off. Kronick, the ex-lawyer, positions him on a stand of rock.

Mike, tell us about Chamonix, says Kronick.

Chamonix is where my eyes were opened to the big mountains. I was a ski-area skier. I had no clue. I had never worn a harness, never worn crampons, had never had an ice ax in my hand.

Why did you come here?

We came here for *Blizzard of Aahhh's*. We'd shot in Squaw Valley and other places in the States where there's some steep stuff. And then we came here, and they told us that on average one person died a week at Chamonix. That blew our minds. You never hear about people dying in ski areas in the States. Maybe one a year. But here, one a week, sixty people a year? I didn't really comprehend how dangerous it was. Go back and watch *Blizzard*. It's pretty apparent how green we were. In the Poubelle, we didn't even know how to rappel. We were lowered by the guide. Plake's on his knees getting lowered. For me, Chamonix was a turning point, my first taste of what it was like beyond the lifts. It was my baptism.

Tell me about Trevor, says Kronick.

I was with Trevor for a week in the Coast Range near Mount Waddington, a couple weeks in Australia and New Zealand, a few weeks in Greenland, and here in Chamonix. When we were here, it was dumping. We couldn't even get up on the Grands Montets. But the whole time he was talking about getting up here and skiing the Cosmiques. That was a week before he died here.

Now you're here with Kye, says Kronick, leading the witness.

Yeah, we're here with Kye, Trevor's son, says Hattrup, his voice lowering, carefully holding on to every word. And we're going to ski the run that Trevor died on.

He stops and collects himself. Kronick waits.

The mountains were superimportant to Trevor. He loved Chamonix. So just being here and skiing that run will probably close the circle for Kye.

But Mike, why, after you've lost friends to these mountains, do you come back? asks Kronick.

I guess the reason I come back to the big mountains and places like this, despite having friends who've died here, is because …

He talks sideways for a while—accomplishment, the chess game of surviving in the mountains—and then comes to it: I don't know, he says, why do you do anything?

Kye's next and he's not happy about it. The sun is bright and he's being asked to take his glasses off so the camera can see his eyes. A grip is holding a reflector, shining sunlight into Kye's face. He's perched on an outcropping of rock and gives me a look that asks, what the hell are you doing to me?

Let's make this quick, I say to Kronick.

Tell me about Plake, says Kronick.

Plake has taught me a lot and hopefully we'll have a good ski down this together.

Fanfan?

Fanfan is an awesome guide. He's always trusted.

Kye's voice is hoarse. The reflector wavers in the wind, the light in Kye's eyes flashes. He's tense, annoyed.

What's the significance of where we are and what you're about to do?

He begins to answer, but an airplane flies over.

Hold for sound, yells the soundman.

We're all suddenly intensely aware of sounds—the grumble of the airplane, the crunch of snow underfoot, the rustle of Kye's coat as he fidgets.

Okay, I'm good, says the soundman.

The importance is that we're going to ski this line where my dad died, says Kye, with thinly veiled impatience. He's squinting painfully.

I've always wanted to ski this line, says Kye. The Exit Couloir and the Glacier Rond. It means a lot to me. It's one of my goals.

Does it scare you?

I haven't skied it yet, so I'll let you know after, he says, giving Kronick a tight-lipped look.

I step past Kronick and help Kye down from the rock.

You okay? I ask Kye.

Yeah, fine, he says angrily. I just want to ski.

I know, it's almost time, I say, putting my hand on his shoulder. He shrugs it off testily.

Let's just get it done, he says.

I know. We're all on the same page. Jordan's just trying to do his job.

Fuck him, says Kye angrily.

I laugh.

Quiet please! yells the soundman.

I turn. He and Kronick are giving me *shut-up* looks. I wave an apology, choking down more laughter, then turn back to Kye. He's laughing as well. After a moment he holds out a fist. I meet it with mine, gloved knuckle to gloved knuckle.

We have been under way since just after dawn. It's nearly two in the afternoon when Fanfan carefully hikes back around the corner of the cliff that leads to the Rond. I look over at Kye. I can tell by the set of his jaw that he is not giving himself an option to back down. I'm not about to give him one either. Any questioning of his confidence will weaken him. Belief is the key to survival; questioning that belief could be disastrous.

Fanfan says its time to go, and I ask Kronick to wrap it up. He says, just one more. I tell him that the skiers need to get up to the wall, climb down it, do whatever they're going to do with Trevor's ashes on the arête, then ski the Glacier Rond before they get to the Exit Couloir, which will get more and more avalanche prone as the afternoon sun bakes it.

He's in place, says Kronick. Ten minutes, Bill.

No, I say.

We're good, says Plake. I can do this quick.

I look at Fanfan. He shrugs.

Just take us a few minutes, says Plake.

Okay, do it quickly, I say.

Kronick doesn't need much to get Plake into it. One word, in fact: Chamonix?

Chamonix puts you in your place, says Plake. You think you're somebody here? You're not.

Plake is a pro, a sound-bite generator. Every nugget has an edge.

In a way it's kind of cool to be in a place where there's no way that you're bigger than you think you are, he continues. It's calming because you don't have to prove ... In the world, everybody's trying to be somebody, but here, you can't be. There are so many things that have been done here that I'll never do. I owe everything in my skiing career to everything that's been done before me. I'm just another link in the chain. I just happen to be here at the moment.

And why do you keep coming back?

I come back for the peace. When I'm down there I'm thinking about all the other garbage. When I'm up here there's none of that. It's peace. And when you're skiing steeps, there's no pressure. It feels like you're floating. You just want it to keep going and going and going. Unfortunately, you only find that in this kind of place.

Is it the adrenaline?

I'm not an adrenaline junkie, he says. I have a respect for visions. I have a desire to visualize something and put it into my body and make it work. But I'm not an adrenaline junkie. An adrenaline junkie is a waste.

Kronick, I realize, has already made a character out of Plake. He has figured out where he fits and who he is. I know because I made the same mistake. With Plake, it's difficult to see beyond the peacock façade and the punk-rock bravado. It's nearly impossible to listen to what's behind the sound bites. I've come to see that he's not merely a huckster. Plake is as complicated and thoughtful as any skier I've ever interviewed. He has deep beliefs about life and death that he's come to the hard way, and I find myself looking for a way to bring that out in the film.

And now Kye is here with you, continues Kronick.

Kye has got a very, very unique situation. He's got a lot of good friends who are going to take him down this thing. We're not only friends of his and friends of his father's but friends of others who we've lost. We can't deny the memory of the friends who are no longer with us. Lots of people are still up here. That's the reality of the mountains. A lot of our friends go and don't come back.

There's a moment as Plake nods his head and looks off to the horizon. Kronick adeptly lets the moment play. The camera rolls, a slight breeze ruffles the long strands of Plake's orange hair.

Glen, what do you believe happens after a person dies? I ask slowly.

He turns his head back toward me and Kronick and our camera.

If they believe in God, they're going to heaven, says Plake.

Where do you think Trevor went? I continue.

I don't know. I wish I did.

If you could tell Trevor just one thing about his son, what would you tell him? I ask.

I'd tell him he's turned out to be a skier, so far.

From the saddle, it's a short hike up to the wall. I join Hattrup on an old stone buttress that once anchored the southwest corner of Chamonix's first tram. We look behind us and watch Fanfan move up the pitch, agile as a mountain goat. Plake and Kye tramp up last.

Hey Kye, take a look at this! yells Hattrup.

Kye kicks his final steps into the snow and climbs onto the cement. He takes a breath and walks over to where Hattrup stands by the tower. The old steel is rusted and pocked, dark red and cold. Affixed to one of the supports is a faded red, white and black sticker. Kye steps up close. Hattrup looks at Kye with an expression that's impossible to read.

No way, says Kye. He stares at the sticker. The edges are chipped away but the letters are still bold. The sticker reads:

Trevor Would Do It
In Memory of Trevor Petersen

The wall is made of heavy stone blocks. It's about a foot wide and six stories high. In the middle of the wall are U-shaped iron rungs leading seventy feet down to the snow.

Plake lashes his skis, poles and ice ax to his backpack.

Hey Kye, gimme your skis, he says. I'll take 'em down the wall.

After lashing Kye's skis to his own, Plake carefully steps onto the cement blocks. He teeters for a moment, then drops to a crawl, slowly lowering himself into a push-up position. He swings his feet over the side, feeling for the ladder, the sole of his plastic ski boot meeting an iron rung like a church bell. Clinging to the wall with gloved hands, he kicks the boots against the rung to make sure he doesn't have any ice on his soles.

Even if he were to survive a fall here, even if he were somehow able to avoid the sharp boulders beneath him, the slope would be too steep to stop himself from sliding. He'd tumble into the rocks of the Cosmiques Couloir, a deadly cheese grater. We're not even skiing yet, and already Plake is in the no-fall zone.

Plake reaches down with one foot, finds the rung, tests it, then lowers his other foot to the same rung.

Construction on this tram began in 1924, which makes this wall eighty years old. Plake climbs carefully, the skis lashed to his pack tilting back and forth like a pendulum.

Okay, it's you now, Kye, says Fanfan.

Kye peers over to where Plake is a small face looking up.

Okay, I guess, says Kye. But I'm not that into this part.

Maybe I should go, says Hattrup, taking note of the uncertainty in Kye's voice.

Yep, maybe it's better, says Fanfan.

Hattrup walks carefully to the middle of the wall, lowers himself to his knees, finds the first rung with his foot, and climbs smoothly down. One foot per rung, he's down too soon for Kye.

You don't like heights? asks Fanfan, tugging at the rope that he's affixed to Kye's harness.

I don't care about heights, but this ladder thing …

I have you on the rope, so you cannot fall, says Fanfan. And anyway, it will look good in the cameras, eh?

Yeah, pretty rad, says Kye, forcing a laugh. He takes a deep breath and starts crawling out onto the wall. The belay line trails behind him. In the middle of the wall, Kye lies down on his stomach and slowly spins his torso. His legs hang in space. He grips the cement block. His dangling legs reach for a rung. *Chong!* Kye kicks his toe in above the first iron rod. He flexes his knee, testing the rung before putting all his weight on it. Solid. He puts his other foot on it.

Nice, Kye, says Fanfan. You're good.

I'm standing behind our cameramen, watching the rope go through Fanfan's hands. I know that he will not let Kye fall, but even a slip here could end our day on the Rond. If Kye were to fall, Fanfan would clamp down on the rope, and Kye would swing into the wall, possibly banging into the rungs, maybe breaking a bone, not to mention what it would do to the young man's confidence. I resist praying. It seems hypocritical. It's been years.

One step down, the other boot follows. One hand, two hands.

Hey Mike, yells Fanfan, can you wait a little bit down here because I think I don't have enough rope for Kye.

Kye shoots a glance up at Fanfan as if to say, not enough rope! What do you mean not enough rope?

Yeah, I'll take him from here, yells Hattrup.

Another step and another. Kye is either gaining confidence or he just wants to get the hell off the wall. He's moving down the ladder quickly now. Light and agile with no pack, no skis, he's a kid on the monkey bars.

Great work, Kye, says Hattrup, as the young man nears the bottom.

As Kye holds onto the last rung, Hattrup takes hold of Kye's harness. He quickly loops a strand of rope around the last rung and ties it to Kye's carabiner.

Fanfan, is it okay to untie him? yells Hattrup.

The shadow of a fat bird drifts across the face of the rock as all eyes look up to Fanfan.

I have enough, yells Fanfan. Keep on both ropes until he gets to the safe place.

Okay, you're safe, says Hattrup. He's got you, and I've got you too.

Okay, says Kye, I'm going again.

Kye kicks more steps into the snow, turning so that he's facing the steep slope. He begins carefully down the slope backwards, just like Plake did. Two, three kicks into the snow. His boots make deep holes. He tests each with his weight, then kicks another hole. There's maturity in his movements, focus. Clumps of snow roll down, bouncing off Plake's pack and disappearing over the edge into the Cosmiques cheese grater.

The wind has formed a knife edge of snow in front of the wall. It begins parallel to the wall, then curves to the west. On one side is the steep ramp of the Glacier Rond, on the other a more precipitous drop into the Cosmiques. Plake steers Kye next to the rock wall away from the edge.

Perfect, says Plake.

I was pretty scared at the top, says Kye.

Me too, says Plake. If you ain't scared, there's something wrong with you.

Hattrup lowers himself down as Plake takes Kye's skis off his pack. He hands them to Kye. Hattrup takes Kye's ski in his hand.

Here, Kye, let me show you a technique for putting on your skis on really steep slopes, says Hattrup. You take one ski and jam it in the snow.

He drives Kye's ski into the snow tail first, almost up to the heelpiece.

Now, you hang onto that one, says Hattrup, as you step into your other ski. If anything happens, you've got a hold of this one. It's an anchor. Then you stand on that downhill ski and take the other one out and put it on your uphill foot.

Kye grabs his ski and holds it like an anchor. Hattrup performs the same procedure with his own skis, narrating each move again. Kye follows every move perfectly. Plake hands Kye his poles.

Also, Kye, when you're not using your poles, says Plake, you don't want to just stick them in up to the baskets. You want to tip 'em upside down and jam 'em way in.

Yeah, a pole falls over in the ski area, who cares? says Hattrup. But if it falls over here and it goes down there, you're skiing the rest of the run with one pole.

And make sure you don't ski onto that cord, says Plake, pointing to the rope that's affixed to Kye's harness.

If you do, let us know, says Hattrup. Then we can check it out and make sure it's all right.

Yep, I've got it, says Kye. He kicks his edges into the snow, testing the texture, readying himself.

Plake sidesteps carefully down the arête, his tips and tails suspended in space. Chunks of snow slide off the top of the knife-edge and explode on the rocks below. He stops and sidesteps back up to Kye and Hattrup, then side-slips down the arête again. He repeats this one more time, each trip shaving the edge of the arête away until he's made a sloping platform large enough for all of them to stand on.

As Fanfan scampers down the ladder, Hattrup sidesteps down next to Plake. Fanfan arrives next to Kye, excess rope coiled over his shoulder, one end tied to Kye's harness. The rope runs through his right hand. In his left hand he holds an ice ax that he'll use to anchor himself in the event of a fall—either his own or Kye's.

Okay, Kye, we go down to Glen and Mike now, says Fanfan.

Kye nervously side-slips down, the knife edge in front of him and the cliff at his back. Plake and Hattrup watch closely, their skis anchored, ready to stop Kye if he falters.

Remember, stand nice and tall, says Plake, pointing to Kye's edges. Be proud, and don't lean in.

Kye stops next to Hattrup. He slides forward a few inches, looks over the knife edge, then backs up as far as he can, the tails of his skis scraping rock.

Did you peek at it? asks Hattrup, pointing down the Glacier Rond.

Yeah, what's that thing going down the middle? asks Kye as he points at a deep groove in the center of the pitch.

That's a gully from a big piece of serac that broke off, says Hattrup. It came off above us and slid down the middle. Whenever it leaves a defined groove like that you know it's a piece of ice, probably serac. Avalanches don't dig a clean groove like that. That thing slid down and then launched off the end of the glacier like a ninety-meter jump.

Except it's a four-hundred-meter jump, says Plake with a wry laugh to let everyone know that the end of the ramp is not something to be taken lightly. Sliding off the bottom of the Glacier Rond is certain death.

It's now past three in the afternoon. Plake turns to Kye to ask whether he thinks the arête will be a good place to throw his father's ashes.

Good, says Kye. It's good.

Who's got the ashes? asks Hattrup.

Plake pulls a steel container out of his jacket and passes it uphill to Hattrup. The small can has a *Trevor Would Do It* sticker wrapped around it.

Hattrup looks at it for a long moment, as if trying to connect the small can with his memory of Trevor. He offers it to Kye, whose hand is shaking.

Thank you, he says, quietly.

Kye brings his hand up to his mouth, bites the finger of his glove, and tugs it off.

Okay, um, I don't know what to say …

For once, none of them do either, not even Plake. Kye unscrews the cap and shakes some ashes into his right hand. They are dust, fine as talcum.

Okay, I'd like to have a moment of silence, I guess, says Kye.

The men lower their heads. Kye makes a fist of the ashes.

Okay, says Kye, his voice quavering. So, I guess I'll blow them right off here.

Plake nods.

Kye holds his palm upright, the small pile perfectly still. Kye inhales, slides forward a few inches, his tips touching the edge of the arête. He holds the ashes up to his face, the heel of his hand next to his lips, his fingers pointed toward Mont Blanc. He blows like he's blowing out birthday candles. The ashes swirl out and up, catching a gust off the Cosmiques, dissolving into thin air.

Hattrup watches the ashes fly into the abyss. Plake drops his eyes to the snow, his head bouncing slightly, jaw moving almost imperceptibly, saying a prayer.

Kye takes three involuntary breaths, short and pained, pushing emotions down his windpipe. The wind grows quiet.

And then Kye is in motion, his hands fiddling with the canister, trying to get the top back on. He stands straighter, ready to begin.

How the hell do I close this, he says.

Plake lets out a burst of nervous laughter. Kye joins in.

Trevor in a can, says Kye.

Well, I tell you what, says Hattrup in a lighter tone. Trevor was always so excited when he was talking about the mountains, but he really lit up when he talked about you and your sister. I know that nothing would make him prouder than to know you're skiing the Glacier Rond. He is beaming with pride right now. I can promise you that.

But I think it's not just your father, says Plake. Fanfan's got friends, Mike's got friends, we've all got friends—

Oh yeah, especially this year, says Fanfan. And I think we do a very good thing for all the friends, and for the big family we are.

Kye meets Fanfan's gaze, then drops his eyes toward the couloir below, over the edge, to where his father made his last turns.

chapter 15

The Exit

Glacier Rond, Chamonix, France
Late afternoon, March 16, 2005

As I'm looking at my watch, fretting over how late it's gotten and how much mountain the skiers still need to ski, I hear footsteps approach. I turn to see a lanky figure hiking up the final pitch.

What's going on? asks Doug Coombs as he lowers his skis from his shoulder. I point over the wall, down seventy feet to where Kye, Fanfan, Hattrup and Plake are standing on the arête. Coombs takes it in. Though he doesn't know about the ritual that's just taken place below, he's astute enough to feel that there's something happening here that he doesn't want to interrupt. We watch quietly. Below us on the arête, Peter Pilafian, the high-definition cameraman, and Brian Whitlock, our soundman, are roped in near the skiers.

Okay, we have to go now because it's very warm, says Fanfan.

Yeah, it's getting heavy, says Plake, lowering his goggles.

Plake is going first, Mike second, says Fanfan. And then, Kye, we go.

Live for the living! Plake yells as he pushes off. His tips hanging off the edge, tails nearly scraping rock, he side-slips down the arête. Where it widens, he makes a hop turn. Landing, he prods with his pole, one stab, two, and then another hop turn. A third. Plake begins to whistle, the notes happy, incongruously carefree.

Coombs and I watch as Plake cuts to his left, edging back up the arête, skis angled against the fall line, curls of snow peeling from edges like hard cheese. Now Hattrup slides down the narrow lane that Plake has packed. Prodding the snow with his pole several times—the feel of the snow under his pole telling him more than his eyes—he spins a cautious hop turn, and another, then traverses toward Plake.

So, Kye, I think we just use the rope for the traverse here, says Fanfan. And then, after, we will see. Maybe the rope again, because it is icy. Okay?

For sure, says Kye.

But for this, you just ski with me, continues Fanfan, slinging another coil of rope over his shoulder. We stay together. You're ready?

Oh yeah. Kye shuffles his skis, grips and re-grips his poles.

Wait, says Fanfan.

Kye sighs.

Where's Bertrand? Fanfan yells up to me.

He's loading more film in the camera, I yell back.

Bertrand Delapierre is an extreme snowboarder and cameraman who we've hired to shoot the descent of the Glacier Rond and Exit Couloir.

I think we need to go now, yells Fanfan. I don't want to be at six o'clock on the traverse with the kid, eh?

I tell Bertrand to hurry up.

Tell them to begin, he says, stuffing the Arri camera into his pack. I will catch up. It is no problem.

As we have plenty of cameras on the top part of the Rond, I tell Fanfan to go ahead.

Okay, Kye, says Fanfan. Now we don't go fast, right?

Yep, got it, says Kye, shuffling his skis fore and aft.

Before he can push off, a low, thudding sound distracts him. A blue-

and-gold rescue chopper banks in low, then hovers over a far corner of the Cosmiques Couloir. This is the gendarme, the same outfit we saw practicing crevasse rescue on the Grands Montets. Only this is not practice. Someone is in serious trouble. Fanfan and Kye watch without comment.

Okay, Kye, says Fanfan. Let's go, duuuude.

Kye manages a smile as he begins sidestepping down the arête, feeling the snow with his poles, his edges. Fanfan holds the rope in his right hand, ice ax in his left. Plake and Hattrup's side-slipping has shaved all the soft snow off the slope. It's a billiard table tipped on end. Kye slides down carefully.

If you make a turn, tell me, says Fanfan.

But Kye is not about to make a turn here. Not just now. Gone is the smoothness, the play. All the talk of his father's fatal run has Kye coiled. He carefully works his way out onto the arête, next to Plake and Hattrup.

Plake stabs at the snow. Stiff but edgeable. He steps into his first turn, comes around, stops, centers, and then carves another one.

I think we have good snow! yells Plake. Hard snow.

Yeah, very icy, eh? We have to go left, hollers Fanfan.

Very hard snow but not ice, yells Plake. He makes another turn, and another. Surrendering to gravity, giving over to the hill in increments, each turn takes him ten meters down the slope.

Oh no, I think it's not good there! yells Fanfan, the alarm in his voice rising. It's not snow. It's ice. Go left.

Plake makes another turn, straight down. And another. He's not moving left.

Careful, huh, Glen! yells Fanfan again. It's very icy here.

Not ice but hard, yells Plake over his shoulder.

Yeah, but just down from you is ice! hollers Fanfan.

Plake proves him wrong with another turn in windblown snow. He nearly stops at the end of each turn, resets, and drives into another. And suddenly his skis skitter. His uphill hand flies into the air as he falls back, a mistake that skiers call riding the bronco. His hip hits the ice. He's sliding. He sets his skis against the fall line. They flap uselessly, edges scraping but not slowing him down. A fine mist of ice crystals blows into the air. Below him there is nothing.

Then his downhill edge finds purchase, and he's on his feet again. He heaves, contracting his abdomen, driving his upper body forward, skis bending, carving. Plake cuts hard to the left into softer snow and stops.

You all right? yells Hattrup.

Yeah, yells Plake. Better go to the left, away from that ice.

Hattrup's skis find hard snow, peanut brittle, but he gets an edge. Shards slide down next to Plake. Hattrup finds a four-beat rhythm. Pole plant, let go, drive the edge, stop. Machinelike, military, he is segmenting the hill one turn at a time. And then he's on his hip, bouncing toward Plake. He throws his hands forward, an old mogul-skier trick, and he's turning again. He regains control and stops next to Plake.

Now it's Kye's turn. Fanfan drives his ice ax into the snow, angles his edges against the slope, and grips the rope. Kye cuts along the top of the knife-edge, steps down, slides a little, and stops. Step down, slide forward, stop. It's slow going, but it's safe. Then Kye slides faster. The rope rushes out. Fanfan closes his hands over it, drawing it out to the side, pulling it against the rappelling ring. Kye is on the ice, too, sliding toward the western edge. The rope twangs tight as Fanfan stops Kye's descent. Kye stays on his feet over the ice, angling, whipping across the slope like a boy on a tire swing. He hits the soft snow and makes a controlled stop next to Hattrup and Plake.

All Kye can do is shake his head.

Shit, says Plake.

Above them, Coombs walks onto the wall, strolling in his ski boots, loose and relaxed, a hundred feet above the skiers. He stops at the ladder and looks down.

Hey Mike, I'm thinking about skiing that with you, Coombs yells. Whaddaya think?

No, I think, no, says Fanfan to Hattrup.

Talk to Bill, yells Hattrup.

Coombs turns and looks over at me. He stands casually on the wall. A slip and he's dead, but his body is as loose as if he were on his own front porch.

What do you think, Bill? asks Coombs.

A tinny voice squawks from my radio. Bill Kerig, this is Greg Stump, can you hear me?

Go ahead, Greg.

I've got a problem, says Stump over the radio. I repeat, I've got a problem. They want me out of here. The tram is closing, and they want me on the last car.

I key the mic on my radio: And you don't have skis, right?

No, I have to take this car down or I'm spending the night.

Coombs looks from me, down to Hattrup, and back to me.

We *do* kind of have our hands full, I say to Coombs.

He looks away from me, down to where Pilafian and Whitlock are roped in next to the skiers, and he slowly nods his head.

Hey Mike, I'm going around, yells Coombs. It looks kinda sketchy anyway. I'll get it another day.

Coombs walks back across the wall with the same loose, surefooted gait. Halfway between the ladder and me, he turns around, as if he forgot something.

Hey Kye, he yells. Have fun!

Kye waves and shoots a look at Fanfan. The best skier in the world thinks it looks too sketchy, but he, Kye, is skiing it.

It's okay, says Fanfan to Kye. We have you on the rope.

You skiing the Rond, Bill? asks Coombs as he puts his skis down next to me.

Abso-fucking-lutely, I want to say. The skier in me wants to ski it, needs to ski it. Now that I've seen the Glacier Rond, all I want to do is slip out from under all the filmmaking pressure and ski. And I want to be beside Kye to make sure nothing goes wrong, or help if it does. But the director has a job to do, and the father in me is remembering the pictures of my kids and the promise I made myself last night. And through all the competing voices comes one clear one that says, know your limitations. You're a good skier but not as good as the guys who are on the Rond with Kye. You have no experience in mountain rescue and haven't prepared yourself to ski something as serious as the Rond.

It's painful to admit, but I'll only be a liability. So I lie to myself, closing my inner dialogue by saying that it's no big deal, I can always come back another day. And then I lie to Coombs, too, if only a little.

I'm not really sure, Doug, I say. Kye's probably got enough help.

Coombs says that Fanfan is one of the best guides in the world and that Kye will be fine.

He steps into his skis and says, Make sure you don't wait too long to go down the Vallee Blanche. That's a long ski in the dark.

And then he's gone. It will be the last time I see Doug Coombs.

It's 3:45 before Bertrand makes it down the ladder and arrives on the arête. He hops his way down, ice ax in hand—hop, side-slip, hop, side-slip—tapping the tip of his ax on the snow for balance.

Fanfan yells to him in French. Bertrand yells something back. Fanfan shakes his head. No, this is no good. I imagine he's telling him about the ice.

Bertrand waves him off. He hops off the arête and lands with the board facing downhill. In a low crouch, ice ax raised, tip facing down, he straight-runs over the ice, suddenly moving faster than anyone would want to go with a fatal cheese grater just below. Then he throws his body sideways, his snowboard scraping against the hill toeside. He drives the ice ax into the slope and disappears behind a curtain of flying ice crystals. For long seconds, it's impossible to know whether he stopped or skittered off the edge.

When the curtain of white settles, he's on his knees, elbows on the ice, one hand holding the ax. His forehead is down, facing up the hill. Another twenty meters—one or two more skips of his board—and he would've been gone. He looks over his shoulder toward the men, grinning madly.

Hattrup just shakes his head. The French, he says.

Okay, we move now, says Fanfan.

Bertrand takes the camera out of his pack and sets up next to still photographer Scott Markewitz, who's made a careful descent around the ice to a spot near the skiers. Kye looks over at Markewitz to see if he's ready.

Never mind the cameras, says Plake. Here we take it slow. On every turn, you stop and center. Nobody here gives a shit what you look like or how fast you get down. This ain't no friggin' eight-minute ski run.

Glen, I need to take your rope, says Fanfan. It is longer and I can rappel him farther. Okay? Kye, stay in this place. Don't move. Now you can put off the rope.

Kye looks at him, his hands moving toward the rope without conviction.

It's okay. You are in a safe place. We put you back on in a minute.

Kye unclips the carabiner and tosses the end of the rope to Fanfan. Plake tosses his coil up to Fanfan, who begins unspooling it, taking out the tangles.

Your rope is like spaghetti, he says. Americans ...

Kye manages a laugh.

Without taking off his gloves, Fanfan loops the rope through Kye's harness and ties a fast figure-eight. He clicks out of his skis and drives them into the snow, tail first. He loops a small rope around one ski between the heel and toe pieces, then clips a carabiner into it.

Okay, I'm ready, says Fanfan. Glen and Mike, try to find a place to stop that's safe for Kye. Kye, I tell you when I have just ten meters more rope and you stop in a safe place, okay?

Hattrup nods and begins to make a long traverse, planting his pole once, twice, three times before making a turn. Then he finds the snow he's looking for. He steps on the uphill ski, twisting to stay square, and the ski comes around under him. Shearing the surface, his momentum pushes him across the hill. He angles against the fall line, away from gravity, up the hill and into his next turn. Getting on the uphill ski early, he plants a pole, letting his hips power the ski, shoulders driving down the hill. His skis find their own path. Steady and controlled, he covers a hundred meters in five turns.

Okay, so next, says Fanfan.

Plake pushes out. He double-pole-plants, an extra-sure technique I haven't seen him use yet. In this section he double-poles every turn. He stops short of Hattrup on the edge of a vertical wind lip.

Ready, Kye?

Yep, he says, poling forward cautiously. Okay, I'm going to turn.

Fanfan pays out the rope. Kye compresses his legs, coiling. He hops his first turn, lands, stops, breathes. He turns again, stops, rests, then makes another.

Fanfan feeds more rope. Kye heaves, overmuscling every turn but making it through three more. It's going to be a long, exhausting descent.

From where Fanfan is belaying, Kye disappears behind the rollover. The slope slants down, then down some more. The rope keeps going out. He knows Kye is still skiing only by the feel of the rope, which is getting near the end.

Ten meters more! yells Fanfan.

The rope keeps going out.

Stop, Kye! he yells.

He looks at the coil of rope at his feet. Less than seven meters. If Kye keeps going, Fanfan will have to stop him. He can't let the end of the rope go through his hands. He'll have to clamp down, force Kye to fall. Another tug, another. Kye is still skiing.

Stop! he yells. *Merde!*

And then the rope stops.

You okay, Kye? yells Fanfan.

Nothing. No pull on the rope. No sound.

It's okay? yells Fanfan.

A long moment.

Yes! yells Plake. It's okay!

I can let go of the rope?

Yes, I've got him, yells Plake. I've got the rope.

Fanfan breathes deeply and throws the rope down. It disappears behind the rollover. Later, as I watch the tape from Fanfan's helmet cam, I see him look down at his watch. The time is 4:15.

The western edge of the Glacier Rond is the steepest part. It's also where the best snow is. Before Kye stops, Hattrup starts down a wind-formed crease, a vertical wrinkle that runs alongside the rocks. If anything sends him to the left—a hooked tip or caught edge—he won't have to worry about making any more mistakes. There is no surviving a fall here.

Standing upright on the hill, Kye can easily touch his hand to the snow without leaning. He's never been on anything so steep. But it's more than the pitch. The vastness of the Rond makes it hard to breathe. It's too big, and he's too small. The enormity is crushing.

I think he can ski alone now, Fanfan says to Plake.

You think? asks Plake, clearly skeptical.

Okay, says Fanfan, changing his mind. Kye, I prefer you ski on the rope now. It's too much exposure.

I'm good with that, says Kye.

Kye looks down the impossibly steep slope beneath him, to the close-out of jagged rocks to the left, and then to the cliff. Straight down is a shower curtain, vertiginous and white, and then a final cliff. A mile below is the brown valley, the snaking green-gray river.

Kye releases his edges, side-slipping. His uphill hand drags in the snow as he stabs the slope with his downhill pole.

Okay, Kye, you can turn, coaches Fanfan.

More side-slip.

You have rope, says Fanfan. Turn now.

Kye can't. He's gripped. He side-slips some more, lurching forward and aft. He plants his downhill pole, getting ready to let go, to let gravity pull him into a turn. And then he pulls the pole out and hop-slips sideways. He is frozen. He can't commit.

He side-slips some more, stops, tries to center.

You can do this, coaches Plake from below. Make a turn just like at the beginning of the Poubelle Couloir.

Now Kye has a visual. His body knows how the turn felt, remembers how it worked. He plants his downhill pole and snaps his skis around. They come around faster than he expects. For a moment, he's on his heels. Planting his pole again, he angles his hip, rolls his ankles, and drives his knee. The skis come around like they're greased.

Another smooth turn, then another.

That's it, turn and center, chants Plake.

He finds a ragged cadence. Turn, center, pole plant, turn. The skis are in the right place, doing the right thing, but there's no slide, no grace. He is skiing against the mountain, grinding against the flow. He grunts to a stop uphill of Plake.

Okay, yells Plake up to Fanfan. He's safe!

From somewhere above, Fanfan's rope flies out into the air and lands uphill of Kye.

Kye looks down. They seem to still have the whole run in front of them.

Shit, this is crazy-long, he says.

Now, on this next part, Kye, says Plake as he begins coiling rope, Mike found some hard snow and cut across.

Kye looks to where Hattrup, Bertrand and Scott Markewitz have traversed toward the east side of the Rond. Hattrup is seventy meters out and not even halfway across. He's stopped there because he knows Fanfan's rope will only reach that far; he wants to be within range to help Kye.

Tumbling snow announces Fanfan's arrival. Hard pellets bounce off Kye's shoulders and helmet. There's no greeting this time, no glib chatter. They must stay focused. You don't hang out on slopes where seracs can fall or where a little slip will send you sliding off a cliff.

Now we have to traverse, says Fanfan. This is too much exposure.

Mike found some hard snow, repeats Plake.

Okay, I am thinking of something different, says Fanfan. Plake, you have to go first and you take the rope. You have one end. I take the other. We stay and Kye goes down it.

Like a zipline, says Plake.

Yep, just in case, says Fanfan. When you get to the other side, you make an anchor. Mike can help. And I have an anchor here.

Fanfan digs in the tail of his ski and loops the rope around it again. Plake takes one pole and lashes it to his pack. He unclips his ice ax and loops the strap around his wrist on the uphill side. Using the ax instead of his uphill pole, Plake begins edging eastward across the ramp. With each step he bounces, testing the snow. After twenty meters, his skis stop leaving tracks. There's no snow coming off his edges. He is on glacier ice, hard as polished marble.

Fanfan plays out the rope. Plake angles uphill of Hattrup's tracks.

No, Glen, this is not good. Stay below his tracks. I think it is no good over there. Go straight to Mike.

This time Plake listens, altering his course immediately. Plake arrives at Hattrup just as the rope pulls taut. He explains the zipline idea, and Hattrup unclips one of the ice screws from his harness. The screw is a hollow, ten-inch titanium tube with a beveled tip and threads around the outside. Hattrup taps the ice until he finds a section that's hard, then twists the screw by using a flat, handlelike loop at the top. The beveled edge bites a half-inch ring, forcing ice out through the hollow tube. Once it's in, Hattrup clips a carabiner to the loop on the screw and ties the rope to it.

Across the slope, Fanfan digs in his pack and pulls out a two-foot strap with a carabiner on either end. He clips one end to Kye's harness, the other to the rope. Fanfan leans back on the rope and pulls it taut, like a clothesline strung across a hill.

Now, Kye, you stay below the line, says Fanfan. You just ski very slowly. It is like, how you call it? The zipline. If you can do this, we can maybe take you off the rope on the other side.

Later, Kye tells me that getting off the rope seems more like a threat than a reward. His palms sweat, and his feet are soaked. Perspiration freezes in his socks. He tells himself to stand tall. Stand on the edge. He pushes off, rolling his ankles in, driving the downhill knee. His skis come up on edge, flexing, holding.

There's ice at the end, yells Plake. Just let up and slide over it. We've got you.

Rolling his feet into the hill, Kye angles up the slope. The carve adds to his speed.

He rolls his ankles out, disengaging the edges. Moving his weight onto his uphill ski, he throws both skis sideways, just like he would when sliding on a rail in the terrain park in Whistler.

He's comin' in hot, yells Hattrup.

Just before he reaches Plake and Hattrup, Kye drives his knees in again, angling uphill, his edges skidding. He stops beside Hattrup.

Greg Stump for Bill Kerig, says the voice on the radio.

Go ahead, I say into the mic.

They let me stay an extra ten minutes, Stump says. But now I'm on the work tram, on my way down.

Did you get them skiing the Rond? I ask.

A little, he says. Sorry. Nothing I could do. It just got too late, he says. Good luck with the rest of it.

Good luck. Right. The kid is down there, just getting to the place where his father was killed, and the only camera we have on him is in the hands of Bertrand, the French snowboarder. I turn to Nate. He's a strong skier and knows the mountain well. A sometime filmmaker, he also knows camera angles.

Any chance you and I can get to a place where we can shoot them? I ask.

Not without a helicopter, he says.

I tried that, I say. It didn't work out.

We could go out on the rafters.

I follow Nate across the wall and up an outcropping. Below us, fifty-year-old beams and boards are strewn like driftwood on a rock shelf.

It used to be the tram building, he explains.

Large support beams and scattered planks hang over the edge of a cliff a hundred feet above the Rond. Nate hops down from the rocks. It's a twelve-foot drop, but he takes it in one leap. *Thwunk.* A hollow, splintering sound shatters the air as he hits the wood. He freezes. The boards quiver, vibrate, then settle. Nate erupts in a manic, deep-throated laugh, not unlike his buddy Plake's. Nate may be American by birth, but he's adopted a decidedly Gallic attitude toward risk.

Maybe you'd better climb down, he says.

I wasn't about to jump, I say.

Turning my back on the timbers, I climb down carefully.

My pack catches on a fin as I try to squeeze through a small, chimneylike formation. I have to hoist myself back up to unhook. Coming around another way, I step gingerly onto the wood. It rocks slightly. Nate is at the edge.

I can just see them, he says.

Can we get a shot? I ask.

Maybe, says Nate. If we set up quick. You gotta check it out.

Flexing my knees, I test the beam I'm standing on. It sways slowly, a giant teeter-totter atop a hundred-foot cliff. Holding my breath, I move toward the edge. The wood groans.

Easy, says Nate.

I stop. The boards don't. I look to where the skiers are clustered far below. Yeah, we could get a shot, but what kind of shot? Even with a big lens, they'll be tiny in the frame.

Let's get off this thing, I say. If this falls it will not only kill us, it'll probably slide down and take them out too.

I take a last look at the skiers far down below. Then I cross back over the wall, put my skis on, shoulder a pack, and begin the long slog down the Vallee Blanche.

Bertrand and Markewitz are tucked into a cavelike depression in a wall on the east side of the Rond. Bertrand has picked the spot. It's safe; there's no snow or ice above them, no seracs to fall on their heads.

It is too late to be here, says Bertrand. It's past five and they're only halfway down the hill.

Yeah, says Markewitz. The sun's heating up everything.

Slides will be coming down from the rocks, says Bertrand. The couloir, the traverse will be bad.

And the bottom is sketchy too? asks Markewitz.

Oui, the traverse, he says. The stuff hanging over will start coming down.

Looks like Fanfan is going, says Markewitz.

Both men raise their cameras. Fanfan rolls off his edge, giving over to gravity, accelerating. He comes across the traverse like a downhill racer, hip angled into the hill—a counter-rotational move that racers use to set up for their next turn. His edges rip at the glacier. The motor on Bertrand's Arri purrs. Twenty-four frames a second of Super-16 film.

Fanfan's momentum carries him uphill of where Kye, Plake and Hattrup wait. He unlocks his hip, carves a perfect button-hook turn, and comes in underneath them. The snow curls through the air like a bullfighter's cape.

There is snow here, he says as he stops. Not bad snow, eh?

Best we've seen, says Hattrup.

I think we can put you off the rope now, says Fanfan. From here on, you ski on your own, Kye.

Kye looks from Fanfan to Plake to Hattrup. *Are you sure?* They're still standing on a sickeningly steep pitch, the cliff edge several hundred meters below.

But don't start freeriding the thing, says Plake. Not in these conditions. This is about as little snow as you could have and possibly ski it.

No mistakes, Kye, says Hattrup. One turn at a time.

I will ski under him, says Fanfan. We will make it, huh?

For sure, says Kye, bolstering himself for the challenge.

I think we go first, says Fanfan. There is just some little bit of snow here and we should use it for Kye.

Fanfan knows that every turn uncovers impenetrable glacier ice. Being the first skiers means better snow. It also means there will be fewer people below to stop Kye if he tumbles. And if he can't stop Kye, or if Kye takes him out—a distinct possibility on a slope this steep—they will both go over the cliff.

Skiing, says Fanfan. He releases his tips and lets gravity pull him into his first turn. The snow is softer here, granular, like wet sand on a linoleum floor. It rolls off his skis in waves. Behind Fanfan, the triangular tracks of his turns glisten faintly. Glacier ice. A bird circles overhead, its dark shadow flitting past the skiers. Fanfan stops and waits.

You're good to go, Kye, says Hattrup.

I'm on it, says Kye.

He steps up with his uphill ski, just as Anselme taught him. As he pushes forward, he re-engages with the slope. The skis come around smoothly, unleashing a wave of a hundred thousand snow crystals. He plants his pole with authority and comes around again, surrendering momentarily to gravity. A third turn. A fourth. Kye is weightless now, every turn bringing him closer to the cliff.

Yes, this is it, Kye, chants Fanfan. Keep going.

Fanfan releases and begins another set of precise, controlled turns, regular as windshield wipers. Every turn pushes the sandlike snow off the surface. He looks over his shoulder on each one, making sure Kye is still in control above him. Kye is stepping it up now, reaching a new level.

Plake and Hattrup watch, small smiles on their faces. Kye is changing before their eyes. Ten, twenty, fifty more turns. Kye is breathing now, letting go.

This is all for me, says Bertrand as he and Markewitz pack their cameras. They are still in the protected nook in the rock, and Bertrand is clearly concerned about the long ski ahead of them. There's the Exit Couloir, where the warm afternoon has made slides possible … probable. And then there is the glacier to cross.

My wife, she is at home with the baby coming, continues Bertrand. And now, my film is finished.

Finished? asks Markewitz.

I'm out, says Bertrand. And besides, it is too late to be here. The snow bridges over the crevasses are warming.

He zips his pack shut, lashing his ice ax to the outside, shrugs it on and clips into his snowboard. He turns to Markewitz.

I must go now, he says. See you later.

Fanfan, Kye, Hattrup and Plake stand at the mouth of the Exit Couloir. Bertrand slows but doesn't stop. He says something in French to Fanfan as he drops into the Exit. Three turns on the apron. It holds. He slows at the choke, checking his speed, then whips through the hourglass.

What did he say? asks Hattrup.

He say his wife is having a baby at home and he must go, says Fanfan. Also, he say, be careful but go fast.

They watch Bertrand make fast turns down the 2,500 vertical feet of the Exit Couloir. They're heartened to see that nothing slides. He's a speck by the time he reaches the base of the chute. No one mentions that he's carrying our last motion-picture camera with him.

Markewitz pulls up to the group. I need to get some shots, he says.

We must go now, says Fanfan.

I just need one shot, says Markewitz. One group shot.

Not waiting for an answer, he begins unpacking his camera.

The men line up across the top of the couloir.

Can I have the ashes? asks Kye.

Markewitz notices a new tone in the young man's voice.

Not now, Kye, says Fanfan. There's not time.

Who's got them? asks Kye.

They're in my pack, says Plake, shrugging it off, unzipping, thrusting a hand inside. He hands Kye the can of his father's ashes. Markewitz focuses on the "Trevor Would Do It" sticker wrapped around the can and releases the shutter.

Okay, now we must go, says Fanfan.

Markewitz zips his pack shut, hefts it.

Wait, says Kye, quietly.

He raises his goggles and pulls off a glove. He unscrews the cap and shakes a small pile of ashes into his palm. The men are still. He doesn't ask for help. Nor is he looking for acceptance. He raises the ashes to his chin and blows hard. There's an assertiveness to it, a finality. He owns this moment in a way that wasn't possible with cameras pointed at him. The fine dark ashes rise up and disappear.

Okay, let's go, he says.

Fanfan starts down the Exit Couloir. Kye's right behind him.

It's heavy in here, says Fanfan. Save your energy. It is very long.

Kye is focused now, pouring every ounce of energy into his turns. They repeat their figure-eight pattern down to the choke.

After this it widens, says Fanfan. I go first and then stop. You wait for the yell, then come.

Fanfan moves carefully through the narrow opening, cutting hard to the right once he's through.

Whoooheeeehooo, he yells.

Dropping, yells Kye.

He comes through the choke like a seasoned pro, pulling up alongside Fanfan.

Within moments Hattrup and Plake are by their side.

We've got spinners coming off and slush slides coming down, says Plake, pointing up at the west-facing cliffs. I know we're ramrodding this mountain experience into you, Kye, and you did your thing up there, which was cool, but you gotta keep listening. It's not as steep here, but don't be fooled. There could be some pockets of snow that are heating and draining onto the slope. So if it looks like I'm skiing slow, or Fanfan or Mike is skiing slow or fast, you might want to look and see what the rest of the picture is. There might be a reason.

Okay, says Kye.

So let me show you what I know, says Plake, pointing downhill toward the rollover. You see how this wind forms that bulge? That wind lip there? You know that's a snow formation that's typically unstable.

Yeah.

Well, we're here in hot, springlike conditions. If you were to put a cold winter day here, with a bunch of fresh snow …

Okay, so that's where it happened to my dad, says Kye.

Yeah, says Markewitz. A friend of his came up here the day after and videotaped the fracture. I'm sure the avalanche broke behind him and he was on this slab riding down.

My dad had a broken neck by the time he got to the bottom, says Kye. He died by injury, not by suffocation.

That little curve at the end, says Hattrup. If he was going fast enough he could've hit the wall.

Kye swallows deeply.

Okay, but this is the thing, says Fanfan. We need to go from here out, right now. This is not good condition to be here. It's 5:30.

If I was guiding this, I wouldn't be here past two, says Hattrup.

Kye, you and I, we go, says Fanfan.

Fanfan drops in first, makes two turns, and pulls to the side. The risk here is not from an uncontrolled fall, it's from avalanche.

Now you go in front of me, he says.

Kye comes around in front, Fanfan behind—the same system they worked out in the Poubelle Couloir. The snow is sloughing heavily. It won't take much to build into a slide.

Faster, Fanfan coaches, ski faster.

Kye grinds his teeth and wills himself through it. He makes turns faster and faster in the knee-deep, slushy snow. This is not fun. It's not play. The heavy snow tugs at his legs. Gravity tears at his torso, trying to pull him over. Kye knows that if they trigger a slide here, there's no getting out of the way. Wet snow tumbles with them. Kye makes three turns and cuts to the side.

Keep going, don't stop, chants Fanfan.

Another slough, this one bigger, barely misses Kye.

I need to stop, he says to Fanfan.

No! Push all the way!

Kye's muscles burn. His lungs scream. The wall hooks in from the left. The couloir finally opens. Fanfan comes around Kye, angling to the right.

The remay! shouts Fanfan. Jump over!

The crevasse where the couloir meets the glacier is mostly filled with sloughs and avalanches. Fanfan and Kye hop over it and cut hard to the right under a cliff into an island of safety.

In the couloir, Markewitz is doing a final setup with Hattrup and Plake. They ski past him—the shutter clicks—and keep going.

Packing up his bag, Markewitz notices another chute that empties into the Exit Couloir. He knows that if the snow in the chute lets go, it's going to take everything in the Exit Couloir with it.

He loads his gear and shoves down the hill, but the heavy pack slows him down. His scalp crawls. This is where his friend Trevor died. He was found right here.

Markewitz needs to go faster. The snow is glop. There's a runnel in the middle from the sliding slush. He's got to get out. He sees the tracks and hops over the crevasse. Angling out of the couloir, he joins the group tucked up under a cliff. No one speaks. A low hiss builds to a groan and then a roar. They look to the sky, scanning for an airplane. But the sky is empty, an impassive blue. And then off to their left, they see it—a wall of snow, a wet-slab avalanche, gushes out of the bottom of the couloir they just skied.

Shit, says Kye.

You see? says Fanfan.

It's not huge, says Plake.

Big enough, says Hattrup.

And going sixty miles an hour, says Markewitz.

I'm glad I wasn't in there, says Kye. Damn, this place is crazy.

Okay, so that's what *is* going on, says Plake. Let's make sure we're watching for this. We're not done yet. We still got lots of glacier to get past.

Kye peers into the maw of the glacier. He's never seen anything like it, even in pictures. There are ice blocks as big as ships, blue-black shadows in between. The only way off the Glacier Rond is a ski track that leads into this frozen nightmare and disappears.

This is the place that Trevor wrote about in his journal, where he fell into a crevasse and barely climbed out.

For some little while now we ski on the edge of the glacier, says Fanfan. It is a strange track but not hard if you stay on it.

It's all crevasses, Kye says.

Exactly, Plake says. That's why you've got to get right behind me. Right in my tracks. Don't do anything I don't do. Right?

Definitely, says Kye.

We'll be right behind you, says Hattrup, so don't worry.

Okay, let's move as fast as we can, says Fanfan, taking the lead. It's past six o'clock.

Kye poles behind Plake. The track is two, three feet wide. Not enough room for turns. Kye starts in a snowplow, but he's losing Plake. He straightens out his skis and picks up speed, once again forced to trust the two men in front of him.

Keep your speed up here, yells Fanfan.

Fanfan and Plake straight-line it. Kye has no choice. The track drops into a deep depression, angles down and then straight up. On either side are black holes. If they catch a tip here, they may never be seen again.

Holy shiiiit, says Kye.

His knees are in his chest. He throws his hands forward, absorbing the compression. His skis leave the ground as he comes out of the hole, cresting the rise.

You're okay, says Hattrup. Nice job.

Skiing fast, they come around toward the north face. Above them are cliffs, seracs, avalanche chutes. Fanfan glances over his shoulder, catches Plake's eye, and jerks his chin up the hill. Above them are two small chutes. Piled at the bottom of both are head-high piles of slush—remnants of sloughs.

Look to your right because there's going to be stuff coming down, says Plake.

Plake's head swivels as he glances at the track in front, then takes a quick look up the hill. All of Kye's focus is on Plake's skis, his knees. He's staying right on his tail. If Plake makes a move, Kye does too. If Plake gets buried, so will he.

They pass under more avalanche chutes, but nothing moves. The mountain holds its breath. The tracks lead away from the cliff and onto the open glacier. The pitch slackens, undulating pleasantly. The track is fast, compressed snow still icy.

Then Fanfan abruptly changes direction. Plake follows. On the outside of the turn is a black gash in the snow. Kye cuts hard, right where the others did. He looks down the long track that leads across the remainder of the glacier. In the near distance are trees, green and friendly.

The last of the day's light falls on a boarded-up building halfway up the mountain. It's a hotel and tram station from the first Aiguille du Midi cable car, abandoned some fifty years ago.

Downhill from the building, in a wide-open field, Kye makes sweeping, lazy turns in pink-tinged slop. The snow is junk now, rotten and soggy, but with danger behind them, it's sweet as cotton candy. The meadow leads into a stand of trees. Kye whooshes past them as he makes quick turns on the narrow trail. He rounds a last grove, and there in front of him is a road. Wide and well-traveled, it leads into the Mont Blanc tunnel, the same one that Trevor and Gordy drove through nine years before.

Fanfan already has his skis off. He holds up an open hand and waggles a thumbs-up.

Kye, you did it, he says.

Kye grins big. He wants to say so much but can't find the words. He shakes his head. Fuckin-A, he says.

chapter **16**

Over the Edge

Chamonix, France
Evening, March 16, 2005

When I get to the Grand Roc bar, Kye and Iberg are at a small table. Kye is rocked back in the chair, half a pizza in him. His eyes are bloodshot.

Bill! he calls out. I walk over, thinking it's the first time he's ever called me by name.

Dude, you should've been down there with us, says Kye.

You're so right, I say, meaning it.

Dude, you've never seen anything like that place. It wasn't just a chute, it was a couloir!

He pronounces it, cool–*wah*!

Now I know the difference, he says. Bill, I am soooo pumped! This is the craziest feeling ever. The satisfaction, the one hundred percent satisfaction from that long mission! I've never done anything that took that long to ski. That much effort. This is really, really cool. And *suuuper* scary. I don't know what kind of words to use, really. The no-fall zones—serious no-fall zones—it's like nothing I've ever done before. Gave me a really crazy feeling of adrenaline. I always wanted to ski this place. To see what my father saw, where he went. Now I've been there. I know now. This is the best feeling, the craziest feeling in the whole world!

And for me, hearing him say it is the best and craziest feeling. I want to hug the kid, but I don't. Instead, I put a hand on his shoulder and give it a hard squeeze. I want to tell him how unbelievably happy and proud I feel, that seeing him light up like this is worth all the bullshit and production hassles, but I know if I start talking I'll embarrass myself. So I take my hand off his shoulder and slap him hard on the back and tell him he was fucking awesome.

Markewitz comes in and asks me to step outside. I'm wondering why he doesn't look as happy as I feel.

Bertrand wasn't around for the final shot of Kye skiing the Exit Couloir, he says without preamble. He said he was out of film.

We sent him down with extra film, I say. What happened?

He said his wife was having a baby and it was too late to be on the Rond anyway.

Why didn't he reload the camera? Hadn't I given him enough film? Later, when I try to get some answers, I'm told he's at the hospital with his wife. She's in labor.

We missed the shot, I say, pulling up a stool next to Plake at the bar. Bertrand's camera ran out of film.

I know, says Plake. He hightailed it out of there.

I don't know why he didn't reload, I say.

He said there was no more film in the bag, says Plake.

What?

But you weren't fully prepared to capture it, either, to get every turn on film, says Plake. You needed a helicopter. And the interviews screwed us up.

It got too late, I say, resigning myself to the reality of my mistakes. We can cover the moment with Markewitz's still photos. If we do it right, it might even play more poignantly.

Plake nods and takes a moment to gather his thoughts.

It's not so important, says Plake, turning toward me now, a light coming into his eyes. What's important is that we had a twelve-year-old skiing down that run! As far as we know a twelve-year-old has never skied down that run. No twelve-year-old ever had a reason to go down that run!

He's fifteen, I say, but Plake pushes on without acknowledging the correction.

But in Kye's situation, there was all the reason to ski it, Plake continues. When me and Fanfan made the decision, when we said, okay, we have the weather, it can be done, I was like, oh shoot, we got the weather, can it be done? The fact that it did take place, that we got him down the run, that's killer. What's important is what that kid over there's feeling.

I nod and order a beer. I believe everything Plake is saying, but that doesn't get me off the hook. I had a job to do, and I didn't get it done. I could blame Obenhaus for not giving me the helicopter or Kronick for doing the interviews or Stump for not bringing his skis up the Aiguille or Bertrand for having a baby. But the fact is, I blew it.

Plake's still talking. Conditions weren't necessarily dreamlike, he says, especially for Kye. We helped him, stepped him down a run that none of his peers have ever skied. I guarantee you that. He never would've gone out there by himself. Chances are he would've left Chamonix saying Chamonix sucks. They don't even have a park.

I don't think he's saying that, I offer.

He was exposed to a form of skiing that he didn't know existed, says Plake. I don't think his peers or his sponsors or his bros even know that type of skiing exists. Now he's aware that there's some other skiing out there other than Alaskan big-face ripping or terrain parks to throw some flips. He found out about the alpinism part of snow skiing, the route-finding part. Most people his age, in the crew that he hangs out with, they just don't know about this stuff.

I look over to see if Kye can hear Plake, but he's blissfully into the pizza, a glob of tomato sauce stuck to his cheek. Plake takes a long pull of club soda. I put back one of the best tasting beers of my life. I try to scold myself again for missing the shot, but it just doesn't stick. Shot or no shot, the skiers succeeded, and we all got down safely.

Plake's still talking, and I'm still nodding.

Another beer arrives, and the bartender tells me it's from the two Americans at the end of the bar. I look over to see Hattrup and Stump, beers in hand, toasting me and Plake.

Plake doesn't notice. He's somewhere else, thinking out loud: I actually felt sorry for the kid. Growing up in the shadow of his father's death. Imagine every year all these yahoos start talking about your dad and reminding you of how great he was and drinking a beer and toasting Trevor. Trevor day! It's freakin' morbid, if you ask me. Let the kid live his own life. Let him get on with it. Now that Kye has actually been to the place, it's over. Said, done, finished, man. It's Kye day now.

And if the kid ever wants to go back and do that run by himself, that might be another threshold. Kye will be here in Chamonix in another five, ten years, hanging out. And he'll go, hey, I got something I've got to go do. I don't want to ski with you guys today. Then all of a sudden he's out there by himself. He's doing his own moment. That might be the next threshold for him and his … relationship with his father's passing.

Later there's dinner over a long table in Argentiére. The Plakes are there, Hattrup and Stump, Kye and Iberg, and most of the crew. Tonight there's no separation between skiers and New Yorkers. Everyone's mixed in, all of us thrilled to know that Kye is down and everyone got off the hill without injury. Gallons of fine French wine come and go. There are toasts and sentimentality. The night is both beautiful and pitiful. Pitiful for trying to recapture the feeling of the day in words and alcohol and food, but beautiful nonetheless for the attempt.

Afterwards, Fanfan, Hattrup and I make a plan to go up the Grands Montets for an easy day, filming some pretty skiing that we can use for B-roll.

The next day, the base area of the Grands Montets is quiet and warm. The lot is filled with cars, but the road is empty. Fanfan is smoking his lunch in front of the ticket window.

Thought yesterday was your last day, I say.

Bought the last ones yesterday, Fanfan says, eyeing the cigarette affectionately. Today I'm just finishing.

Those things will kill you, I say.

Fanfan laughs, and for a moment I feel very American.

Fanfan tells me that the snow is still nice in some places, and with the strong sun it's a good day to shoot. We decide to spend time with Kasha Rigby and Meg Oster, two American pro skiers who are in Chamonix and available to film. Kasha, a pioneer of women's ski mountaineering, has made first descents in Asia, Russia and South America. She's thirty-four and the closest thing she has to a permanent address are two storage units—one near Snowbird, the other near Chamonix. Meg is younger, all enthusiasm and ambition. She skis fast and loose, like she's made a secret agreement with the mountain. At twenty-one, she watches Kasha closely, learning from the more seasoned veteran. They walk up to Fanfan and me like they're already in a film shoot. There are Euro-style cheek kisses all around. It's going to be a fun day.

Where are we going? Kasha asks.

I will show you from the top, says Fanfan.

Then he's moving toward the tram, his arm around Kasha. The two are old friends. Meanwhile, Meg is charming the soundman. Kayce is with us, too, plus two cameramen, a still photographer, a soundman, two camera assistants, two porters, two guides, and me. All these bodies just to get some pretty skiing on film. Pro skiers have a term for film shoots with too many people and too much gear: junk shows.

Where's your green, Kerig? yells someone from the back of the tram line.

I turn. Mike Hattrup's ducking the rope, cutting the line, catching up with us.

St. Patty's Day and you don't have green on? he says. What kind of Irishman are you?

Realizing for the first time that it's March 17th, I say: I'll buy tonight. Any place we can get a Guinness.

Plenty of places, says Nate, who's carrying camera gear for us.

Hear that, Fanfan? Bill's buying in the bar tonight, says Hattrup.

Whoohoo, big night for everyone, says Fanfan. Maybe we start early?

On the tram, men jockey for position next to women. Perfume mixes with sunblock and sweat. No one is planning to tempt death today.

I think, Bill, this piece here is good when the sun is coming, says Fanfan.

We're in the tram terminal at the summit of the Grands Montets. Fanfan is pointing out a window. To the west lies a small glaciated area with large blue seracs, tongues of untracked snow between. In an hour, maybe two, the light will be just right.

It's safe? I ask.

It is nothing, he says. But it *looks* like something, eh?

That's the idea, I say, and we start to move the convoy.

Shit, says Fanfan. He turns to his brother, Jean-Luc, who is working as a porter. He asks him something in French. His brother shakes his head.

Merde.

There's a problem? I ask.

Someone stole my helmet off my pack while I waited in the line at the bottom, Fanfan says.

We can get you another one, I say.

It's okay, he says, palming the Tibetan scarf that's tied to his backpack. This protects me more than any helmet.

Lighting a cigarette, he tells Meg and Kasha about the scarf, how it was given to him by a monk in Tibet. The smoke, the accent—if Fanfan weren't the real deal you might be tempted to hate him, but he's not faking a single bit and you can't help but love him.

He leads us into the glaciated area we saw from the window. Sure enough, there are blue seracs, black crevasses. *This is nothing?* I'm thinking. There's a gray cornice as big as a battleship looming over the whole area. It looks like it's been there for years, but I wonder what the odds are that it's going to fall today? Beneath the cornice is a long bulge in the shape of a nose, covered with untracked snow. The pitch looks sane, but it ends in an ice cliff.

You sure? I ask him.

I will go and check it, says Fanfan.

I slide down the hill underneath the nose to scout camera angles. The snow is two feet of powder over pearly ice, curved and bulbous like neglected molars.

Fanfan slides into a pocket below the cornice, above the nose.

It's good, he yells.

Alrighty then, says Kasha.

I'm not asking you to ski this, I say to Kasha and Meg as I hike back up. This is just B-roll stuff, so don't ski anything that looks sketchy.

We'll ski, you shoot, okay? says Kasha.

I grin. I've known her for years, long enough to know that her confidence is justified.

Okay, I say, let's wait for the light.

We set up two cameras, and Kasha gets into the pocket. Then we wait for the sun to move to just the right angle to make the shot sing. Fourteen people sit in the snow. There are stories, jokes. Fanfan and Hattrup take turns recounting their adventure on the Glacier Rond.

At the bottom, Fanfan is saying, we pull out to the side, and *vroom*.

It let go, says Hattrup. The chute flushed.

How long after you got out? asks Meg.

Not much, says Fanfan.

Few minutes, maybe, says Hattrup.

You guys were lucky, says Meg.

So, now the light is coming, says Fanfan.

With that, the mood changes. The skiers hike into position and for a moment the joking stops. While this is not an especially dangerous spot by Chamonix standards, a mistake could send a skier off a forty-foot ice cliff and onto a flat, packed landing. I count Kasha down and she slices hard telemark turns into the bridge of the nose. Platter-sized slabs of snow tumble off the end. She slides around the cliff and cuts her final turn as the snow cascades behind her.

Hi there, she says to our cameraman, Pilafian. Her tone is light, bubbly, as if she just ran into him in a coffeehouse.

Meg's next.

Dropping, she yells. She makes fast turns, pushing through the heel in the way that very good skiers do on very fat skis. Snow flies, blond hair streams. She smiles through it all.

Hattrup takes it closer to the edge of the cliff, driving into a telemark turn just above the highest point. His skis skitter; the tails slip on hard snow. Moving sideways, just feet from the edge, he heaves backwards and makes a stabbing pole plant. The effort is just enough to change direction away from the cliff.

Jesus, he says, as he arrives next to us. You'd better not use that one.

Fanfan skis last. He angles in even closer to the edge than Hattrup. The sun hits the spray coming off his skis like an arc light. For a moment he's wreathed in diamonds. He jumps the corner of the cliff.

Yeah, Fanfan! yells Kasha.

Damn, I'm thinking, *damn, he's good.*

There it is, says Hattrup. That's how it's done.

Fanfan leads us deeper into the glaciated terrain. He stops at a long, narrow ramp of powder bisected lengthwise by the dark shadow of a vertical cornice. Below it, a large serac forms a bench—a perfect place to set up cameras and keep everyone out of the shot. Bodies move slowly into position. It's a sunny day, and no one can be bothered to rush.

Fanfan sidesteps up into the shadow of the cornice, taking care not to track the snow where the sun is shining on it. He prods the snow with his pole, hikes up some more, and prods again. He shakes his head and moves farther up the slope, angling in for a better exposure.

It's no good, yells Fanfan. It's ice under ten centimeters of powder.

Okay, I say. Let's go find another place.

I'll just give a few turns, yells Fanfan. If you want, you can film it.

We are *sooo* lucky to have Fanfan as a guide, says Kasha. He's the man.

Our cameras focus on Fanfan poised on an apron of untracked snow. Behind him is a ragged wall of ice. Behind us is only pale sky and far down below, already falling into shadow, the town of Chamonix.

Sound? I yell, my breath forming a cloud in the chill air.

Sound's rolling, answers the soundman. Quiet, please.

Camera's rolling, calls the cinematographer.

The crew settles. Small movements cease. All eyes are on Fanfan's orange jacket and blue hat. He lowers his goggles and clicks his poles together three times, snapping snow off the baskets, focusing his attention.

I count him down. Three, two, one … He plants his poles, rolls his shoulders, and pushes off. Angling into his first turn, his edges bite nicely, a light touch to stay in the soft new snow without driving into the glacial ice below. A fine white spindrift roils over his boots and shins, flaring behind him in the glazing light. He snaps his turns, quick and precise, yet somehow carefree and light, the disciplined dance of one of the world's best skiers.

Two turns, three. His power is immense. He moves smoothly, with authority. He speeds into the transition between the steep pitch and the flat shelf where we stand. Our lenses follow him as his weight shifts slightly forward. One of his ski tips dives below the crust. The ski stops. He cracks at the waist, bends as if taking a bow. He drives his knee, trying to power the ski through. The ski tip plunges deeper, jerking his leg backward. Heels rising, he flies past our cameras, hands reaching into space as he disappears over the edge.

For a moment there is nothing but silence. We're frozen in time by the impossibility of what we've just witnessed. Then the moment shatters, and everyone is in motion, cursing, clicking into bindings—the chaos of sudden disaster.

As Hattrup and Nate ski around the cliff, I skate down the bench, stop, and inch out toward the edge. Digging my downhill pole in, I peer over. Seventy feet below is a deep crater, a hole of evil curves and furrows. At the bottom of the hole is a crevasse. The eastern edge opens into blackness, but in the middle is a thick ice bridge. On it is Fanfan, face down, legs and arms splayed, motionless.

Nate is the first one to reach him.

Call the rescue! he screams. Call the helicopter!

Hands dig into jackets. Cell phones come to ears. Who do we call and what's the number and, shit, who has a signal? Then one of the grips, Fanfan's brother Jean-Luc, makes the connection. He speaks slowly, his French precise and measured, getting the details straight for the gendarme on the other end.

What thoughts flood a skier's mind as he feels death approaching?

Does he wonder why he was drawn to the mountain life? Or does he understand that a life lived fully, lived at the edge of disaster, is worth losing everything? Does he feel satisfied, peaceful, or does he think that it was all a hollow fiction?

Something moves behind me and I turn. Two skiers pull up: Pilafian and Markewitz. There's a moment. Something passes between us. It's a look of caring but trying not to care, fear but swallowing down the fear.

Are we shooting it? Pilafian asks.

I have no answer. I'm living the nightmare I've been having since this film began. A skier, a friend, is badly injured and possibly dead, and I'm responsible for it. If I hadn't ginned up this whole thing, he wouldn't be lying at the bottom of a hole.

It's your call, says Markewitz.

The shooters just want to do their jobs. They look to me for a decision, and I look for a way out. I want to stop it, shut it all down. Nothing is worth losing a life. I think of all the other skiers and crew members I've put at risk. And for what? To make a film?

In the beginning I'd set out to tell a story that would shake the sleepers by their lapels, that would show what it means to live big in the face of their fears. I wanted real, not some sneaker slogan or soda-pop tagline. And this is as real as it gets.

If I were a real filmmaker, a hardened director, we'd already be rolling. Real filmmakers shoot first, ask questions later. But I'm not a hardened director. I'm a skier, just like the guy down there in the hole.

The *thwop* of helicopter blades echoes far down in the valley. A navy blue speck appears in the sky. The thudding grows louder as the rescue chopper banks in from the east. For a long moment everyone on the mountain looks skyward.

Everyone, that is, except me. I'm looking at two guys with cameras, seeing my reflection in the lens.

Shoot it, I say. Shoot the hell out of it. If he's dead, we throw the footage away.

Pilafian is already setting up his tripod.

Brian, Hattrup has a mic on, doesn't he? I ask.

Yeah, he does, says Brian Whitlock, our soundman.

Peter, turn on that camera and just keep rolling. I want to hear what's going on down there.

Pilafian turns on the camera, and we pick up audio from the wireless pinned to Hattrup's collar. I slide over to Whitlock and put the headphones on. The sounds are wonderful and horrible. The voice is Fanfan's. He's alive but badly injured and moaning in pain.

Make sure those legs don't move, says Hattrup to Nate.

Don't move, Fanfan, says Nate. Don't move.

And then a welcome sound, words, in French: *Qu'est-ce que j'ai fait?* What have I done?

Hattrup: Don't move, Fanfan.

J'y crois pas, Fanfan moans. I can't believe it.

Hattrup: You're okay. Don't move.

Fanfan: *Arguuhhh, qu'est-ce que j'ai fait?* What have I done?

Hattrup: Don't move.

Comme je suis idiot. Qu'est-ce que j'ai fait? What an idiot I am. What did I do?

They're coming, says Nate. The rescue is coming.

Je ne peux pas respirer. I can't breathe.

A ski patrolman in blue and yellow appears. Fanfan's brother Jean-Luc knows him. He calmly directs him into the hole. I listen to Fanfan as I watch the rescue helicopter coming toward us.

Déplace ma botte gauche. Take off my left boot.

The chopper banks in from the east.

Le pied gauche, s'il te plait! The left foot, please.

The side door of the helicopter is open.

Qu'est-ce que j'ai fait? What did I do?

Three figures lean out, assessing the scene.

C'était tellement stupide. That was so stupid.

The ship flies slowly past, banks a tight arc, and comes around again.

Espece d'idiot. What an idiot I am.

Now a man is on the helicopter's skid. He holds a blue body board.

Qu'est-ce que j'ai fait une connerie. I really screwed up.

As the chopper rises over us, the gendarme steps into the sky. Revolving slowly on a cable, he is lowered into the hole. Rotor wash churns the snow. The crater is a raging blizzard. The Tibetan silk scarf, still affixed to Fanfan's pack, dances madly in the wind.

The line comes up. The gendarme stays in the hole. The helicopter is directly in front of us. I'm close enough to see the pilot's face.

The ship banks away. Through Hattrup's microphone, more yelling. There's incomprehensible French over the wireless, and then this: *Je suis blessé.* I'm hurt. *Mes maux de dos. Vraiment maux.* My back hurts. Really hurts.

Arghuuuh. Ce maux. That hurts.

The crackle of radios. Clipped speech.

The helicopter cuts a hard circle, and then two more people step into space. The pilot lowers them into the hole. They are quick but calm.

Now a woman's voice comes over the mic. She's a doctor, taking charge. More French.

They're putting in a morphine I.V., says Nate, translating for Hattrup.

Another burst of French.

What did she say? asks Hattrup.

The helicopter is back, hovering at eye level with our camera. The pilot lowers the line again into the hole, then hovers the ship for long minutes. Through the headphones I hear many voices down in the hole. The rotor wash blows stinging ice pellets into my face. I cover my eyes and say a silent prayer, the words familiar from childhood.

The line rises up. Fanfan is on a body board. The doctor is clipped in next to him. She's steadying him, holding his head as they rise, spinning, into the sky. The line drops again and retrieves the other two gendarmes, and then the ship heads west, toward Geneva.

I've still got the headphones on. Through them, I hear Hattrup's voice.

What did she say? repeats Hattrup. The doctor, what did she say?

She said the leg is broken, says Nate.

I caught that, says Hattrup.

And the neck is broken too, says Nate. She said his neck is broken.

chapter 17

Candles

Argentière, France
March 18, 2005

It's early morning in Argentière and warm enough for a T-shirt. The Chamonix sun is relentless. I'm sunburned and sweating. We are gathered on the deck of a café, waiting for news of Fanfan. He's in a hospital in Geneva, alive, but that's about all we know. He needs surgery to prevent paralysis, but the procedure has been postponed twice for more serious cases. A broken neck and he's waiting in a queue. Kronick has been phoning updates from the hospital waiting room.

Yellin presses a cell phone to his temple, holding it there like a compress. He's talking to New York—to doctors, lawyers and his boss, Peter Jennings. Kye is quiet, eating at a table off to the side, watching.

Plake and Hattrup are planning their next adventure, apparently undeterred by their friend's accident. They're going to ski the Y Couloir, an avalanche-prone trophy line above Argentière. Kasha Rigby intends to join them. It's steeper and more dangerous than the Glacier Rond. Plake and Hattrup say it's too dangerous for Kye, and the young man doesn't argue. Now they're poring over a description of the Y Couloir in Anselme's book.

Over the course of the morning I help arrange a helicopter drop at the base of the couloir. I'm going to climb part of it with them, then film the descent from the chute. This time we'll also have a camera in the helicopter as well as a camera at the top of the couloir and one across the valley. I'm determined not to miss a frame of the descent, but I can't seem to shake the feeling that I'm forgetting something crucial.

Kronick calls to say Fanfan just went into surgery.

Say a prayer, says Plake, lifting his head from the book.

He nods once, twice, then drops his eyes back to the book. No one else says a word.

That night I meet Plake and Hattrup in the Grand Roc bar. There are more logistics to take care of. I write everything down on a notepad. My brain can't absorb any more information. Still, we press on until Plake has to leave to pick up Kimberly, who can't drive a stick shift with her leg in a cast. Hattrup and I finally give up the planning, and he puts a pint of Guinness in front of me.

Happy St. Patty's Day, he says. A day late.

We clank glasses.

A few minutes later Kronick calls and says the surgeons have replaced Fanfan's crushed vertebrae with a piece of his pelvis.

And? I ask.

And he's not paralyzed, says Kronick. But he may never ski again.

How is he taking it? I ask.

He says he's going to go fishing in Corsica, says Kronick.

I hang up and repeat the fishing line to Hattrup.

We'll visit him after we ski the Y, says Hattrup.

Sure, I say. We'll bring him a fishing rod.

My phone rings again. This time it's Yellin.

Tell me what's happening tomorrow, he says.

I walk out of the bar to spare him the music and tell him about our plans for the Y Couloir and the helicopter.

They are free to do it, he says quickly, but we're not shooting any more skiing. No helicopters, no fucking crevasses, no more action. We're done. Period. Finished with anything even remotely dangerous.

Silence on the line. I'm thinking.

Don't argue with me, he says. This is my decision, and you can't change it.

My mind moves slowly as I absorb this new directive. Yellin keeps talking. He tells me that we could be sued, and even the threat of a lawsuit will effectively shut down any further fund-raising, which will shut down the film. Then there's the possibility that someone else will get hurt. How would that look? What if it's an American, with the American legal juggernaut behind him? So, judge, these reckless filmmakers broke a guy's neck and nearly killed him, and then went out to film more just two days later!

I hang up and walk back into the bar to tell Hattrup. The news is not greeted with enthusiasm.

Shit, he just doesn't get it, says Hattrup. He doesn't understand that these things happen. You can't quit just because one guy got hurt. We all get hurt. You don't just stop.

I know, Mike, I say. But we've exceeded his risk threshold. Maybe it's a miracle I ever got them to agree to this in the first place.

The next morning, two rental cars pull up to a small chalet perched on a bench on the north side of the valley. Iberg and Kye get out of one. Hattrup gets out of the other. The three of them stop and look up the hill. The chalet has a snowflake motif in the pine lattice on the soffit and across the front deck. The house has an unobstructed view of the Aiguilles du Midi and the Glacier Rond. This is Anselme Baud's home. The morning sun is just finding Anselme and me on the deck.

Anselme waves to Kye and heads down the stairs. I follow him, filming with a small camera. Kye wears a dun hoodie, sweatpants, and unlaced sneakers. He carries a large book. Anselme comes out the door to greet them. He wears a corduroy button-down shirt tucked into wide-wale trousers. The snowbanks are neatly shoveled. The flagstone path is wet with melting snow.

Hattrup explains that he and Plake are going to ski the Y Couloir, and he's come to ask Anselme for some advice.

The Y Couloir, says Anselme. Yes, Patrick Vallencant first skied this in 1972. I think it was much later in the year, though. July, maybe. You are going when?

Plake and I were thinking about tomorrow, says Hattrup.

For the film, says Anselme.

No, they're not shooting any more skiing.

Ah yes, with Fanfan … It's okay, I think. This is a serious thing. Maybe it might not have ended so good with Fanfan still alive.

So, you think it's a bad idea to do the Y tomorrow? asks Hattrup.

No, I think it's okay.

Hattrup asks him details about the couloir—which side of the Y is more prone to avalanche and how to tackle the entry. Anselme answers in simple, declarative statements.

You get a good feeling of accomplishment from this one, says Anselme in summary.

Hattrup thanks Anselme.

And you, Kye, you are going to the Y?

No. I came over to say goodbye, says Kye. I have to go to La Grave to do another film shoot.

The name of the French resort gives me pause. Kye's trip is unfolding in the reverse order of his father's.

Ah yes, says Anselme, patting him on the shoulder. And you brought something.

This was my father's book, he says. The one you wrote. I was hoping you could sign it.

Anselme takes the book, *Les Alps du Nord*. The cover is tattered, the binding broken. This is the book Anselme wrote twenty-five years ago. For Trevor and Plake it was their bible. Anselme takes it and sits down on a low wall. Kye sits next to him.

You did it, huh? says Anselme. You skied the Rond and the Exit Couloir.

Yes, says Kye.

And how did this feel?

The best feeling in the world. I've never felt so …

Stoked? offers Hattrup.

Relieved, says Kye. Pumped.

You do good, says Anselme. Your father, I think he would be proud, hmmm?

I hope so, says Kye.

And you will come back to see me again? asks Anselme. You will call when you come.

For sure, says Kye.

I would like that, says Anselme. You have my number? I will write it down. Maybe you can come in? Have a coffee?

Sure.

I don't have iced tea, says Anselme, smiling slowly.

Anselme takes a pen from Kye and opens the book to the title page. He tests the pen on the palm of his hand—a blue curlicue across the skin—and then he begins to write:

Pour mon jeune ami skieur Kye. Avec tous mas souhaits de belles descentes a Chamonix en homagges a ton papa et avec mes sinceres sentiments. See you soon, Anselme. [For my young friend Kye. All my wishes for beautiful, wonderful descents in Chamonix in honor of your dad. With my strongest feelings.]

So, now you come in, he says.

The back door is heavy, on springs to keep the wind from blowing it open. The light inside is dim. We're in a basement with racks of neatly organized equipment—skis and poles, jackets and sleeping bags, ropes, ice axes, crampons. It's as well stocked as a mountaineering shop. Anselme leads Kye up a staircase to a living room of blond wood with a stone hearth, framed ski pictures, and a pair of ancient, wooden skis in the corner.

How old are those skis? asks Kye.

They are my father's first skis, says Anselme. From when he was maybe twelve.

He hands them to Kye, who fingers the bear-trap bindings.

He was skiing in the World Championship in 1938, says Anselme. He win a silver medal at Aspen in 1950. Silver medal in downhill.

And his father was a guide eighty years ago, says Anselme, pointing to a small, framed photograph of a skier with a wool sweater and a rope slung across his shoulder.

That's amazing, says Kye. And this, this is your son?

Kye nods at a large photograph of a young man. It's a head shot, taken in the mountains, of a young man in a red jacket with sunglasses perched in his dark hair.

Yes, Edouard was twenty-four.

The enlargement is bordered by a hand-made wooden frame.

He was in good shape. A very good skier. Very good worker. Very sporty.

The frame is draped with a gold Tibetan scarf.

He have everything, continues Anselme. And he get killed by a serac. The Gervasutti Couloir.

You showed me that couloir on the very first day.

Ah, yeah. Sorry.

It's all right, says Kye.

Today is his birthday, says Anselme. The nineteenth of March.

Whoa, says Kye.

You can see the candles, says Anselme, pointing to a small deck at the front of the house where a row of short votives are lit. Clustered behind the candles are bouquets of flowers. In the middle is a platter-sized piece of shale with a photograph of Edouard lacquered to the surface. Red flowers are painted on the stone.

Today would've been his twenty-fifth birthday, says Anselme. It is okay, he says. We are still alive, no?

Yeah, says Kye. Yeah, we're still alive.

Into the Light

Geneva, Switzerland
March 21, 2005

Hattrup, Pilafian and I walk out of the rain and into a tall, dark building with yellow windows—the Hôpitaux Universitaires de Genève. We stop to read a sign: *Hueres de visites 12h.30 a 14h & 18h a 19h.30.* I look at my watch. It's eight o'clock. Visiting hours ended half an hour ago.

We walk past the front desk, down a long green hallway, and after thirty minutes of wandering around we find Fanfan, lying under blue blankets in a nest of tubes and wires. A large plastic neck brace angles his head into the pillow. His black hair is matted, but his face is tanned, still filled with surprisingly good color. He can only look straight up. He rolls his eyes toward us as we near the bed.

This is stupid, no? says Fanfan.

We're so sorry to see you in here, I say.

Then we each recount the accident, telling it from our different points of view. The details differ, but the result, the last beat in the story, is always the same: Fanfan on a body board, slowly spinning into the sky as the helicopter flies away.

But I think I'm lucky, eh? says Fanfan. This is the third one this year.

The third injury? Pilafian asks.

The third time I almost die, says Fanfan. Maybe now, I'm thinking a little bit. Maybe now I'm wondering. It comes in threes, you know. This is maybe a signal.

It would be easy at this point to say, Yes, my friend, this certainly is a signal. It's a billboard, a giant flashing neon light telling you to back off or die. But I don't say this. Nor do I try to take the burden off Fanfan by apologizing for having brought him up there. We were each playing our respective roles: him guiding, me following. He made a mistake and got hurt. That's the simple honesty of the mountains. It's why we go to them for answers. They tell us the truth. It's something that none of us need to restate in a dim hospital room in Geneva.

We brought something for you, I say.

Hattrup pulls a fishing rod and reel out of a plastic bag.

For Corsica, I say.

Fanfan laughs softly.

Yeah, this is good. I think the fish, maybe they should watch out now, eh?

We all laugh, throaty with relief. A nurse appears, dowdy in a washed-out blue smock. We don't understand her French, but it's clear she wants us to leave.

You go back home now? asks Fanfan.

I tell him that we are headed out the following day, but we'll be in touch. I ask him if I can take a picture before we go.

Sure, why not? he says.

I raise the camera and press the shutter. The flash lights up the dim room. In the photograph, Fanfan's eyes are slits. The neck brace jams his head into the pillow, but he's raising both arms, his thumbs and pinkies outstretched in a surfer's gesture—hang loose.

A day later, I'm wrapped in white airplane noise. The peaks are behind me and the horizon has shrunk dramatically. Brian Whitlock, our soundman, gives me a sleeping pill, but it seems to have the opposite effect. Suddenly I'm wired. I pull out my laptop and begin writing an e-mail to Peter Jennings.

> *Peter,*
>
> *Missed you in Chamonix. Hope you are well. On my way home now, trying to sort out our trip. I'm sure Kayce told you of our good luck and our bad luck too. I think back now on the questions that you posed that night we had dinner at your house. What's the story really about? And why do I need to tell it?*
>
> *The answer is family. The story is really about how this great and extended family of skiers, this tribe—with a language, costumes, rites and rituals all its own—takes care of its members. How and why it continues and what it means to be part of it.*
>
> *Through the eyes of young Kye, I wanted to see what it is that makes this mountain life so special that people are willing to die in order to live it. I wanted to see selflessness, the loyalty of family, tradition and respect. I wanted to see men risk their lives to help a boy become a man—a better man than themselves, perhaps.*
>
> *I think that if we can re-find the special something of coming together to live fully in the face of death, maybe we can deliver it to an audience of skiers and non-skiers alike. Now that I know what it's truly about, I'm even more committed to telling this story well. I hope that together we can make something great. I plan to go home, spend some time with my family, and come to New York soon.*
>
> > *Best,*
> >
> > *Bill*

Even before I finish the message, I know I'll never send it. It's too much, too revealing. And besides, Yellin and Obenhaus will think I'm going around them to curry favor with Peter. So I click save and close the file, figuring I'll use it to organize my thoughts when I talk to Peter in New York.

But that conversation never happens. Two days later, Peter announces that he has lung cancer.

I call Yellin.

I don't know what this means, he says. I really don't. You should take some time off.

I send Peter an e-mail very different from the one I'd composed on the plane. It's about how I know he'll beat cancer, how I look forward to working with him soon. I receive one back a week later. It's a mass e-mail that he's sent to his well-wishers.

Dear Bill,

I hope you can understand what your message meant to me. I abhor the idea of one response for all—but it is really important for me to say thank you in a timely way to all of you who have expressed your support. Some of you have made me laugh like hell—thank goodness that doesn't hurt.

Some of you—many of you—have made me cry, in the very best sense—which out of a slight sense of embarrassment I immediately blamed on the steroids. Some of you have reached out of the past so distant that it is nice to know we are both still kicking. Others, not always strangers, have reminded me of connections unknown or forgotten by me until now. These are the ones that often make me cry—which I promptly blame on the steroids. As one friend said quite accurately, it is like being hit by a truck. He then said he was glad that I was willing to stand here and slam right back. Truth be told, I think you have given me more strength than I thought I had. I write as I begin chemo-

therapy because I want you to know that—and to say thank you.

As for the steroids … they have given me an appetite for calorie-intense ice cream. Damn, we need a bigger freezer.

As always …

Peter

I wait. I take my family on vacation to Baja California. Even floating on a surfboard between sets at a mellow surf break called Raouls, forty-five kilometers south of Tijuana, I can't get it all off my mind. Through the surfing and the sand castles, fish tacos, and diaper changes in the rented RV, I can't stop thinking about the film. I need to find a way to tell this story. I come back across the border a few weeks later and call Yellin from Barstow, California.

I don't know anything about the movie, he says. We're all really busy. Kayce is completely involved in caring for Peter. I'm working on something that I can't tell you about. Mark's taking some time off. Just hang on. We'll get back to you.

The weeks slide by and turn into months. I wait for the call that will tell me to come back to work. June passes, July, and no calls from New York. I take a full-time job helping my father-in-law revive his struggling Internet company. Finally, in early August, a call comes that changes everything. It's not from New York but from British Columbia.

Hi Bill, it's Beth Stewart, Trevor's mum.

Hi Beth. How are you? How's Kye?

We're both fine. We really appreciate the trip and what you did for Kye, she says. I called to offer my condolences on the passing of Peter Jennings.

The project that Yellin couldn't talk about turns out to be a two-hour memorial for Peter. ABC had asked him to begin planning it before Peter died. I watch the broadcast with Bel. It's touching but not sentimental.

Yellin did a classy job.

I call and tell him as much. We talk for a while about the funeral, and he tells me that he lost not only his friend and business partner, he's on the brink of losing his company. Without Peter, almost all the projects his production company had lined up have evaporated. And unless he can pull something together, Obenhaus, his top director, is going to leave and find other work. That's when I realize that our ski film is one of the only projects that doesn't need Peter's involvement to complete. And mine is the only job that Obenhaus can walk in and take over.

For a few weeks I hold out hope that our friendship will prevent Yellin from taking the logical course of action, but I know that he didn't get to where he is by being sentimental. And then the call comes.

The road to making this film is like a long journey through the mountains, Yellin begins. You were the guide to get us up the first few mountains, but now you're going to have to hand it off to another guide to get it the rest of the way.

The film is Obenhaus's now, I guess.

You'll still get your money and your credits, and you're free to keep working on it, says Yellin. Just talk to Mark.

So, I can audition for a job on my own project?

You could look at it that way, but that would, in my opinion, be a mistake, he says calmly. You were the right guide to get the expedition moving, and you're still on it. There's just someone else leading now.

I hang up and punch the wall. That night, I recount the conversation to Bel.

Tom can't do that, can he? she asks. It's your film, your project.

I explain that I sold all rights to my treatment and entered into a work-for-hire agreement, which means they can sideline me any time they please. I summarize the situation with a maxim I learned from a veteran director years earlier: If they're paying your ass, they don't have to kiss it too.

I call Obenhaus and leave messages a couple of times, but he doesn't call back. It's clear that he wants to handle the material in his own way, without my involvement. A year passes. Yellin and I talk often, but our conversations are short and strained. In time my anger recedes. In its wake I come to understand the difficult situation Yellin was in and even come to respect, if not agree with, the decision to replace me. The foundation of his working family was breaking up, and he found a way to keep it together. All the while I knew that he was still committed to our initial goal: to make a great film that would show the courage, nobility and passion of the skiing tribe.

On April 9, 2006, *The New York Times* runs a story about the death of Doug Coombs. Nine days earlier he was skiing with friends in La Grave, France, near Chamonix, when one of his companions, Chad Vander-Ham, fell in a couloir and disappeared over a cliff. Coombs skied to the edge of the cliff to begin a rescue but apparently hit ice, lost his edge, and also disappeared. Both men fell about 500 feet. A rescue helicopter arrived shortly after the accident, but Coombs was pronounced dead on the scene. VanderHam was taken to a hospital but died soon after. Coombs left behind a wife, Emily, and a three-year-old son, David.

About six weeks later, on May 17, 2006, *The Times* runs a front page story about Coombs' death and the dangers of extreme skiing in the Alps. The headline: "Skiing Beyond Safety's Edge Once Too Often."

It's a year and a half before I see Kye again. He calls me in Salt Lake City on a warm April day. He and Iberg are in town for a preview of a ski film that Kye's in and how about we meet for lunch? Kye's a head taller than the last time I saw him. When we shake hands, we stand eye to eye.

Your hair's longer, I say.

I can't wait till it's long, he says.

Growing a ponytail again?

Fuckin'-A right, he says, grinning.

We sit outside at a restaurant near my office and eat burritos. Kye is animated, excitedly telling me about the new ski film and his numerous other projects. He talks like a pro skier—sponsors to please, commitments to meet—and then he turns the conversation to Chamonix.

So, like, I really wanted to say thanks for taking me over there, he begins. It was full-on. I mean, it was, like, one of the best things ever in my life.

Over the phone I'd already told Kye that it didn't look like he'd be in the Obenhaus film, but as I hadn't seen more than a few scenes, I wasn't sure. Before meeting Kye, I'd called Yellin to find out whether anything we shot in Chamonix was in the final cut. He told me there was a clip from the Fanfan rescue, but that Kye wasn't in the film at all.

I break the news to Kye, and he doesn't miss a beat.

Yeah, I figured, he says. They haven't called. It's okay. Cham was like nothing I've ever done before. I never would've known about that world and those guys and the whole big-mountain scene.

I ask him if he felt like he was part of that world now.

I'd love to be, he answers. In a while, but not right now. Chamonix was a place where I could test whether I was ready, a place to take a step back and see. And I know I'm not ready for that on my own. I'd like to go experience some more places, really learn the mountains and the climbing skills. Then I'd like to go back to Chamonix, go back to the Rond again.

I tell him I'm glad that it meant something to him. What I don't tell him is how hearing him say it makes me feel. Kye is well on his way to becoming his father, to taking the same risks that Trevor took, and though that gives me pause in the same way that I fear for all my friends who live lives of great daring, it also gives me a profound sense of happiness.

In March 2007, Yellin calls to tell me that the film that Obenhaus made, entitled *Steep*, was accepted into the Tribeca Film Festival and in light of all we'd gone through to make this movie, I had to be there for the premiere. I agree and book a ticket to New York, but as the day of the premiere draws closer I waffle. Then the day before the screening, I call and leave Yellin a message: I'm not coming to New York; I'm going skiing instead. He calls back a few minutes later, angry with me for not coming.

I've made my decision and you can't change it, I say, so don't try to talk me out of it.

He tries anyway.

You can ski any day! he says.

That's right, I say, that's why I live here.

The following night, the night of the premiere, he calls to report on the scene—the ski journalists and the featured skiers and the full house of expectant moviegoers. He tells me the film was well received and he's confident we'll get a distributor. Congratulations, I say, and mean it.

As I say the word, I feel a weight lift off my shoulders. Throughout the three years of working on the film, I'd been assessing whether my own life decisions (where to live, what to do for money, etc.), which were driven mostly by a desire to keep skiing in my life, had been dead-end mistakes. By deciding not to go to New York for the premiere of the film, I'd unconsciously recommitted to the mountains.

Early the next morning, I'm standing at the top of Alta ski resort where I've been teaching my children to ski. The sun is warm and the snow is soft. My four-year-old daughter, Grace, holds my hands. C'mon, Dad, let's go, she says. We push off and the mountain rushes at us. Standing confidently between my legs, Grace makes turns that clack her skis off mine as I snowplow to keep her from going too fast. The run is thigh-burning and magic. Though I've had a lifetime of thrills on skis, nothing compares to these simple moments of sharing something I love with my children, who seem to love it as much as I.

At the bottom, Grace and I ski up to Bel as our two-year-old son, Liam, pushes off on his own little skis. He straight-runs down a small hill, screaming with delight. Then he crashes into a heap.

There is nothing safe about the sport of skiing or a life in the mountains. Injury is virtually assured for those who spend enough time on skis. Even accomplished skiers make critical and potentially tragic errors. So why do it? Why keep coming back? And more important, why share this life with the people I love?

As I ski over to my fallen son, I'm holding my breath. I wipe the snow out of his goggles, see that he is giggling, and realize that today I have found a balance between acceptable risk and a parent's responsibility. I've allowed the mountain to teach my children that our actions have consequences, that life isn't a dress rehearsal. And I was there to help them recover from their falls. Yet, just as surely as I know that today I found a balance, I have no doubt that tomorrow it will elude me.

Maybe, like Trevor, I'll make mistakes and my luck will run out. Expertise, equipment, and experience offer but thin insurance policies. Seeing a skier like Fanfan make such a costly error is a reminder that tragedy can happen to anyone, anywhere. We were lucky in Chamonix. Though we surrounded Kye with good people and took all the right precautions, his experience could have been—and almost was—much different, much darker.

There are no guarantees. This is a lesson that the mountains teach. Humility and gratitude are the benefits of such an education and may be the best reasons for sharing this life with others. I think Anselme was right. It's beautiful, sometimes, and anyway, the mountains are here. We must take the best of the mountains and follow life.

Epilogue

Kye Petersen has continued to advance his skiing career. In April 2009 he beat out twenty of the best big-mountain skiers in the world at the invitation-only Red Bull Cold Rush competition at Retallack Lodge, British Columbia. With starring roles in several of the most popular ski movies, as well as appearances in magazine stories and advertisements, he's solidified his status as one of the world's elite skiers. He returns to Chamonix every year, learning more about the big mountains and his place in them.

Less than a year after his accident, Fanfan stepped onto skis again. In weeks he was skiing at full speed. Still regarded as one of Chamonix's top guides, he performs in films and commercials and says he is skiing better than ever. He never did take a fishing trip to Corsica. Lately he's been pioneering new ski routes on Russia's Kamchatka Peninsula.

Glen and Kimberly Plake continue to promote skiing all over the world.

Mike Hattrup still heads up K2's Telemark division and guides backcountry ski trips through the Alps. Both of his children are avid skiers.

Anselme Baud still lives in Chamonix, teaching young men and women how to stay alive in the big mountains.

In 1998, two years after Trevor's death, Beth Stewart founded Parents of Lost Skiers (www.polsonline.ca), a nonprofit organization dedicated to supporting those who have lost sons or daughters to the mountains. In 2008, Beth moved from Vancouver Island to the mainland to be closer to her grandchildren, Kye and Neve Petersen.

In 2007 Eric Iberg released his fifth ski movie, entitled *Idea*. Different from other films of the genre, it strives to tell a coherent story and develop interesting characters.

Greg Stump has moved back to the mountains, where he is working on a semiautobiographical film that chronicles the birth of extreme skiing. His first ski film since 1999, its working title is *The Legends of Aahhhs*.

Steep, the film that Obenhaus and Yellin made, is centered on the life and death of Doug Coombs. After premiering at the Tribeca Film Festival, it was purchased by Sony Pictures Classics, the same company that distributed *Dogtown and Z Boys* and *Riding Giants*. It opened on 120 screens nationwide and received good reviews.

Just after *Steep* premiered, Yellin's oldest daughter, Chloe Yellin, graduated from her father's alma mater, Harvard College. Rather than follow her father's footsteps into the television or film industry, she went skiing. Her father greatly encouraged the move and helped her find a job in Vail, Colorado.

The company that Yellin ran for Peter Jennings found a new life as The Documentary Group. Headed by Kayce Freed Jennings and Yellin, it produced four successful documentaries in its first two years. One of its films, *Operation Homecoming*, was nominated for an Academy Award.

I still work in a flat-roofed office just down the hill from Utah's Wasatch Range, but the money I was paid to work on the film allowed us to buy into a bit better neighborhood, away from Meth Boy. I spend more time on the hill than I have in recent years, much of it skiing with my family.

In the spring of 2008, Yellin sold me the rights to all the film footage that I directed in 2005, including everything that happened in Chamonix. As this second edition of *The Edge of Never* goes to press, I am finishing the film that I started to make in 2005: a simple father-son story about Kye and Trevor Petersen. Rather than sell it to a distributor, I am managing the distribution myself. In the fall of 2009 we will travel to ski-friendly cities and towns all over the country, renting theaters and showing *The Edge of Never* to the tribe. Find more information on www.edgeofneverfilm.com.

Acknowledgments

Without my family I would find little reason to get out of bed in the morning, much less write a book. My wife Bel, my daughter Grace, my son Liam, and my father Huck were and continue to be inexhaustibly supportive. I love and thank you all.

If writing a book about real events and people requires an ironclad adherence to detached objectivity, then I am a failure. The people I've written about in this book are all dear to me. They allowed me into their homes and lives, endured cameras and recorders and all manner of tedious questioning. I am deeply grateful to all, especially to the following:

First and foremost, I'd like to thank Kye Petersen for sharing his journey with me. He is a very special young man with a powerful story that he was generous enough to let me tell. Kye comes from a strong family. His mother, Tanya Reck-Petersen, and his sister, Neve, never failed to welcome me and patiently answer my questions—even the dumb ones—trip after trip, visit after visit. Kye's grandmother, Beth Stewart, a writer herself, was unflinchingly honest and courageous in recounting her life and the life of her lost son, Trevor Petersen. Kye's uncles, Rick Petersen and Lindsay Dakota, were outstanding in their forbearance. Trevor's longtime skiing and climbing partner, Eric Pehota, was a pleasure to speak with and chase through the Whistler backcountry powder. Dave Nagel was a wealth of information about heli-logging. Gordy Peifer was precise and patient when recalling his last days with Trevor.

Glen and Kimberly Plake were terrific and dedicated, their enthusiasm an endless font of inspiration. Anselme Baud is a fine and wise gentleman who generously shared his time, knowledge and personal feelings. Stephane "Fanfan" Dan and Mike Hattrup are the kind of guys I'd want on any adventure: competent, composed and congenial. Thanks to Kasha Rigby and Meg Oster for grace and patience during a difficult time.

This book would not exist without the film project that grew into the documentary feature *Steep*. As with any large, collaborative endeavor, the film represents the talents of far too many people to name here. A few, however, stand out. Tom Yellin was the first person to believe in this story. The second person was my Snowbird ski buddy Brian Beck. Not only did he sign on to help raise the money for the film, he remained steadfastly optimistic through the darkest times. Brian's brother Monte Beck was the first to put his money where his heart was and underwrite the film. The unfailing generosity of urbane and imperturbable Stuart Horsfall made it all possible.

I'd also like to thank Kayce Freed and the late Peter Jennings for their willingness to take a flier on me, and the dynamic Gabrielle Tenenbaum and diligent Jordan Kronick for their tireless work to make the Chamonix trip a reality. I'm also indebted to our talented film crew: Eric Iberg, Peter Pilafian, Brian Whitlock, Beat Steiner, Greg Stump, Bertrand Delapierre, Scott Markewitz, and Nate Wallace. As always, Steven J. Goldfisher offered sage legal advice and services.

After the initial draft was written, there came a time of immense self-doubt. Fortunately, I found a wonderful editor to work with. Dorothee Kocks threw herself into this book as if it were her own. She was a godsend, and her work elevated the text to a level I could not have reached alone. After her came editor and publisher John Gattuso, who also dove in headfirst. Complete commitment is a hard thing to find these days. Both Kocks and Gattuso had it in spades.

And then there were the many friends whom I imposed upon to read the manuscript. Of these I owe the greatest debt to Peter and Guthrie Schweitzer, who were indefatigable supporters. The Wasatch Writers' Alliance (Melissa Bond, Betsy Burton, Chris Cokinos, Teresa Jordan, Christy Karras, Dorothee Kocks, Jana Richmond and Steve Trimble) was an invaluable source of critique, camaraderie and insight. I am also grateful for the generous help of Rob Baker, Francois Goulet, Dennis Gaspari, Steve Dudley, Scott Beck, Dave and Melissa Fields, Laura Shaffer, Susie English, Paddy Kaye, Bill Grout, Elizabeth Brown, Marc Peruzzi, Keith Carlsen, Mark Kozak, Rachel Odell, Shawn Stinson, Emily Stifler, Thomas Cooke, Mark Wheadon, Porter Fox, Peter Shelton, Guy Morris, John Calhoun, Lito Tejada-Flores and Adam Barker.

End Notes

Writing *The Edge of Never* was a complex and rewarding challenge. On the one hand I wanted to write a factually accurate book that stands up to the highest standards of journalism. On the other I wanted to tell a tale that lives up to the best traditions of storytelling.

Much of the story was captured on Super 16 film, high-definition video and MiniDV. Background information was drawn from written records and photographs as well as published stories. I also conducted numerous interviews in person and over the phone. Some were recorded on audiotape, others on a MiniDV video camera. Telephone interviews were documented with contemporaneous notes. In every instance the subject was informed of the presence of a recording device or my own intention to transcribe the conversation. In most cases, if making contemporaneous notes or an electronic recording was not possible, I wrote copious notes as soon after the event as possible. Scenes that I didn't personally witness (such as those involving Trevor and the Petersen family) are based on interviews with people who were present.

Much of the dialogue is transcribed from electronic recordings and edited only for grammar and clarity. In some cases, dialogue has been reconstructed from my notes and memory. As a journalist, I believe that quotation marks should be used only to represent exactly what was said. In a previous draft of the book, I placed recorded dialogue inside quotation marks and presented non-recorded dialogue without them. I found this arrangement confused and distracted readers, so I chose to remove quotation marks altogether. While the absence of quotation marks is unconventional, I feel it is the best method of handling the varied source material, and, as I discovered later, tends to speed the eye across the page. As this book is about freedom and speed and risk, I believe this is the right and only way to tell the story.

Technical information (about ski techniques, snow composition and avalanche activity, for example) is based on my own experience and research and interviews with experts in related fields.

The following notes document sources for each chapter:

The events related in the **Prologue** were recorded on film and high-definition video. The recordings were supplemented by my own recollections and recorded interviews with Mike Hattrup, Kye Petersen, Peter Pilafian, Beat Steiner, Kasha Rigby, Meg Oster and Scott Markewitz.

Chapter 1 A Madman's Scheme is reconstructed from my own recollections, augmented by conversations with my wife Bel and recorded interviews with Glen Plake. I also received help from Tom Yellin and my father, Huck Kerig, who checked relevant sections of the chapter for accuracy.

Chapter 2 Kye is based upon my recollections of the events and supplemented after the fact with video that I shot in the Petersens' apartment with a handheld camera. Kye Petersen, Tom Yellin, Beth Stewart and Tanya Reck-Petersen read this chapter for accuracy.

My dinner with Peter Jennings in **Chapter 3 Jennings** was reviewed by Tom Yellin and Brian Beck, both of whom were present. The scene between Kye and Tanya is based on recorded interviews with Kye and Tanya. After Eric Iberg arrived on the scene, all action and dialogue were recorded on videotape.

Chapter 4 Trevor: Journey to a Strange Land was assembled from several in-person recorded interviews with Beth Stewart and phone interviews with Trevor's brothers, Lindsay Dakota and Rick Petersen. Beth Stewart also accompanied me to the Shawnigan Lake School on Vancouver Island, a visit that I shot with a video camera. The details of Trevor's logging days were obtained in recorded interviews with Beth Stewart, Eric Pehota and Dave Nagel. Details of Trevor and Tanya's trip to Chamonix were taken directly from their journal (which Tanya graciously lent me) as well as two recorded interviews with Tanya and one with Glen Plake. Beth Stewart read the chapter for accuracy.

Chapter 5 Death Sport Capital of the World is based on personal recollections and videotape of Glen and Kimberly Plake.

Chapter 6 Trevor: Return to Chamonix is from recorded interviews with Glen Plake, Tanya Reck-Petersen, Gordy Peiffer, Mike Hattrup and Scott Markewitz.

With the exception of my recollection of phone conversations with Anselme Baud and parts of a brief conversation with Jordan Kronick, the details recorded in **Chapter 7 No-Fall Zone** are from film and video shot on location in Chamonix.

The first scene in **Chapter 8 Small in a Strong Place** is taken completely from my recollection of the conversation, recorded in my journal later that evening. I interviewed Tom Yellin after he read this section to verify its accuracy. The remaining action and dialogue in the chapter are from film and video shot on location.

The first scene in **Chapter 9 The Eagle's Lair** is from my recollection of the event, confirmed later by Yellin. The scene in which the skiers scout the Poubelle Couloir is taken from film and video shot on location. The final scene, which occurs at the Grand Roc bar, is based on personal recollection, recorded in my journal immediately after it occurred.

Skiing action in the Poubelle Couloir in **Chapter 10 The Cheese Grater** is taken directly from film and videotape. The scene that occurs later that evening in the Grand Roc bar was documented in my journal and confirmed in interviews with Glen Plake and Tom Yellin.

While there is no way to know the exact circumstances surrounding Trevor Petersen's death, my narrative of the event in **Chapter 11 Trevor: Exit Couloir** is based on recorded interviews with his closest ski partner, Eric Pehota, as well as with Gordy Peiffer, Tanya Reck-Petersen, Mike Hattrup, Rick Petersen, Beth Stewart, Lindsay Dakota and Scott Markewitz. I also referenced the paperwork, including the death certificate, generated by the French authorities concerning Trevor's accident.

The scene in **Chapter 12 Into the Mess** in which Plake and Kye discuss the planned descent of the Glacier Rond was recorded on videotape by Eric Iberg in the room that he and Kye shared. The details of Greg Stump's story were drawn from conversations with Stump in Chamonix.

Chapter 13 Ascending the Spire is from film and videotape shot on the Aiguille du Midi.

With the exception of a short conversation with Kye concerning our mutual stomach issues, **Chapter 14 The Wall** is taken directly from film and videotape shot on the Glacier Rond.

Most of the action and dialogue in **Chapter 15 The Exit** is from film, still photos, and videotape shot on location. The only exceptions are parts of the conversations I had with Doug Coombs and Nate Wallace. Pieces of these conversations were caught on tape. I filled in the remainder from memory. Conversations between Scott Markewitz and Bertrand Delapierre were re-created from a recorded interview with Markewitz. The dialogue between Fanfan, Plake, Kye and Mike Hattrup was taken from an audio recording made by Fanfan's helmet camera and later corroborated in interviews with Plake, Hattrup and Kye. The scene in which Kye scatters Trevor's ashes a second time was photographed by Markewitz. The descent of the Exit Couloir was reconstructed from recorded interviews with Plake, Kye, Hattrup and Markewitz.

The first scene in **Chapter 16 Over the Edge** is based on memory and notes that I wrote that night and later corroborated by Plake in a recorded interview. The next two scenes, in which we ascend the Grands Montets and get into place, are reconstructed from memory and interviews conducted afterwards with Kasha Rigby, Meg Oster and Hattrup. The ski action and accompanying dialogue, including the crash, were drawn from film and video shot on location. My brief conversation with Pilafian and Markewitz is not recorded on film. I re-created the dialogue based on personal recollection and interviews with Pilafian and Markewitz. The rescue was recorded on film and videotape.

The first two scenes of **Chapter 17 Candles** are reconstructed from memory and interviews with Plake, Hattrup and Yellin. The dialogue and action at Anselme's house is taken from MiniDV video I shot on location.

The hospital scene in **Chapter 18 Into the Light** was re-created from memory, interviews with Pilafian and Hattrup, and still photographs I took at the time. The airplane scene is based on personal recollection and the e-mails I wrote (but, in one case, didn't send) to Peter Jennings and the e-mail he sent to me. The remainder of the chapter, with the exception of a recorded conversation with Kye, is drawn from memory.

www.stonecreekpublications.com

www.theedgeofnever.com

Also from Stone Creek Publications

TALKING TO GOD
Portrait of a World at Prayer
Winner of the 2006 Nautilus Book Award and Foreword Book of the Year Award

The Dalai Lama, Karen Armstrong, Desmond Tutu and other celebrated writers of faith explore the universal significance of prayer in this inspiring volume, illustrated with more than 100 photographs chronicling the diversity of the devotional experience in all of its intimacy and mystery.

"A sumptuous feast of beauty and wisdom."
—Philip Zaleski, editor of *The Best American Spiritual Writing*

"Rich with powerful images and thoughtful reflections."
—Sharon Salzberg, author of *Lovingkindness: The Revolutionary Art of Happiness*

Hardcover, 176 pages, 12x9 inches, 100 photos, $39.95, ISBN: 0-9656338-3-7

SHADOW BOXERS
Sweat, Sacrifice & the Will to Survive in American Boxing Gyms
Winner of the 2004 Dorothea Lange–Paul Taylor Prize

At one time there was a boxing gym in every sizable town in America. Today, they are found mostly in big cities, tucked away in shabby lofts and basements. Those that survive are the repositories of a centuries-old tradition of pugilistic knowledge that encompasses not only the physical mechanics of the sport but a code of respect and discipline that, at its best, transforms raw aggression into "sweet science." Award-winning photographer Jim Lommasson and a team of veteran boxing writers capture the fierce beauty of these vanishing institutions, giving readers an unflinching look at the brutality of the sport but also its grace, poetry, and blood-and-bone humanity.

"Affecting, intricate and sometimes just glorious."
—*Time*

"Evocative."
—*Sports Illustrated*

"Gritty, grimy and gorgeous."
—*The Oregonian*

Hardcover, 176 pages, 9x12 inches, 180 photos, $39.95, ISBN: 0-9656338-2-9